Personalizing
Evaluation

ML1

Personalizing Evaluation

Saville Kushner

SAGE Publications
London • Thousand Oaks • New Delhi

First published 2000

Apart from any fair dealing for the purposes of research or private
study, or criticism or review, as permitted under the Copyright,
Designs and Patents Act, 1988, this publication may be reproduced,
stored or transmitted in any form, or by any means, only with the prior
permission in writing of the publishers, or in the case of reprographic
reproduction, in accordance with the terms of licences issued by the
Copyright Licensing Agency. Inquiries concerning reproduction
outside those terms should be sent to the publishers.

 SAGE Publications Ltd
6 Bonhill Street
London EC2A 4PU

SAGE Publications Inc.
2455 Teller Road
Thousand Oaks, California 91320

SAGE Publications India Pvt Ltd
32, M-Block Market
Greater Kailash – I
New Delhi 110 048

British Library Cataloguing in Publication data

A catalogue record for this book is available
from the British Library

ISBN 0 7619 6361 8
ISBN 0 7619 6362 6 (pbk)

Library of Congress catalog card number 130147

Typeset by Mayhew Typesetting, Rhayader, Powys
Printed in Great Britain by Athenaeum Press, Gateshead

Contents

Acknowledgements

Unfortunately, the way we publish books lays undue emphasis on individual authors, and masks the accomplishments of critical academic communities. Where do academic ideas come from if not from exchanges within professional cultures? The success I do claim for myself is in having discovered a rich and challenging community of practitioners in applied research and evaluation with whom to develop some worthwhile thoughts. For the most part this has been at the Centre for Applied Research in Education under the Directorship of Lawrence Stenhouse, Rob Walker, Barry MacDonald and, most recently, John Elliott. But the first draft of this book was compiled under a Visiting Scholarship from the University of Malaga in Spain. There, I held rich and formative conversations with the excellent research group at the Departamento de Didáctica y Organización Escolar – Miguel Sola and Angel Perez helped me especially. My critical community extends across the 'pond', too, where it was Bob Stake and Michael Quinn Patton, in particular, who kept this book alive when its health was looking decidedly flaky.

Had Barry MacDonald not changed his mind 20 years ago and reluctantly conceded that I had something of the evaluator in me, I would not have benefited from his tutelage and, latterly, stern critique of drafts for this book (which publication is unlikely to stem). Had Nigel Norris not been there throughout as an intellectual brother-in-arms and friend, what scholastic rigour and self-confidence I can muster would long since have evaporated.

It must go without saying that much of the strength of an evaluation argument like mine must rely on the quality of data and evaluation experience – and this is down to respondents. Though they have been anonymized for this book (not a customary practice for me) their words and thoughts remain with me. The quality of their expression lends much to whatever quality you will perceive herein.

However, those who contributed most directly to the ideas in this book have been research students – mostly mature professionals in their own right – with whom I have spent as much time as I could manage. They are the research students who have the most immediate sense of the complexity of field-based enquiry, for it is they alone who work at the leading edge of constructive confusion. So thanks to Lim, Chow, Lingan, Rosanna, Wafaa, Jackie, Masha'el, Sofi, Fernando, Kath, Sister Alies and others who should not feel disregarded at not being named.

. . . but it all, one way or another, comes back to Lawrence Stenhouse.

Overture

Program Evaluation – the Heart of the Matter

At the heart of London lies a financial metropolis – the City. Its wealth burgeons visibly in new tower blocks, pretty flower boxes under solarized windows and the natty designs in which pinstriped suits are cut these days. Once merely a drab place of work, the City has luxuriated in the policies of the past 20 years to switch the country's wealth-creation base from manufacturing to financial services. Many of the thousands of millionaires who live in London have made their money here, so much so that wages in the City alone distort national statistics for average earnings. For some years this has been a place of serious chic.

At one edge of the City, astride what was once the river that separated it from the poor East End of London, lies an ostentatious expression of this vast wealth – the Barbican Centre. Built as a residential complex, it is dominated by high-rise blocks of expensive apartments. At their feet lies an arts centre and concert hall – the home of the London Symphony Orchestra – shops and cafes, a church, car parks, a school – the complex even hosts a conservatoire, the Guildhall School of Music and Drama. Perhaps one day someone might be born here, grow up here, be schooled, music trained, married, employed and have their funeral here. Moreover, this urban village has been designed so that it has no major entrance leading directly to the street. Instead, its main entrances have their own tunnelled access roads. There is a facade to the Barbican, but this is in its core, facing inwards to a courtyard of brown tiles and rectangular pools, and towards its own residential community. From the street the visual impression of the Barbican is of what appears to be a continuous brick wall.

I am sitting in one of the Barbican cafes with a young woman and we are drinking coffee. I am interviewing her. She is a student at the Guildhall Conservatoire and I am evaluating an innovatory course there which she is taking as an elective. We are talking about her background in music – one in which she had to compete against adults to choose her own identity as a musician. She wanted to be a flautist, her teacher wanted her to be a pianist. She explains that she peaked early in her career; she was principal flautist with a national youth orchestra in her mid-teens and even attracted the attention of James Galway. I get up to buy more coffees and invite her to a piece of the rich cakes served here. She demurs, smiling and telling me that she is overweight, as it is, so best not.

When I return with the coffees (and a piece of cake for myself) I pursue the chance remark and ask why she thinks she is overweight. She tells me she is bored with her music at present. At the level at which she plays, learning opportunities come few and very far between, so the routine of practice has little compensation and is hard to maintain. She carries her flute around with her and goes for days without practising – in the disciplined culture of the Conservatoire she feels guilty about this and overeating is her comfort. This bothers her – 'God, I'd like to be sylph-like.'

Our interview carries on – I have never switched off the tape-recorder. She mentions in passing her frequent dreaming. There is a recurring dream she has in which she is famous. She is not playing the flute in these dreams but receiving accolades in the Green Room following a performance. This, she says, is what 'turns me on'. Recognition. 'But also, along with that, I dream about maintaining my integrity.' The goals, she says, are impossible – 'just playing the instrument – I'm always faced with failure'. I ask her a whimsical question: would she prefer to be 'sylph-like' or famous? She stares into the middle-distance for a moment and turns back to look at me. 'You know,' she says, 'I think I envisage the two together.'

She lives with these and other preoccupations all the time and she joined the innovatory course which I am evaluating to see if it might help her work through them. The course takes students out of the Conservatoire to interact with local communities in music workshops, to reconnect with their creativity.

This vignette was challenging for me and, in hindsight, probably marked a turning point for me in this evaluation and even in my career as a program evaluator. I find myself recounting it a lot – some reading this will recognize it. It demanded some sort of analytic resolution and I could not ignore it. The disturbing fact was that our conversation had never left the ambit of the innovation. But its significance was so personal and idiosyncratic that it was hard to incorporate into my emerging theory of that innovation – other than in the blandest of terms, that educational innovations like this have to respond to the realities of these personal struggles. This fell short of being formative for the innovators.

The problem was that the personal drama of the piece threatened to overwhelm the somewhat more prosaic view I held of the innovation. I used the vignette in a report without making a great deal of it – without fully understanding its implications, until I had talked of it often enough. Then it became compelling to portray this young woman (and others like her) as a context in which to understand the innovation, rather than the other way about. This was not a solution, but offered a direction to move in. It required a great deal more working out – much of it accomplished in the writing of this book. But there was more complexity to come.

At some point I wrote of the innovation that in order to fulfil one of its primary aims – 'to break into community' – it first had to break *out* of the Barbican. Historically this had meant crossing the river that divided the City rich and the East End poor, and the fact that this river now ran underground did nothing to diminish that obstacle. Not many of the Conservatoire students were wealthy, but their institutional heritage and the symbolism of their music was. However, the Conservatoire could take advantage of a historical precedent.

One of the sponsors of the innovation was a traditional London brewery, whose offices were yards away from the Barbican. The Director of the brewery, who saw to it that charitable money went their way, had a particular reason for sponsoring this innovation.

In the nineteenth century, some in the wealthy community of philan-thropists from the City of London discovered exotic societies – no longer in the far-flung corners of the world reached by the National Geographic Society, but on their doorstep in the East End of London. In Tower Hamlets, Hackney, Bow, Stepney, Whitechapel, the world of poverty produced forms of life and humanity substantially different and strangely primitive. Many Victorians, newly committed to the distorted theory that was Social Darwinism, saw little that could be done about poverty itself. This was, after all, an evolutionary state created by the inevitable coincidence of development with intelligence. Poverty was immutable other than through further evolution. Not so culture. Why should the poor have to be deprived of appreciation for the more uplift-ing aspects of life and morality? So the philanthropists built philo-sophical institutes and concert halls where the poor might seek diversion from their hunger. These were, if the literature is to be believed, honourable acts, a seeking to share the cultural wealth of the City of London with their poorer neighbours.

Not all of those philanthropists were solely concerned with cultural palliatives, however. One whose work went further was Sir Charles

Booth, first President of the Royal Statistical Society – the man who coined the term and the concept 'the poverty line'. Booth combed the streets of the East End of London documenting poverty, painstakingly, house-by-house, street-by-street he produced a diet of statistics so undeniable as to be digestible for whichever government. In so doing, he generated rich fuel for those social reformers who managed to set aside the convenience of Social Darwinism for long enough, within the century, to create a welfare state. Now, that brewery Director sits in his office facing a bookcase with the complete works of the great statistician – his grandfather.

He has many reasons for distributing this money – philanthropy, self-interest, social obligation (the brewery boasts outlets in almost all of Britain's village and town communities), and, of course, a personal sense of duty or of worthwhile action. But he looks at his grandfather's books every day and is influenced by that same mission. The Conservatoire innovation is making that same journey as did Booth and the philan-thropists, albeit in a contemporary style – he sees the value of the innovation in developing personal and social skills in the schoolchildren it works with.

I moved between the intellectual, political and historical contexts implied by these (and other) stories looking for where and to whom my responsibilities lay. The young flautist wages her struggle beneath the towers of the Barbican, steeped in the culture of the Conservatoire. At stake is nothing less than her capacity to define herself. To my knowl-edge, she never met the brewery Director who was, in his own way, using this innovation to construct a legitimate version of himself. But their life projects became, somehow, linked. Together, in a small way dependent on each other, they were elements of a challenge to the insti-tutional wealth of which they were a part – bound, in unpredictable ways, into a small attack on privilege. Knowingly, unknowingly they were bound up in historical currents and economic cycles. I had, some-how, to make sense of these things through my evaluation while doing justice to the values and aspirations of the innovation itself. Like waking from a dream remembering disparate images and events but none of the logic that bound them together this melee has no obvious inferential base – no clear thread of coherence with which to string together these pieces of evaluation data.

But always in the background were those people in the streets of London's East End whose relative living conditions have barely changed since philosophical institutes were first offered to them and who will now receive music workshops – and the patients in the hospitals and hospices where these students worked, and the youth clubs and schools and prisons and community theatres. Here were the 'real worlds' that were constantly being invoked against elite groups and professionals who were being urged throughout the period of this innovation to reform their projects. There are problems of scale, mutual exclusivity and selection here. The legitimate, highly consequential personal struggles of the middle classes are played out against a backdrop of social injustice. Squaring the circle of self-esteem and recognition is important to this young flautist – but what can it mean to the people of Stepney, and to the schools, prisons, hospices and youth clubs the students worked with? Again, there had to be points of analytic contact between East Enders and the retinue of innovators in and around the Guildhall School, for these people were, claimed the innovation, what it was all about. Loosely lumped together they were the 'community' everyone was trying to make contact with; in a general sense, these were the concert hall audiences of today and tomorrow without whom music-making would be an unprofitable and fruitless activity; but above all, it was felt that if music could not be made meaningful to these people and their children, then music-making faced a crisis of legitimation.

But, once again, the idiosyncrasy of these diverse social contexts made it difficult to find threads of coherence with which to talk about all these players in the same paragraph, so to speak. The people who were one way or another embraced by this Conservatoire innovation lived in discrete contexts of action, advantage and hope – the music student, the brewer, an Asian child, a dying woman, a prisoner on a life sentence, a conservatoire manager . . . a university evaluator. All were, indeed, linked together in one sense, but possibly through the least common denominator of all, that is, that they were all part of an educational evaluation. Other than to the evaluator and the main players in the innovation, this counted for little.

Fortunately, there is no resolution to these confusions, and so evaluation retains its intellectual challenge. We might, of course, take refuge in the view that all can be resolved in the context of program aims and values – that the Asian child and the conservatoire manager and the dying woman and the poor of London achieve adequate meaning as 'stakeholders' in the program's evaluation. But this offers only temporary respite, for pretty soon that alibi runs out and the program ceases to explain enough about their lives to understand its relevance to them – or lack of relevance. A dying woman and her doctor, or an Asian child, may be, in some sense, stakeholders, but so fleetingly as the program rushes into and out of their lives as to make the concept a virtual irrelevance. Even then, the benefits afforded them by the innovation relative to those that accrue to the Conservatoire, for example, are too often negligible – there is a hidden asymmetry in the notion of stakeholder. After all, the working classes of the East End cannot mount projects disseminating their culture to the Barbican.

This book is about program evaluation. I do not offer a comprehensive survey of program evaluation theory, rather I draw from my own experience to make some observations about particular aspects of it. Principally, I am concerned with the confusions highlighted above and with the difficulty of finding the appropriate backdrop against which to construct a meaningful analysis of the value of a program of innovation. It starts with an assumption – and this is important for the reader to be aware of – that to measure a program against its objectives or against an externally imposed set of indicators is a meaningless exercise in itself, for those objectives and indicators relate to the lives of the people I have mentioned in very different ways. There are no singular measures to compare, for example, program outcomes with initial objectives; the worth of a program is too subject to situational interpretation and contested meanings. We merely find ourselves back into the problem of how to measure one life against another. The question of 'standards' – that is, criteria against which to measure the worth of events – is one of procedural principles or indicators of how a journey is going – it is not one of end-states. As Glass (1978: 259) says in his argument that the assessment/evaluation movement corrupted the debate over criterion-referencing when it opted for criteria as exact measures, 'In education, one can recognize improvement and decay, but one cannot make cogent absolute judgements of good and bad.'

The second assumption which the reader is invited to share here is that it is more educational to read about problems and issues in evaluation than about models and solutions. There is no evaluation model offered in this book – everything I propose falls within pre-established rubrics of case study evaluation, principally the Democratic Evaluation model of Barry MacDonald (cf. MacDonald, 1987). If readers identify with anything here it will have to be with the messiness of doing evaluation, the inevitable uncertainties and imprecisions of its practice. To reiterate, I do not analyse program evaluation theory; I offer a personal account of the messiness of doing program evaluation. But, then, that is something that is not often on show in the evaluation literature. There are many useful texts on program evaluation still being published which are instructional, in that they do not require the reader to bring their own experience to bear in order to understand. But this one does, and without having some experience or foreboding of a problem, this book may make little sense. Indeed, it was developed entirely in seminars with research students and grew out of conversations regarding the confusing experiences we were all having with fieldwork.

Early in the development of case study evaluation – in the 1960s and 1970s – people were confronting and having to account for stories much like the ones reproduced here. They were reaching for legitimate ways of representing people's lives, and then of using those lives to bring authority to their evaluation reports. At one point Barry MacDonald dedicated himself to writing about issues associated with the 'portrayal of persons as evaluation data'. He argued (MacDonald, 1985: 51) that the evaluation task was 'to display the educational process in ways which enable people to engage it with their hearts and minds'. He was clear where the deficit lay: 'The "heart" of judgement is rarely acknowledged in conventional definitions of evaluation purpose, which speak clinically of providing decision data for the continuation, revision or termination of a program.' This book tries to get to the heart of the matter.

I have written this book in such way as to carry the reader through an argument which is laid out in the first three chapters and illustrated with practical examples in subsequent chapters. The book is 'of a piece', best read, I think, from Overture to Coda. Nonetheless, the first three chapters do have a particular identity; they are intellectual, historical, philosophical and political contexts to what comes later. In these terms they lay out a case for a form of methodological individualisms 'personalization'.

Chapters 4 to 8 (inclusive) provide more practical expressions of the argument and invite the reader to take an intimate look at the practice of program evaluation – bearing in mind all the time the tension between person and program. These chapters deal with observation, interview, forms of representation, ethics and reflexivity. In contemporary parlance they deal with 'participation' and 'inclusivity' – though this is *not* an argument for 'participatory evaluation' *per se*.

1

Personalizing Program Evaluation

Item from an evaluation report:

A leading arts administrator was considering making an award to support a policy seminar for the arts. They had received a request from the Director of an ambitious and radical innovatory course in a London Conservatoire who was looking for opportunities to extend his innovatory reach. The administrator wrote a letter which ended – 'we consider that the seminar should be concerned not only with "providing a starting point for deriving guiding principles" but should also seek to determine the units in which the benefits of art to education and indeed to the wider community can be expressed.'

At about the same time I, as the evaluator of that same Conservatoire innovation, was sitting talking to two young women students who, as part of the innovatory course, had recently been running music workshops in a hospice for the terminally ill. Lucy was saying that she had been touched and changed by the experience, whereas Ann said she would probably not think about it were I not asking the question. But Lucy reminds us that in a rehearsal of their string quartet, shortly after leaving the hospice one time, Ann had sat crying and unable to play. So was it, I ask, an experience worth going through? Was it a 'good' experience? 'How can you say it was a success or a failure,' protests Lucy, 'when that sort of thing took place?' She raises her hands from the table in a gesture of insistence – 'She couldn't play!'

Lessons:

(a) There is no reason to suppose that having an evaluator around makes the issue of measurement more resolvable. (b) Lack of resolution does not presuppose failure of understanding. (c) Some people have more leverage than others over what counts as a reasonable measure of success and failure.

There is no ethical standard which says that the needs of the administrator (above) for guides to productivity have to take precedence over the need for Lucy and Ann to resolve their moral confusions – or, indeed, our need to learn from that. These are competing demands for evaluators,[1] and though we often try to service both there are strong political and contractual pressures on us to give priority to the former. And, also, we have to live with the methodological contradictions they imply and resolve them in our work and with limited resources. The field of program evaluation is well served by advice on how to achieve the former, that is, how to support administrative decision making and judge the productivity of programs; less so with advice on how to withstand the complexities and demands of accomplishing the second, that is, making sense of the experience of Lucy and Ann. This book is a small contribution to righting that balance.

I do not propose a new methodology, much less a paradigm – indeed, I will argue that a large element of methodology is personal construct, and so resists generalization. What I am concerned with is to offer a *stance*, a way of mobilizing a concern with people in the practice of program evaluation. In fact, I will argue later that to pursue such a concern, that is, to assume that there may be a divergence of interest between programs and their participants and to prioritize the dilemmas of the latter, will sometimes involve freeing evaluators from the narrow constraints of methodology. Of course, evaluators are usually bound by contracts and we can rarely avoid that. But these are not the only bindings; there are other, more subtle ones, which are more tractable, and these are the ones I am concerned with.

PROGRAMS

By a program, I mean an attempt to put certain policies or ideas into action by dedicating resources to a specified purpose, creating responsible roles, giving it a management structure and a form of organization – usually encompassing multiple sites – and, sometimes, by giving it a chronological shape, if only start and finish dates. I am talking about programs of reform or innovation. A program is a significant event.[2]

---

1 Stake (1977: 161) has always been unequivocal about the tension between focusing on product and process: 'What the evaluator has to say cannot be both a sharp analysis of high-priority achievement *and* a broad and accurate reflection of the program's complex transactions. One message crowds out the other.'

2 Rossi and Freeman (1989) talk of social programmes as *'laboratories of change'* – emphasizing the enthusiasm with which social scientists realized that in housing, education

Examples of educational programs might be: government introducing a literacy curriculum to schools; a national curriculum for teacher training; the sector-wide development of information strategies in higher education; the devolution of budgets to schools for local management. The Conservatoire innovation of which Ann and Lucy were members started life as a small innovatory course but grew in scope and influence to become a program. We will hear more of it later.

A key element of programs is that they are sites of learning – for individuals and professsional groups who are embraced by them, but also for society at large, usually represented by administrative systems or political representatives. Educational programs are educational in themselves as well as dealing substantively with educational issues, for through observing their workings and their fate we learn much about the tolerances and, therefore, the limitations of the democracies which host them. Programs often embody visions of social futures – or, at least a receding view of flawed pasts.

There is a vigorous publishing market for program evaluation as this has emerged and expanded as a profession and a discipline. Many of the methodological advances made in the field of educational evaluation have grown out of and into our experience of working with programs – that is, at this level of social action – often in confronting the limitations of scientific method. This is partly because evaluators, like other social scientists, have been intrigued and heartened by the opportunity of working with significant units of social action – units, that is to say, which are large enough to constitute a meaningful experiment and which, in themselves, are complex enough to represent society at large. Programs are microcosms of democratic society in that they have power structures, advocate policies, embody relations between citizens and elites, reveal political priorities through their resourcing decisions and have cultural characteristics – each evaluation, therefore, is a case study of the social contract.

Early in the emergence of program evaluation Weiss and Rein (1969) argued that social and educational programs are best characterized as having 'broad aims', which make them inappropriate for simple

---

and community development programmes they had what the natural scientists had always enjoyed – controlled experimental conditions for observing cause and effect relationships. No wonder the social programme was, in the earliest years of evaluation, defined within the limits allowed by what passed for scientific method; and no wonder, too, that by the methodologically stormy decade of the 1970s evaluators were beginning to reign in their enthusiasm, somewhat unnerved – at least in the USA – by the mismatch between the frailty of their conclusions and their legislative clout (Cronbach, 1975; Rivlin, 1973).

comparative tests of achievement against objectives, or for assuming that their variables can be controlled through experimental artifice. The kinds of dilemmas posed by Lucy and Ann, the tension between our need to assure the productive value of social spending, on the one hand, and the frailties of measurement on the other, point to the inevitability of broad aims and demand complexity in the assessment of social value. They strike at the heart of our continuing attempts to sustain the innovatory project of liberal democracy, for this tension reflects the central tension of political culture – the competing needs to sustain systems while respecting individuals. While remaining faithful to our responsibilities to fulfil our contracts, that is, to report on the particularities of a program, there is no need to limit either the range of learnings available from it, nor to limit the potential range of interested audiences, for program evaluation has the obligation to work at both sides of that cultural tension – to serve an instrumental and essentially economic purpose, but also to ease humanistic understanding.

PLURALIST APPROACHES TO PROGRAM EVALUATION

The attempt to pursue broad aims started relatively early in the emergence of evaluation as a discipline and as a discrete field of political action. Norris (1990) and House (1993) document the broad history of what House calls 'pluralistic' approaches to evaluation, that is, those approaches which seek to generate and publicize as many program perspectives as possible and which Norris (using Michael Quinn Patton's term) labels 'situationally responsive'. There were, throughout the 1970s and 1980s, a series of transatlantic invited seminars[3] held at Cambridge University, England which were dedicated to synthesizing the early encounters of evaluators with these methodologies.[4] Their broad methodological aims were

---

3 For an account of the first of these see MacDonald and Walker (1973).
4 This was a period of widespread repositioning in educational enquiry and these seminars, though clearly important and influential, were not unique. In the USA, for example, the North Dakota Group was busy holding their own evaluation meetings to question some conventional evaluation approaches; the 'Reconceptualists' were meeting to discover a radical position on curriculum theory and created the *Journal of Curriculum Theorising*; shortly into the period Lee Cronbach assembled his team to produce the influential text on the 'Reform of Programme Evaluation'; in Britain, again, the sociologists and the educational psychologists were busy repositioning themselves in relation to the curriculum reform movements and these new methodological and political developments – Rob Walker (1980) had written 'you can study children, teachers or schools without necessarily engaging in the study of their pscyhology, sociology, history, anthropology or ecology'.

summarized in a manifesto that was produced following the first flush of enthusiasm at having apparently spawned a movement, and are quoted by Helen Simons (1980: 5), a participant at these seminars and one of the documenters of the emergence of case study:

to be:
- responsive to the needs and perspectives of different audiences;
- illuminative of the complex organisational, teaching and learning processes at issue;
- relevant to public and professional decisions forthcoming; and
- reported in a language which is accessible to [their] audiences.

In today's terms these might sound unassuming – indeed, render each in its negative and there would be few supporters. In 1972 when they were written, however, they represented a fundamental challenge to evaluation (and research) canons, for they were to lead to radical approaches to validation, generalization, sampling and theorizing – four key pillars of scientific enquiry. They came to imply an erosion of confidence in internal validity in favour of external (respondent/practitioner) validity – as well as confusing issues of reliability and verification with case study precepts of idiosyncrasy and uniqueness of context; they took generalization out of the realms of formal procedures for inference and comparison and into the unchartered territory of the 'science of the singluar'; they were to lead to developmental (as opposed to pre-ordinate) sampling, and to sampling as a process of questioning rather than confirming the relationship between a case and its class; and from the very start they generated a scepticism with formal theory in favour of practical, situationally located theory.

Principal among the early British expressions of such enquiry values was the influential paper by Parlett and Hamilton (1977), which introduced 'illuminative evaluation' to recapture the missing complexities of program process – 'it becomes imperative to study an innovation through its medium of performance', and the SAFARI publications which emanated from CARE at the University of East Anglia. These publications (MacDonald and Walker, 1974; Norris, 1985) emerged from a program of evaluation of curriculum reform which itself provided a basis for methodological development. Out of his early experiences of developing and using case study, Barry MacDonald (1987, but reprinted from an earlier paper) generated his model of *Democratic Evaluation*, which set out a core of political ethics that remains influential today, dealing with negotiation, confidentiality, impartiality and information exchange. MacDonald contended that evaluators had to find their place in the interplay of power and interests that characterizes programs, and argued forcibly for an impartial (i.e. 'neutral broker') stance. Though developed in contrast with two other ideal-types – Bureaucratic and Autocratic Evaluation – it is worth quoting at length MacDonald's (1987: 45) characterization of Democratic Evaluation:

> Democratic Evaluation is an information service to the community about the characteristics of an educational program. Sponsorship of the evaluation does not in itself confer a special claim upon this service. The democratic evaluator recognises value pluralism and seeks to represent the range of interests in his issue formulation. The basic value is an informed citizenry, and the evaluator acts as broker in exchanges of information between groups who want knowledge of each other. His techniques of data gathering and presentation must be accessible to non-specialist audiences. His main activity is the collection of definitions of, and reactions to, the program. He offers confidentiality to informants and gives them control over the use of the information they provide. The report is non-recommendatory, and the evaluator has no concept of information misuse. The evaluator engages in periodic negotiation of his relationships with sponsors and program participants. The criterion of success is the range of audiences served. The report aspires to 'best-seller' status. The key concepts of Democratic Evaluation are 'confidentiality', 'negotiation' and 'accessibility'. The key justificatory concept is 'the right to know'.

There was a natural fit between this political ethic and case study methodologies. Much of the early work on developing evaluation case study was conducted by Rob Walker, who worked closely with MacDonald. He wrote 'from the commitment to the belief that the subject being studied can impose its own authority on the sense that is made of it by the investigator' (Walker, 1980: 224). Simons (1987) gives both a historical account of these developments and a detailed account of the stresses and strains of taking a case study approach in evaluation. It was this community of evaluators – many of them worked together at the Centre for Applied Research in Education – in which I was trained, and which represents my invisible college.

The invisible college of evaluation pluralists is wider, of course, and in the USA these works paralleled those by other Cambridge seminarists – Bob Stake, Louis Smith, Myron Atkin, Howard Becker – and, of course, seminal contributions from such as Lee Cronbach, Gene Glass, Ernest House, Carol Weiss, Elliot Eisner and later Egon Guba with Yvonna Lincoln, Michael Quinn Patton and others. The people who contributed to this 'movement' were not just theoreticians – they tested and developed their ideas in practice. It should be no surprise that they received, often substantial, sponsorship to mount case study evaluations, for while they were appealing to values in social justice – not frequently an operational priority for evaluation sponsors – they were also deeply concerned with utilization (as the extract from the manifesto above shows).[5] Much of the argument for case study or naturalistic evaluation approaches was based on a failure of conventional approaches to, in Parlett and Hamilton's terms, 'articulate with the varied concerns and questions of participants, sponsors and other interested parties'.

There is an implicit thread which runs through case study theory, infrequently addressed and rarely exploited for the challenge it makes to conventional theory, and this is where I locate my argument. Case study is rooted in existentialism, especially the existential commitment to description of current states and the assertion that pasts and futures only have meaning in the here-and-now (the 'ever-present present', as it is sometimes put). Existential philosophy is suspicious of general theory for its attempt to extrapolate beyond the particularities of· the present (see Schon's expression of this principle[6]). And, too, the existential concern to discover more authentic states than those forced upon us by social life was transferred to case study evaluation. This became expressed in concerns such as to look behind the role to the person; to conduct 'real time' field-based studies; to assert the particularities of context; and by the urgency to use interview and observation to reveal the dilemmas of program people to drive evaluation theorizing with direct experience.

Though these new approaches[7] were often articulated as 'alternative' or 'complementary' approaches to, for example, the dominant experimental design, they were, in practice, enmeshed in oppositional struggle with them – principally through the attack on general as opposed to

---

5   So, for example, in the 1970s, Stake was sponsored by the National Science Foundation in the USA to mount a major evaluation of science education which was based largely on 11 school case studies; MacDonald was sponsored by the British education ministry to evaluate the largest ever multi-ministry programme for the development of educational technology – the National Development Programme for Computer-Assisted Learning.

6   'The here and now provides the test, the source and the limit of knowledge. No theory drawn from past experience may be taken as literally applicable to *this* situation, nor will a theory based on the experience of this situation prove literally applicable to the next situation. But theories drawn from other situations may provide perspectives or "projective models" for this situation, which help to shape it and permit action within it. However, this process of existential theory-building must grow out of the experience of the here-and-now of this situation, must be nourished and tested against it' (Schon, 1971: 231).

7   For example, 'Responsive' for Stake (e.g. 1975); 'Democratic' for MacDonald (1987); 'Goal-free' for Scriven (1974); 'Illuminative' for Parlett and Hamilton (1977); 'Policy-oriented, Reformist' for Cronbach et al. (1985); 'Stakeholder' for Weiss (1983); 'Utilisation-focused' for Patton (1997); 'Connoisseur' for Eisner (1985); 'Empowerment' for Fetterman (1997); 'Constructivist' for Guba and Lincoln (1989).

situational theory-building. To propose radically new methodologies is to challenge power bases among academics and researchers. People build careers on experimental design and research council funds are limited. So, conferences were split in controversy, reputations were attacked, sponsorship was hotly competed. This was healthy insofar as it exposed debate between competing views on the ethics and politics of evaluation; healthier, perhaps, than where such debate is suppressed by too easy an assumption that the two schools can be integrated in a methodological melting-pot.

THE 'FINE-GRAIN' IN PROGRAM EVALUATION

Thomas Cook (1997), one of the principal US actors in the reform of experimental approaches to program evaluation, picks up the struggle between what he terms 'quantitative' and 'qualitative' approaches – what has, elsewhere, been called a 'paradigm war' (Guba and Lincoln, 1994). Cook argues that qualitative approaches have achieved legitimacy and, he says, it is time to move on from what is perhaps too simplistically thought of as the 'qualitative-versus-quantitative' debate – in fact, towards better evaluation theory, more synthesizing studies drawing together findings from program evaluations, and a continuing preoccupation with methods. He calls for a repositioning of evaluation in relation to the methodological debate.

His concern is principally with the failure of program evaluation to match up to its social obligations to help understand, for example, ways of better tackling poverty. Compared, for example, with our persistent failure to evaluate the commercialization of public services, continued debates over the merits of 'quantitative' versus 'qualitative' methodologies are distractions.[8] Nonetheless, it is worth noting that recent

---

8   This is not an uncommon position in the late 1990s. Pawson and Tilley (1998), for example, are dismissive of paradigm wars as irrelevant to the issues of program evaluation. They claim that significant differences in evaluation emerge in design – that it is only when one evaluation design 'rubs up against' another that we can engage in meaningful comparison and contrast. There are flaws with this empiricist argument. It is a conservative position to argue that design and methodology are coterminous, and few would deny that at least some aspects of evaluation methodology need to be 'responsive' and, therefore, emergent (as I argue extensively later in this book). Evaluation cannot (as Pawson and Tilley themselves acknowledge) ignore context. But, like Cook, they overlook what House and others whom I also explore later have written – that methodology is informed by social justice values. The whole point of paradigm wars is that this is precisely what they are – struggles between worlds of meaning, epistemological systems. Of course design

methodological conflicts around constructivism and postmodernism have had some impact on the way we view the individual, and there has yet to emerge a robust response from the evaluation community. Later, for example, I will look at the problem for social justice of the recent attacks on key notions of the integrated self, authenticity in experience and the coherence of judgement across contexts.

Cook's argument about synthesizing studies is important, and rests upon an interesting paradox. The tendency for individual evaluation studies, he says, is to paint pessimistic pictures of what is possible and achieved by programs; whereas studies reviewing the experience of many programs – often meta-evaluations – tend to reveal positive impact, albeit smaller than wished for. The question, presumably, is whether the synthesis study is more accurate by virtue of screening out biases and narrow focuses in individual, small-scale studies; or whether, on the other hand, the broad review is too coarse-grained to pick up the subtleties of program complexity and, itself, constitutes a methodological bias on a grand scale.

I am, too, concerned to move beyond the quantitative/qualitative debate and I want, principally, to focus in on shortcomings of the 'qualitative' tendency. Unlike Cook, however, I want to do this by looking in more fine-grain detail at program experience and not by moving to an aggregate level of analysis or even to the notion of program success or failure. I will be arguing for evaluators approaching programs through the experience of individuals rather than through the rhetoric of program sponsors and managers. I want to emphasize what we can learn about programs from Lucy and Ann. This does not mean ignoring the rights of program managers and sponsors with access to evaluation. There is no case for using evaluation against any stakeholder group; though there is a case for asserting a compensatory principle in favour of those who start out with relatively lower levels of access to evaluation. I don't think there is a serious risk of evaluators losing touch with their contractual obligations to report on programs and to support program management and improvement; I don't think there is a danger that evaluators will ever lose their preoccupation with program effects. There is always a risk, however, that evaluators lose their contact with people; and a danger that in our concern to report on programs and their effects we

---

reflects those same struggles, but the quantitative/qualitative or positivistic/structuralist or structuralist/constructivist debates are important as major conflicts over competing definitions of social justice – albeit the instruments of war are blunt and poorly crafted for the task.

lose sight of the pluralism of programs. So my arguments will robustly assert the need to address 'the person' in the program. For me, the solution to Cook's paradox is clear: the further away we are from individuals the easier it is to be decisive and to assert precision. The finer the grain of the methodological capture – that is, the closer to the individual – the closer we draw to the impossibility of closure.

Indeed, this is an area in which program evaluators have lagged behind methodological developments elsewhere; evaluation has not yet repositioned itself in relation to influential debates stimulated by post-modernism and post-structuralism (Adelman, 1996).[9] In so doing, I want to pursue another of Cook's sub-themes. He argues that evaluation has failed to provide a public voice in debates about social programs and social justice – partly through the fragmentation of the evaluation community into those preoccupied with education and those with economic concerns.

> Public rhetoric about social programs is more global, pessimistic and poor-bashing than is warranted by the cumulative social science evidence, yet there is no countervailing voice from the evaluation community, myself included. Should we not play a special role in public debates like these, given the close correspondence between the issues being debated and evaluation's core function of generating cumulative knowledge about social programs? (Cook, 1997: 39–40)

One of the key arguments of case study advocates has been that what has been too frequently missing in program evaluation has been the voice of the program participant and the citizen and that this has a tendency to erode the ethic of the evaluation enterprise. It is significant, for example, that MacDonald almost immediately followed up his seminal paper outlining a Democratic approach to evaluation with a paper (1985) entitled 'The Portrayal of Persons as Evaluation Data', in which he argued that evaluation should take 'the experience of the program participants as the central focus of investigation'.

In the persistent difficulty evaluators face in accomplishing this lies a latent source of unfairness and injustice built into the fabric of program evaluation for it tends to favour the voice of those few for whom programs are useful instruments to advance their careers and their economic power. For the majority of people implicated by or involved in a program, the concept 'program' is barely understood and may

9 Although feminist discourse is having some impact – especially in the USA.

even be irrelevant to their lives. Or, more to the point, it represents an opportunity irrelevant to their interests and their opportunities. It is not hard to see, for example, that the concept of 'program' is likely to be more meaningful to the arts administrator who seeks 'units of benefit' than to Ann and Lucy – or, indeed, to the terminally ill patients they worked with. The value invested in the notion of a program has a negative effect on the distribution of both resources and opportunities – perhaps more significantly, it has a negative effect on what Berger (1974) calls 'the calculus of meaning' – that is, the distribution of opportunities for people to live in what to them is a meaningful world. For some, to be embraced by a program is a reaffirmation of what is meaningful while for others it is merely falling into the embrace of someone else's dilemma. But what is, perhaps, worrying is that meanings represented by programs sometimes might only exist in certain contexts because evaluators persistently evoke them through their questioning.

One of the costs of this (necessary since contractual) focus on programs rather than on experience has been that evaluation has been strongly influenced by the forms of thinking and discourse of program managers and has, as a result, been restricted in its purview and intolerant of others' rights to meaningfulness. For example, a powerful metaphor that has underpinned the emergence of program evaluation has been that of 'service' – service, that is, to decision-makers and other 'stakeholders'. For some writers on evaluation this has led to a dominant focus on the 'use' or the 'utilization' of evaluation by administrators and by the political community (Patton, 1997); for others it has led to seeing evaluation as an alternative form of social action. When the two are combined there can be discerned a tone sometimes of indignation or at least dismay in response to successive claims that key decision makers rarely succumb to the influence of reported evaluations.

Our tendency to focus on the image of social organization as represented in programs has led to the loss of the image of the individual. What might program evaluation look like and involve were we to invert the conventional relationship between individual and program – that is, rather than document the program and 'read' the lives of individuals in that context; to document the lives and work of people and to use that as context within which to 'read' the significance and meaning of programs? Program evaluation voicing the concerns of individuals (and groups of individuals) can be an instrument for giving pause to policies that seek to apply universal treatments. Here is an alternative to the 'service' notion of evaluation. There are times – certainly in response to Cook's concerns for evaluators to be more engaged with the distributive impact of policies – when the most useful outcome of evaluation is the overwhelming of decision making with the complexities of human experience, for example, when social justice is served by delaying action.

In one sense, this might be timely for evaluation theory, which has, to some extent, been bypassed by contemporary interest in biography and the marginal voice. However, it is important to say – and I will explain this – that when I talk of focusing on the individual I am not talking of biographical enquiry or of the mere application of life-history research. There are two principal reasons for this. First, questioning the methodological bias towards reading experience through the lens – that is, the priorities and the values – of programs does not mean losing the social program as the principal focus for evaluation analysis and critique. To reiterate, I am not advocating subverting contracts – though I would advocate educating sponsors and negotiating more freedom within contracts than we might otherwise do. Evaluation as an applied form of policy research is principally interested in those organizational forms we create to package new ideals and innovatory strategies. We should seek to understand programs through experience – not displace them with it. I am assuming that evaluation sponsors and program managers have as much to learn from personalized accounts as anyone else.

My second reason for not simply conflating biographical research and life-history with program evaluation is that these methodological tools are precisely that – tools. They cannot – in spite of occasionally ambitious claims – replace methodology *in the field of evaluation*. What I am interested in are individuals in their institutional and political contexts. I seek to focus on individual experience, but as an element in the interaction of institutional cultures – the tension between individualism and collectivism, between action and context. Barry MacDonald (1985) chose to develop Stake's notion of 'portrayal' as portraiture of people-in-context – that is, people in their contemporary institutional contexts rather than merely in the context of their lives: people as keyholes through which to discern power structures, for example.

We need to know more about Lucy and Ann – and about the arts administrator – and we need to know them as individuals. To understand something of their lives and values may help us understand, not just the significance of the program they are part of, but something, also, of its potential, for programs can only work through their participants, and they are generally frustrated by their resistance and conservatism. But what I think we need most of all – since this is an evaluative and not a research context – is to know something of how they arrive at judgements, how those judgements are mediated through association with others, and are prejudiced or favoured by the way individuals relate to power.

I will argue later that this refocusing of evaluation methodology involves a significant theoretical inversion which, briefly, looks like this. Any evaluation pursues a given logic (House, 1980). A key feature of that logic is a *theory of coherence*, that is, what makes a piece of data look more like a piece of evidence (towards an argument); what makes one piece of data relate to another. The telling point behind the story of the arts administrator and Lucy and Ann is that meeting their distinct information needs and portraying the different worlds of meaning they each live in does not imply discrete analyses – separate, as it were, evaluation projects. Their stories are contingent one upon the other, they are part of the same analysis – that is, the problem of measurement of impact. (Hence, portrayal rather than biography.)

This theory of coherence is often, in evaluative enquiry, taken from the innovation theory carried about by the evaluator or by the rhetoric of the program or by a mix of both.[10] Evaluators share with program managers and sponsors a value in programs and the logics that hold them together – we all make our money and careers through them (Weiss, 1987). But to refocus evaluation on individual experience involves yielding that theory of coherence in favour of a sense of coherence drawn from our respondents in evaluation. Seemingly unconnected events and phenomena may be quite coherent in the life and against the values of the individual whose life is momentarily embraced by the program's activities. The challenge for evaluation is not to lose sight of innovation theory and program rhetoric – that is, what we use conventionally to make sense of data – but to seek out and then to understand their reciprocal forms in the lives of those we evaluate. A unified theory of coherence, as it were, combines both.

METHODOLOGICAL CONSERVATISM AND RENEWAL

In advocating the 'personalization' of evaluation, I have in mind both the person of the evaluator and that of the individual being evaluated. In

---

10 'Program theory', says Weiss (1998: 321), 'includes the processes of program implementation . . . and the desired outcomes . . . and then hypothesises about the mechanisms that link processes to outcomes . . . the evaluator can use the program theory as scaffolding for the study.'

each case I place a premium on intellectual autonomy which I argue is constantly threatened by a conservative approach to evaluation methodology. The specific audience for the book is those who might make a difference in evaluative enquiry. This implies those who have not yet been socialized into evaluation convention – that is, research students, young evaluators and those professionals who may have substantial field experience but who come to evaluation anew. 'Young' research often takes place within powerful systems of patronage; supervisors have interests. This is a common limiting factor in the methodological independence of doctoral or post-doctoral research. In contract research the issue can be rediscovered in a more political form. Methodology can be a focus of struggle for ownership of the research between the 'patron' (the research director) and the (usually young) contract researcher. Either way, PhD and contract research are not flawless instruments for methodological renewal.

The condition of methodological independence for young researchers is important. Professionalism and specialization in educational enquiry inevitably leads to a domination of enquiry practices by powerful interest groups – professoriates, research sponsors, research managers, theorists – and such groups do not always favour methodological adventure.[11] This is to state little more than the commonplace that educational enquiry is conducted within a discrete community of values and interests regulated by power groupings, whose practices are suffused with the competitions and struggles typical of any such community. Norris (1995) shows how the interests of these power groupings in social research are increasingly being proscribed by narrow economic interests and coopted by government and official agencies.

This does not diminish the necessity for evaluation fieldworkers to be methodologists – not merely practitioners of methodology. We need to be able to think independently of methodology so as to use it as a site of reconciliation between our personal values as evaluators and the volatile characteristics of the field we are observing – and that ought to be part of the professional preparation of young researchers and doctoral students. We need to make methodology a striving to combine justice with intellectual autonomy, and to some extent this requires us to find our

---

11 Indeed, in the late 1970s Lawrence Stenhouse convened a conference at York University on Case Study – with the explicit purpose of foreshadowing the problem of a field of enquiry which would produce students faster than it would produce people to supervise them. His claim that this would generate a conflict of power with methodological development was strongly contested by a prestigious education professor who was present at a plenary session.

own 'voices' in enquiry, as well as continuing the search for better ways of giving voice to those we evaluate and acknowledging the changing complexities of their lives. We should be especially concerned with voices which are otherwise marginalized.

To balance the expression of our personal values with the discipline required to sustain a viable ethic with being responsive to the experience and the values of those whose lives and work we observe is no mean feat. It is, though, an essential strategy to free the professional practice of evaluation from the constraints of its own methodological orthodoxies and systems of patronage. New evaluators are more likely to produce methodological innovations than are veterans. To seek our own 'voice' in enquiry blows us in the direction of personal advocacy; while to seek merely to 'give voice to others' risks abandoning responsibility for the discourses we help to create, and threatens to dislocate our actions from our values.

I am not, then, arguing merely for advocacy. Stake (1997) struggles with the overwhelming reality of the drift in evaluation in this direction. His backdrop is a society in which education is valued less and less, and where educational argument is losing its persuasiveness in the face of more direct (e.g. advertising) appeals to the citizenry. Despairing of the demise of the authority of educational argument we evaluators are reluctant to 'separate . . . findings from yearnings' (Stake, 1997: 401), and so use our studies to nurture what we see as wholesome and worthwhile activities and ideas. In seeking to protect, we argue.

I do not deny the allegation. However, I see this neither as presaging the inevitable 'fall from grace' of the impartial evaluator, nor as a trap that cannot be avoided with an appropriate political strategy.[12] The problem persists and has to be managed through practice. The intrusion of our values is a condition of our work which has to be taken into methodological account. I accept the reality of personal advocacy but not necessarily its legitimacy.[13]

---

12 An alternative is given by Donald Campbell (1999: 79), who is concerned that 'reforms are advocated as though they were certain to be successful,' and who wanted to put them back on an experimental footing. 'The problem can be reduced by two shifts in attitudes . . . One involves a political shift from the advocacy of a specific reform to the advocacy of the seriousness of the problem.' This is surer ground for the impartial evaluator.

13 Scriven (1999) recently wrote about the nature of bias in evaluation and distinguished 'affective' from 'effective' bias. The former was the psychological or emotional pre-disposition we have; the latter, its impact on our actions. To neutralize the impact of the way we hold a prejudice, e.g. to legislate against racist practices – is more realizable than seeking to eradicate the bias. It is possible to be a racist but to not act in a racist way.

Just as intriguing may be the case of evaluators who may use instruments of enquiry that do not express well either their own reasons for engaging in it or the nature of the enquiry field itself. 'No problem', argues House (1990: 23), 'is more difficult and complex in the social sciences than that of how values are embedded within the research methodologies that we employ'. His argument is that we cannot be neutral as to social justice for our methodologies will inevitably take a stand on our behalf. Rather, we need to examine our methodologies to understand better how they help to create options to enhance or erode social justice. His example is drawn from methodologies linking cranial research to theories of human development and intelligence. It might as well have been an example of cost–benefit analysis, say, applied to the question of class-sizes.[14]

Hence, there may be cases where an evaluation driven by a desire to enhance social justice employs instruments and methods which are, in themselves, unjust and promote inequality – standardized language tests in bilingual education programs; school improvement measures applied universally across diverse contexts; quantifiable performance indicators applied to social services.

Danziger (1990), on whom I will draw extensively in a following chapter, reminds us that forms of investigation have to be understood as forms of social organization – they do not happen outside of our institutions, our social relations, our politics and economics. Both argue that psychology has furnished us with archetypal research relationships – that is, between researcher and subject – but that these have been limited and distorted by institutional contexts in which psychology emerged and grew as a discipline. Research is cast in the image of the institutions which bear it and which husband it. These organizational contexts are not necessarily natural homes for methodological enquiry, or even, perhaps, for taking risks in pursuit, for example, of social justice. This refers to both the commercial research or consultancy firm and to the modern university, each of whom are vulnerable to their market reputation and generally lack funds to support researchers who might have taken a risk that back-fired.

Writing as far back as 1965, Harvey Brooks, Harvard Professor of Physics, noted that 'the whole trend of modern scholarship has been towards greater conservatism in deciding what can be legitimately

---

14 Carol Weiss (1987) argues that where evaluators employ methodologies which give them partial – blinkered – views of complex events they lose control of the political nature and implications of the assumptions they make.

inferred from given evidence' (p. 71). His concern was reinforced in the field of educational enquiry by, for example, Cronbach's (1975) influential critique of the attempt to marry experimental and correlational research, and Glass's (1978) attack on the standards movement – both of whom pointed to the constraints on educational understanding of a hegemonic belief in precision and an insistence on significance filters. More recently we have endured a further wave of conservatism in relation to inferential practices from the sceptics of postmodernism and post-structuralism who promote scepticism about the construct validity of all evidence.

Of course, conservatism is a product of growing respect for evidence, as Brooks points out, but it also has something to do with growing sophistication in the *use* of evidence. The more we are accustomed to working with evidence, to ground our investigations in practical concerns, and as our work is acknowledged as 'useful' (i.e. utilizable), so we seek to classify it and protect it – we mark it out and stake claims to it. The evidence and access to its sources can become interlaced with our careers because there is a living to be made out of useful knowledge. Differentiation and specialization in enquiry can lead to territoriality which, itself, encourages a patrolling of the boundaries of a discipline – this is *psychological* knowledge of classrooms, this is *mathematical* knowledge of them, this is *educational* and this *sociological*. Here are some roots of the patronage system within which young researchers are inducted into research. The combination of patronage, a disciplinary base and a conservationist view of methodology is not conducive to risk-taking.

Another element of the context which threatens the independence of young researchers is the growing commercialization of enquiry – a result of the declining economy of higher education, government pressure to make social research serve the interests of wealth creation, and the rapid growth of competition for research resources from the private sector. Partially as a result of all of these, the research manager has assumed a prominent role. This is a person for whom methodology has to have both an epistemological and an economic justification; we often have to balance the needs of the enquiry with the needs of the contract researchers we employ – and these with the political economy of our organization. This means we tend to look for problems that suit our approaches and try to construe other problems in a similar way. The research manager seeks to control her resources to squeeze best value for money, and this has led to increasingly demanding conditions for young researchers (in exchange for fragile contracts of employment) who, as a consequence, have little time for methodological adventure and little confidence for risk-taking. These are very different conditions to those under which I completed my own evaluation training. Universities, in any event organized for undergraduate teaching rather than for research, are not, by nature, comfortable homes for researchers. As strapped for cash as universities currently are, neither are they always friendly places for the aspiring dissenter.[15]

House (1993) gives an account of the growth of evaluation as a discipline and envelops it in a theory of the development of scientific disciplines (drawn largely from Toulmin). In his view, ideas belong to generations and adapt to the tastes and demands of new generations, each of which has to earn its spurs in the regulatory framework of peer review, argumentation and persuasion – 'each generation re-creates the discipline anew', and he talks of young researchers as 'apprentices'. Where a new generation comes up with new ways of thinking about the discipline – to respond to new problem-definitions – 'it is necessary,' he argues, 'to have professional forums to generate and discuss the various concepts, to discuss how to attack new problems and what new concepts are worth accepting' (p. 83). Here is the patrolling of boundaries.

We can, of course, use the same evidence to talk of power systems.[16] Those forums House talks of can also function as conservative agents capable of distorting and frustrating change *in unwarranted ways,* just as much as they play that essential function of disciplinary quality assurance.[16] The apprenticeship model – an appropriate descriptor of doctoral research – emerged in industrial society as a pedagogy of conservation designed to replicate the teaching of the fathers. It was not the job of an apprentice to look for new ways of doing things.

House does not account for the micropolitics of contestation – how apprentices and their potential contributions are too often suppressed, or, as often, engage in self-suppression. They are sometimes excluded from those forums House mentions; some will tend, by the very nature of social enquiry, to be moving a methodological step ahead of their supervisors and either constitute a threat or risk being misunderstood;

---

15   See Schratz and Walker, 1995: ch. 7 for a similar argument. They focus on problems of sustaining fair supervision of research students.
16   See Danziger (1990), for example, for an account of how the discipline of psychology was hijacked by powerful insider groups and distorted to meet the narrow interests of educational administrators determined to bend schools to social differentiation; Karier, Violas and Spring (1973) on the same theme but portraying psychology as serving the corporate state; and, for sheer enjoyment, read (Hazen, 1988) for an account of how the forums House speaks of – in this case leading international journals – are commonly used by researchers, in this case in the lucrative field of superconductor research, to conceal theoretical advances for financial gain.

they are usually economically vulnerable and dependent on patron-age; they are vulnerable to being overwhelmed by the accomplishments of their supervisors. In the current economic climate in which research funding is cut to the bone young researchers' salaries are falling and the demands made on them so as to cut the costs of research are rising. In short, the conditions of much doctoral supervision are more those of control than sceptical and paternalistic curiosity in their alternative views.

LOSING THE DOTS: METHODOLOGICAL IMPROVISATION

A key instrument of control is methodological discourse. House (1993: 83) follows Toulmin by describing evaluation learning as 'enculturation' and argues that 'novices cannot become proficient without knowing how to use the techniques and procedures'. Hence, methodological texts tend to be written as prescriptions – sometimes as proscriptions – and the doctoral student tends to meet them as a broadside of powerful advocacy. Theses and dissertations are screened by examiners for their grasp of the relevant research literature and for consciousness by the student of how her research is located within the general field. This is, of course, a quality assurance mechanism, a reassurance that advances are grounded in what is already known. Although it inevitably acts as a drag on innovation, a historical grasp is essential to its full and proper conceptualization. But we cannot lose sight of the essential contradiction which this implies. Let me explain with the use of a salient (to this book) metaphor and a reference to music improvisation.

We require of young professional music aspirants that they are proficient at both playing from the score and at improvising, and this expresses a more fundamental requirement that they have been immersed in music traditions to a point where they are 'comfortable' with them; and that they can be capable of music innovation, that is, that they can express their ideas as well as others. (For many professors recognition is a constantly resurgent need, not an accomplishment.) But there is a peculiar cognitive effect, it seems, which is familiar to many conservatoire teachers, in which proficiency in playing from a score comes at the price of dependency.[17] This tension has been one of the

---

17   This cannot be minimized as a problem; when Yehudi Menuhin recorded those jazz albums with Stephan Grappelli he purportedly had to script his 'improvised' solos. And, too, there are few pianists who have the confidence to freely improvise those Mozart cadenzas left for personal interpretation.

commonest sources of discomfort for musicians – professional and trainee – throughout my music education evaluations.

The problem is a serious one, for it has more to do than with just the motor skills of learning to read 'the dots' and then learning not to read them. Music scores are sources of authority and ownership, they are the creations of others – there is moral ownership involved – and the nearest a musician can get to ownership for themselves is by contributing a personal interpretation. This is achieved successfully (students are frequently told) by only a chosen few – and these are people who, as they play, can forget the score, shift to a higher cognitive level and *improvise* (that is, with the mood or the spirit of the piece). The score is a constant reminder to most musicians how weak they are in the contest for ownership of original music: how their creative talents have to be ignited by the expression of others.

Let me stay with this analogy for just a moment longer so as to illustrate it with the use of an example – though you can probably already see the shift I am about to make back into methodology. This is drawn from the evaluation I conducted at the Guildhall Conservatoire. A student, Val, is considering the experience of being asked by the innovation course to perform without her music stand. This presents her with an emotional challenge, but also with an opportunity. She searches to explain the feeling, and finally says that it is almost as though she saw herself afresh from the audience perspective – not sitting *with* the audience, but *behind* the audience, watching herself.

> It's easier to see it from the audience point of view – it just breaks down all the barriers and all the tensions – and the nerves become nerves for different reasons. Not because you'd like to play well, or it's just a big occasion and there are lots of people out there . . . 'I've got to play that A Sharp' or 'the reed is not working' . . . you get down to what really matters, which is playing to the people and sharing something and making it work.

We can read into this a sense of gaining some personal stake in the music that was not there beforehand. The music stand, as well as propping up the score, served to remind the student of the distance between her and the audience – that is, she belonged to the culture of music (was, perhaps, owned by it) and not to the public culture. We could take this further into an exploration of what improvisation means in identity terms – perhaps it would emerge as something more akin to taking responsibility for oneself. Whatever the case, we can see that having and losing the music score has implications for how we see ourselves as musicians.

I think a similar problem goes for evaluation methodology. For the reasons cited above we tend to teach young researchers to 'play it by the score' – at the very least, we are bound to induct them into the history of ideas, especially if we nurture hopes in them of methodological advancement. This means more than that we simply give them methods and ask them to apply them. As with musicians who learn their loss of independence from the score, so young researchers learn from methodological 'scores' about the accomplishments of the 'major composers' of theory; they learn that ownership of issues – even those as intimate as social relations in research, ethical dilemmas and reflexivity – has already been staked. This, while perhaps sometimes creating a sense of outrage and inciting a struggle for methodological freedom, also has a tendency to create a relationship of dependence. Quite apart from anything, the supervisor or research manager are members of the methodology 'owners club'. Why provoke them?

More worryingly, embracing young researchers within our culture of methodology (what Danziger calls *'methodolatry'*) runs the risk of reminding them that they are not of the public culture. The music stand for the music student, perhaps the research textbook and observation schedule for the research student, all have a tendency to take away from the individual a degree of responsibility for their own actions. In particular, I argue in this book, it takes away from people the responsibility to ensure that there is as close a match as conditions will allow between personal beliefs and methodological action – and, of course, that the two change and develop as far as possible in concert.

THREE EXEMPLARY EVALUATION PROJECTS

The argument of this book is set in the context of three evaluations I have conducted. What I try to achieve is to saturate that argument in the experience of doing evaluation and, of course, having it done to you. In later chapters you will read a lot of evaluation data. Notwithstanding the specificity of the examples I draw from, the aim is to generalize to program evaluation in whatever substantive area. I have conducted program evaluation in Higher Education, school curriculum, bilingual education policy, IT development and police training – I would maintain the same values and views in each one, and I could find similar exemplars in them. For purposes of consistency, however, all my examples are drawn from one field – music education – and from program evaluations for which I was responsible at the London Guildhall Conservatoire, the Royal Opera House and the City of Birmingham Symphony Orchestra. This allows me to draw data from a wide range of respondents – young children, students, professionals, senior administrators – all talking about similar events.

In each of the programs I was evaluating musicians, and music trainees were engaged in outreach programs, usually including school workshops. To reiterate, this is not a book on music education and nor is the argument confined to arts evaluation. Rather, the grounding of the argument in specific cases emphasizes a key part of my argument, which is that evaluation methodology is embedded in direct experience. Giving the reader some insight into one particular field of action allows me to exemplify the process of methodological construction. From there on I rely on 'naturalistic generalization'[18] – that is, the process by which this account provokes recognition and bump-starts thought and reflection in the reader.

For example, at one point I will give an observation of a young woman singing in a music competition and argue that this is an exemplary or essentialist observation on which I begin to build – through inference – a view of the conservatoire as an organization and then as a social institution. This is, of course, highly specific to the case of the music college – but it is not hard to think of other organizations (schools, hospitals, police stations) where highly focused observations of key practices help us to see images of organization. What I offer here is an exemplary analytical strategy – an archetypal observation.

Although my intention is not to confine my arguments to a substantive field, it is important to know something of the context from which data will be drawn. Though I can only give a brief sketch here, this will suffice to locate some of the ideas to which the evaluation was responding in each case.

(1) The Guildhall Conservatoire, London   This was an evaluation of the MPCS program. MPCS stands for Music Performance and Communication Skills. This was an innovatory program carried out (and evaluated by me) over a three-year period. It was designed to introduce curriculum and pedagogical changes to the music training culture, and from there, to begin to stimulate changes across the music-making professions. At a practical level, this program was centred on an elective course which required students to leave the Conservatoire to devise collaborative workshops in community institutions – schools, hospitals, prisons, youth

---

18 See Stake's (1995: 85–8) explanation, and the original reference. But see, also, Norris (1990: 131–5) for an extended critique.

clubs. The educational rationale was that through reflecting on these workshops students would discover alternative – more independent – ways of relating to their music and their creativity. At the political level this was intended to be (and to some extent proved to be) a challenge to established forms of power and organization that were structured around more conventional notions of creative production. (For example, one target group for the innovation was the professional orchestra, whose then crisis with their creativity was attributed in part to power inequalities which tended to suppress individual creativity among musicians.)

As radical and potentially destabilizing a force as this innovation was to be (and which was recognized at the time), it was embraced by the Guildhall Conservatoire. These were difficult and competitive times for the British conservatoire movement, which was facing cuts and possible closure by a crusading government intent on cutting educational spending. As controversial as the innovation might prove to be, it marked out the Guildhall as an innovatory and entrepreneurial institution. This was likely to give it – and it did – a competitive edge in the market for students.

This innovation reflected much of contemporary changes and movements in the music world at that time: the Thatcherite challenge to elite institutions; the assertion of community rights; the rise of notions of 'reflective practice' in the professions, given substantial impetus by the work of Donald Schon. It shares, therefore, many of the features (though pre-dating them) of the other two projects.

I spent the best part of three years evaluating this innovation, sponsored independently by the Leverhulme Trust. I shadowed the course on its travels, speaking with students, staff and those who came into contact with them, writing case studies of its work, observing its operation and the conservatoire in which it was hosted and I published reports. Barry MacDonald was the Director of this evaluation and it was his model of Democratic Evaluation which I sought to adapt to this context. My fieldwork was, in turn, influenced greatly by the pioneering and creative work of Rob Walker, who had been one of the group at the Centre for Applied Research in Education (CARE) which, in Britain, laid the foundations for evaluation case study.

(2) The City of Birmingham Symphony Orchestra (CBSO) The CBSO had an education outreach department run by an administrator. The core of its work was a program called the 'Adopt-a-Player Scheme'. Somewhat akin to the Guildhall innovation, this program was part of the movement which saw leading arts institutions seek out a working base in

local communities. Here, a collaborating (primary) school would 'adopt' an orchestral player who would run workshops in that school based around the theme of a major work. Once children had created and performed music pieces associated with the theme, they would visit the concert hall to hear the orchestra perform the whole work – one such example was a performance of *A Midsummer Night's Dream*. The rationale was that once the children saw their adopted player in the orchestra in the concert hall and related them to the person who had worked with them in workshops at school, this would de-mystify the orchestra and symphonic music. The educational rationale was not so developed as at the Guildhall and, for the most part, its sponsors and managers (including the local education authority/school district) had in mind the limited objective of building concert audiences for the future.

Most of the work of this project was carried out by school teachers who continued to work on the themes between visits by the orchestral players, whose main role would be to monitor and stimulate the music creations. Much of the educational impact of the scheme lay beyond their reach, as teachers sought ways of using the music theme to give a binding rationale to cross-curriculum activities. A broad conclusion of the evaluation was that the Adopt-a-Player Scheme had greater educational impact than was envisaged by its sponsors and participants.

I was commissioned by the Calouste Gulbenkian Foundation to write an evaluative story of this scheme, which I accomplished over a period of four or five months. The story was based on observation of workshops and meetings which formed the basis of conversations with teachers, musicians, administrators and, especially, young children.

(c) The Royal Opera House/Royal Ballet This prestigious institution also had an education department – here, very extensive, well-resourced and with an operational reach which spread across the whole country. The Education Department ran school workshops, large-scale opera projects in schools and the community, dance access schemes and workshops, open days and a range of other events, drawing from the performing companies for musicians, dancers, costumiers, singers and the like. This work had an uneasy and sometimes critical relationship to the core activities of 'the House', as, for some in the Department, was intended.

The relationship between the evaluation and the Education Department became uneasy, as the evaluation was seen to be avoiding the issues which interested the Department and, indeed, the House. The evaluation focused increasingly on the structural relationships between the Department and the performing companies and associated issues in the professional development of artistes; while the Department wanted a thoroughgoing analysis of educational interactions.

The evaluation was funded independently by the Esmeé Fairbairn Charitable Trust. Most of the fieldwork (once again, observation-based interviewing and shadowing the 'workshoppers') was conducted by my friend and colleague Richard Davies.

2

Love and Death and Program Evaluation

I want to look more closely at what educational programs represent and how we, as evaluators, relate to them. To do so I will come at the issues from a rather oblique angle – through a consideration of mortality. This is not merely an artifice, a playful disguise, as it were, for a more serious argument. It is, rather, based on a view that our sense of mortality and our fears of it are an understated but significant theme in our continuing struggle to construct a democratic society. Our fears and general avoidance of mortality are a rehearsal for our avoiding other forms of incompleteness and failure in life. Social programs are vehicles for the cooption of people into ideal, even utopian, political states, that is, states which too often represent the denial of complexity and shortfall. As Dollimore (1998: xxvii) puts it:

> In the last century fears of failure have intensified in proportion to the conviction that the social order can or should be engineered. These fears have been expressed as a heightened concern about the threat of social death – the fear that society is endangered . . .)

The difficulty we have of confronting the reality that programs will most often fall short of their desired goals is partly conditioned by our reluctance to concede failure – which is itself a condition of a collective denial of mortality represented in that notion of 'social death'. 'Modernity now intensifies and refines, now struggles against, now seeks to nullify that merciless immanence of death' (1998: xxviii), but has come to realize that 'change – or at least social change – can be controlled through praxis'. Praxis – taken to large proportion and extremes of ambition in Marxist and other revolutionary theory – is a form of action represented in a social program – what we evaluators evaluate.

This chapter is based on a presentation titled 'Love and Death and Responsive Evaluation' made to the Bob Stake Symposium on Evaluation in Urbana, Illinois, May, 1998.

Such deceptions as that we can stave off failure, incompleteness and mortality are accommodations enjoyed by society at large, for whom the very fabric of their relations is made up of artificial and diversionary tactics – but these are luxuries that cannot be enjoyed by evaluators, whose social responsibility it is to put these things into perspective. As evaluators we cannot entirely escape the absurdity of role, nor can we stand outside of the society that is founded on fictions. We live in the quotidian world as citizens, parents, consumers. But we can momentarily stand aside from society's praxis and, through acts of cognitive discipline, assume an impartial perspective – if not entirely independent, certainly more authentic and procedurally more objective by degrees.

DEMOCRACY

'The walls of society', wrote Peter Berger (1963), 'are a Potemkin[1] village' erected in front of the abyss of being . . . a defence against terror.' As the existentialist would have it, we are bound by our fear of mortality into society as an artifice – an avoidance. Society is merely a set of diversionary tactics made up of inauthentic roles and forms of organization which all represent flight from moral responsibility – the responsibility, that is, to face up to our mortal frailty and the inevitability of failure. The grandest artifice, perhaps, is the Hobbesian state, the Leviathan, founded on a social contract agreed with a people in flight from the terrors of non-society – society is the single largest expression of a 'praxis' designed to combat 'social death'. This image and representation of society continues to underpin much social consciousness in Britain in respect of relations between state and citizen. Unrestrained by society, that is, regulatory structures such as government, argued Hobbes (Macphereson, 1968), we are exposed to the threat of our mutual greed and fear, condemned to a life that was 'nasty, brutish and short'. The state is, as it were, the embodiment of our fear of death. Society and its restraints on *laissez-faire* behaviour is an unfortunate necessity, to be reassessed and limited wherever possible. Margaret Thatcher was, perhaps, the most recent and forceful advocate of Hobbesian principles.[2]

---

1 Admiral Potemkin constructed artificial Russian villages to create the impression of a populous – and therefore well-defended – society to an invading armada.
2 The contrast perhaps most salient for evaluators would be with Thomas Paine. Whereas Hobbes saw the social contract as one between government and people, Paine saw it as one among the people themselves with government as a bystander and servant. Here, government as an outcome was a positive resource for society, standing less for constraint

For Seery (1996) the failure to escape from or to reform a Hobbesian social contract founded in the main upon the fear of death has tainted democracy and made of it 'a second-best compromise, a calculated risk'. The Hobbesian contract is the secular version of the religious exploitation of mortal fear on which is constructed the unimpeachable authority of churches – the outer limits of freedom. Seery condemns the absence of thought and debate about mortality, for this is what prevents the emergence of more positive and sophisticated (e.g. rights-based) versions of democracy.

The significance of this analysis lies in its explanation of the problematic relationship we have with our institutions – our apparent inability to define them in such a way that they stand for support and freedom rather than tension and constraint. Berger's analysis – a mix of humanism and existentialism – rests on an argument about social psychology. It is that social institutions are, as it were, the architecture of our fears; they are constructed in such a way that we can adopt roles, relationships, patterns of thought and action that are free of those terrors. It is not as though without being able to call ourselves 'teacher', 'manager' or whatever we would find ourselves on our backs kicking our legs in the air in desperate and perpetual recognition of mortality. It is that mortality stands for all sorts of smaller as well as larger 'deaths' – that is, the deaths of successes, hopes, projects.

For example, if we were to accept the fragile nature of truth and certainty, the impossibility of cultural renewal, limitations on what we can know and the moral dilemma involved in coercive schooling, then the role of 'teacher' as contrasted with that of 'pupil' would be problematic and more difficult to sustain than it already is. We would have to face dilemmas we can more comfortably set aside, for example, that there is a tension between education and achievement in schooling – that is, that the striving for autonomy is irreconcilable with compliance. So, in flight from uncomfortable realities – from moral obligations – we go along with the artifices of role and institution. The moral dilemma of coercive schooling is not resolvable and is, under contemporary political conditions, inevitably corrosive of freedom and the equitable

---

and flight from fear and more for opportunity and strength. When, for example, the early United States were reassessing their constitution to broaden its remit, Paine argued that the Federal Government had no role to play in this. Their role was to await the decision of the people as represented by their state representatives (see Henry Collins (ed.), *Paine: Rights of Man*, London: Penguin (1969), esp. p. 213). We can see that the role of an evaluator under these two regimes would be substantially different, as would be their freedom for critical movement.

distribution of opportunities. But we continue to act as though this were not the case, and condemn ourselves to the fictions of reachable standards, equal opportunities, consensus policies. Few, for example, are the curriculum programs that bring controversial issues into class-rooms, that are based on conflict management or that concern them-selves with social change.

For Berger, concerned with humanism more than specifically demo-cracy, social enquiry cannot be so bound into the artifices of role and organization. Social science exists to monitor the state of these social compacts and the extent of the fictionalizing. Through engaging in the act of enquiry we face – we are obliged to face – the terrors; that is the closest we come to objective truth. As evaluators we do indeed occupy a role – another social construct, but one that is privileged by its search for authentic expression and by standing somewhat outside of normal social relations. Part of the unpopularity of impartial evaluation, the hesitancy on the part of evaluation sponsors to fund an independent brief, has to do with our capacity to raise questions about the nature of the group mission represented in the program – that is, to stand for the possibility of not being coopted by program values.[3]

Death – in its corporeal, most mundane form – is urgent and real enough a theme for educators and educational evaluators. Read Martha McNeil's (1996) critique of an emerging US National Curriculum which starts with the words of a young boy saying school is a refuge from killing and being killed on the streets. (Reality – another word for death – is another poverty disease: artifice, evasion and inauthenticity come easier for the middle classes.) But dismayingly, what awaits that boy in school is hardly the kind of confrontation with those realities that will eventually allow him to cope with them. School is in the vanguard of the Hobbesian flight from moral obligation. Under the punitive regime of test-based accountability and its success being mandated by politicians, schools can barely even publicly acknowledge the realities of poverty, racism, sexual behaviour, government corruption, inter-generational conflict, gender tensions – let alone address them meaningfully. Death in its many forms – corporeal as well as conceptual – barely stands a chance.

---

3 Part of that, of course, is to do with the politics of the immediate situation and a protective instinct towards policy on behalf of politicians and managers. But part of it, too, might be protection of certain implicit assumptions about the 'social contract' – for example, that authority should not be questioned since in itself it represents tacit popular sanction. Implicit in Hobbesian philosophy is that authority (the State) is justified by its very existence, that is, it is proof of its own history and its enduring rationale.

My interest in this theme was first sparked when I conducted a case study in a hospice for the terminally ill which I will discuss in some detail in a later chapter. There, my evaluation was limited by the fears and tolerances of those who lived and worked in the hospice. The Mother Superior, the Chaplain and the senior medics were all people who were touched by mortality and who transferred their fears – each in their own way – into forms of professional practice and forms of exchange with patients and families. Where my questioning and my writing threatened to articulate those fears – just to give them form – my work was disciplined with recourse to our confidentiality contract. Where I insisted on exposing the interaction between fear and action – publishing a full account – there was an attempt at suppression.

Where, then, lie the sources of such avoidance and fears of failure? What might be the nature of the threat?

Death (says Mellor, 1993) is a threat to the modernist project, since it puts a limit on personal projects and, thereby, to our commitment to societal goals – it reduces the attractions of change. Reflections on mortality remind us of the incompleteness of all projects and so the worthlessness of 'reflexive planning' – they render us more resistant to cooption into innovatory programs which trade on utopian and con-sensus ideals. Hence death is, as they say, privatized – hidden from view, outlawed – as, nowadays, are non-compliance, dissent, failure to meet targets and other sources of important learning. Death in the context of our educational concerns stands for incompleteness, failure essential for learning, intractable authority – the ever-receding and non-reachable standard. Doctors in the hospice, for example, knew well that medics traditionally reject the death of patients as sign of their medical failures, of the limits to medical knowledge, and so marginalize it (and the terminal patient) from their professional lives. One key mission of the hospice movement is to recover confidence in medical practice, that is, learn how to come to terms with the limitations of knowledge and self. Politicians have barely started to address a similar condition in our education system.

Nor am I claiming that we need to take a lugubrious and negative view of what stands for death. Quite the contrary: the insistence on inauthentic compliance to the policy plot is a kind of death in itself and a denial of life – that is, a denial of diversity and idiosyncrasy.[4] In its own

---

4 'All plots', writes Don DeLillo (in his book *Libra*), 'lead to death.' He constructed a story in which an intention to 'almost' assassinate Kennedy developed its own momentum and was overtaken by the logic of the ostensible plot.

way, the hospice accepted and promoted death (comprehensive pain control allowed the Mother Superior to claim that a dying person was 'the best audio-visual aid we've got'); the theory was that its acceptance brought a liberation which itself allowed a dogged celebration of life. The problem for my evaluation was that we never achieved a shared view of how the aims of those working in the hospice to confront realities might coincide with my role as evaluator – so there were always layers of artifice to be protected. Another way of thinking about this – again, I will look at this in detail in a later chapter – is to think of the ethical and political gap that is created when there is a divergence of interest between the evaluator and her respondents.

Let me return to education. If we were not haunted by the ephemeral nature of our accomplishments we would not, perhaps, be so obsessive about promoting them in schools. The situation is serious for children who lie on the wrong side – albeit the fortunate side – of a fundamental paradox in schooling. Here are many young people whose consciousness of mortality is barely ignited, but whose same consciousness is being tampered with by adults for whom mortality is an ever-simmering reality. This is not to ignore teenage depression and suicide and the early stirrings of mortality in young children, but to make an argument about degree. It is largely true of youth, broadly the case with adults.

The sensitivity of this situation can be intense – there is the danger of an accidental scuff creating an explosive spark in a young mind. A doctoral student of mine – an English teacher – talked to me of the personal pain of trying to teach Beckett to his pupils. How, he asked, do you explain *Waiting for Godot* without contaminating that luxurious moment of immortality – and without preemptively introducing adolescents to existential nausea? But then I frequently recall a moment in one of my evaluations when a young (eight-year-old) Muslim girl explained to me why, when she joined music workshops in schools, she risked inheriting a narrowing grave for her sin. Children, in the end, face many 'deaths', big and small, as they juggle with competing orthodoxies – failing parents, failing teachers, failing moral authorities and, of course, failing politicians.

I noted this last datum about narrowing graves on the evaluation of an orchestral outreach program, and the story raised a question about how we view educational programs themselves in relation to those who people them. It raises the issue of how we might invert the relationship between program and individual in such a way that we might 'read' the significance – even the scale – of a project in the life of a young girl. Here, the potentially terrible consequences of breaking a religious taboo make us look at the music program in a particular – moral – light. At about the same time I asked another child, Richard, from the same school what it was like to be a pupil: 'I don't know,' he said, 'I ain't never been a teacher.' Intentionally or not, Richard makes us think of how we confine children in our own educational Potemkin villages, intrigued more by the gravity of our campaigns than with the experience of living in inauthentic states; how we so consistently fail to measure the significance of that campaign in the immortal life of the child, but how easily we assume the place of that child in the significance of our ephemeral strategies.

Of the existential tricks Berger counts among the Potemkin buildings, the social program stands tall. Here is the bulwark against failure, the key vehicle in the modernist forward-moving convoy. Programs, the mythology goes, once were the social scientists' long-yearned-for laboratories of change; the observed experiment writ-large, where social process could be dissected and analysed, bombarded and altered and then announced to a waiting world. Small wonder, and for good reason, were social investigators attracted to them. Carol Weiss in 1987 wrote of the cooption of evaluators into program realities and their being career-enmeshed with them. One of the underlying biases we live with is our frequent assertion of program status over that of the individual. Look at the contents page of almost any educational evaluation report. Context comes first, and that almost always means program and policy contexts. Children and youth (where they appear) come later.

This situation would not be so perilous if programs were the speculative theatres of observation they once supposedly were. Now, however, they are more like purposeful 'colonizers of the future', demanding loyalty to progress, intolerant of hesitancy in respect of change. They are the harbingers of Donald Campbell's 'experimenting society' – the society committed to endemic reform through waves of experiments led by scientists (Campbell and Rosso, 1999: ch. 1). But we lack the 'honesty' (that is, the willingness to confront experimental failure) which Campbell saw as the essential moderating ingredient for that society. For, elsewhere (Campbell, 1999: 78), he talks of a 'tangle of advocacy with administration' in which social programs are presented 'as though they were certain to be successful'. This is a society thoroughly imbued with the ideology of progress and political/scientific authority; saturated with inauthenticity through its intolerance of incompleteness. We live in a world where there is no longer a 'Plan B'.

My claim of inauthenticity has a particular meaning in relation to social programs: it concerns the avoidance of questions to do with social justice and the democratic contract. Where each social and educational program can be seen as a reaffirmation of the broad social contract (that is, a re-confirmation of the bases of power, authority, social structure, etc.), each program evaluation is an opportunity to review its assumptions and consequences. This is commonly what we do at some level or another. All programs expose democracy and its failings; each program evaluation is an assessment of the effectiveness of democracy in tackling issues in the distribution of wealth and power and social goods. Within the terms of the evaluation agreement, taking this level of analysis into some account, that is, reviewing part of the social contract, is to act more authentically; to set aside the opportunity is to act more inauthentically, that is, to accept the fictions.

Our tendency to 'read' children's lives through the lens of the 'school' or 'curriculum program' – to use the program to shed meaning on the work and lives of so-called pupils – signifies further cooption into 'Plan A' and a flight from mortality and tolerance of failure. When evaluators believe in the social status of a social program and use it as a template of meaning placed on individual thought and action, that is, when evaluators go along unquestioningly with the concept of role – this one a 'teacher', this a 'pupil', that one a 'manager' – we risk being coopted into the artifice and becoming part of the exhortatory machinery that drives people on.

LOVE

The alternative is to document people's lives and to use these as contexts in which to read the significance and the meaning of the program – to invert the relationship between program and person. In particular, researching the lives and views of young people is of central importance. Not, as I will argue, to continue to scrutinize the powerless, but to attempt to see power structures through their eyes and against their criteria – that is, to subject power structures to their judgement. This means a key evaluation task is measuring the significance of programs in the lives of people, especially young people, rather than the inverse of that – and, of course, documenting how educational programs consistently (and in important ways) fail them. We need to spend more time in interview with young people. We need to hold educational programs more to account for their success in meeting the needs and desires of young people.

There is an argument to be heard about the strength of this piece of advocacy. In earlier drafts of this chapter I wrote this last paragraph as follows: 'If I am hard-headed about anything it is this – that in educational evaluation almost all that is intrinsically worth researching are the lives and views of young people – most of all else is avoidance and cooptation.' One or two people who read the draft objected to the strength of the statement, arguing variously that our contracts usually require us to report on professional action and that is where our focus should lie; that young people have a tendency to conservative if not authoritarian views and tend to remain unaware of professional responsibilities of teachers; that in a world of generally disastrous educational practices our responsibilities should be to collaborate with professionals to identify and disseminate good practices; and that both students and teachers reveal themselves more through their practices than through what they say.

I do not wholly accept the thrust of these arguments, though I ought to be more circumspect about privileging the voice of youth against the voice of other vulnerable and marginal groups, including victimized teachers, the disabled and poor parents. Though our contracts generally require us to observe the work of professionals, there remain two caveats. First, that as contracts are (in Britain, at least) increasingly restrictive and prescribing of methodology[5] we must be aware of the argument that we are vulnerable to cooption into program realities. Secondly, that there is more than one way to skin a cat: we can be legitimately creative in designing and conducting our evaluations as well as in educating our sponsors to accept more flexible contractual relations. All is always possible.

But in any event, my argument is precisely about fulfilling our obligations to evaluate programs – to bring judgement to bear upon them. Such judgements emerge from the *informed* views of youth, though the 'informed' element calls for complex methodologies, not simply serial interviewing and profiling.[6] Views of youth regarding educational standards, treatments and ideas, that is, in the crude language of commercialism, the 'client view', are less deniable and carry more potential for interrupting policy discourses than the same coming from teachers.

---

5   See (Norris, 1995), who reports on an extensive interview-based survey of researchers' grim experiences with government contracting. He concludes: 'The new contractual order gives added emphasis to the oligopolistic nature of control over the supply of social research resources and the relative economic weakness of contractors . . . The institutionalisation of evaluation, driven by the goal of efficiency, creates a lack of reciprocity by stressing narrow economic interests at the expense of other values and considerations.'

6   An increasingly popular research practice is sharing data with young people to bumpstart analysis, but also to share control over inferential procedures with them. In a project I am involved with we aim to engage young people in a learning process through data-based workshops in which they read and discuss the meaning of reported experiences of peers.

I still advise, therefore, as strong a focus as is feasible on the views of young and marginalized people in the conduct of educational evaluation. Here we walk in less familiar territory for it requires evaluators to engage in an immersion program – immersed, that is, in the lives of the recipients of policy[7] rather than its conceivers, implementers and other stakeholders. But the point is to break the link between program and progress – to search for Plan B – as often, to frustrate in order to best serve decision making. We need, as one of my students once alleged of me, to be 'in love' with our respondents.

This was a moment when I asked one of my teaching groups to research an archive of my Conservatoire evaluation. I had spent almost three years with music trainees on that evaluation and had explored rigorously the option of reading programs and events in collaboration with young people. I asked my group to identify me and how I appeared in various guises. 'It's obvious,' said Ed, 'you were in love with the students!' And so I was – though I have to say in a social-cognitive form of the affliction, which is how Ed meant it.

I will discuss this in detail in a later chapter so I will not dwell too much on it here. What Ed did mean was that he noticed evidence of mutual dependence, mutual exploitation, joint celebration and a fascination with the emotional precipice of social intimacy. Here was evidence of engagement, an intermingling of interests – but, ultimately, as in all good tangos, of final betrayal. I talked as a friend but slunk off to write as a scientist: 'the face of a sinner, the hands of a priest', as Sting's lyric goes.

This is one version of what can be involved in the privileged role hinted at by Peter Berger – the social enquirer who cannot enjoy the luxury of inauthenticity, who comes at program analysis from the angle of immediate perception, whose training, preoccupations and social warrant equip her to look beyond the fiction, and to enlist our respondents. To document the lives of young people involves an essential betrayal – a drawing close and an eventual distancing.

---

7 Of course, many of my terms are problematic, and there is an inevitable degree of licence involved in using them. The notion of a 'policy maker', for example, is meaningless, given the range of people and roles and the complex processes this embraces. Teachers set classroom policies and, in so doing, determine, to some extent, the lives of children. A government minister may be powerless to resist a general policy drift. And yet we would want to include teachers in the category of the marginalized. Look at Cronbach et al. (1985), Lindblom and Cohen (1979), Wildavsky (1979) and Cohen and Garrett (1975) for an induction into the complexities of the notion of 'policy making' – that is, that policy making is a community, rather than an elite activity; that it is a process and a discourse; and that it is based in common rather than specialized knowledge.

I started out on this tack, actually, encouraged by Bob Stake's (1967) notion of portraying 'the mood and even the mystery' of a program as he counselled evaluation to pause from offering (interrogative) stimuli to programs (that is, regarding the program as an experimental site) so as to be 'stimulated' by it, and adopt a more 'responsive' posture. 'Mood' and 'mystery' – two words I least expected to read when being inducted into program evaluation. I still consider this to be a radical aspiration yet to be widely realized in the field of evaluation. Here – to love and death – is where this has led me, for here lie program mysteries. Once again, this is not to renege on our obligations to measure the significance of programs; quite to the contrary. The significance of a program in the life of a citizen promises more accurate and relevant measures of significance than we conventionally opt for. And, too, we ought to do more of a job to locate programs as iterative renewals of the social contract and to see each, thereby, as an opportunity to re-evaluate that contract and to expose its artifices.

So I worry that in treating the program as the primary source of data (rather than, for example, a life) we are dealing with the surrogate, and that what we need to do to properly understand programs is to forget about them for a while and be stimulated, instead, by the lives of program participants – not as role-incumbents (that is, as defined by the program), but as people and citizens.

EVALUATION AND SOCIAL JUSTICE

I have given a view of programs as the 'object' of evaluation enquiry, and now I will give a view of the kind of evaluation which relates to it, one which will be elaborated throughout this book. Since concerns with social justice are at the heart of my arguments I will also make some brief comment about that. I have presented a general view of programs as being sites of political and moral negotiation between government and people – places and times when it becomes appropriate and opportunistic to reflect on society, its contracts and its limitations. This has defined a role for evaluation in intensifying those reflections by confronting and extending the boundaries of social tolerance, especially in respect of failure and incompleteness.

The privileged role I ascribe to program evaluators in moving beyond those boundaries of tolerance does not imply their disengagement from program participants; quite the contrary. The relationship between evaluator and program participant is one of dependency. The data the evaluator needs to generate extends beyond the descriptive and merely informative into the speculative, the judgemental – the metaphysical – and these are only accessible through interaction.

In general terms, therefore, I follow MacDonald (1987) and Walker (1974) in distinguishing evaluation from research as an activity that (a) reduces the freedom for the pursuit of personal agendas of enquiry, and (b) is saturated with political and ethical consequence. MacDonald notes that the researcher is relatively free to construct an agenda so as to match the 'problem-solving techniques of his craft'. For the evaluator the situation is somewhat reversed, in that the techniques of the craft are available as a repertoire to respond to problems conjointly discovered with program participants. Walker, in setting out some of the foundations for case study evaluation, argues that evaluation is distinguished by the intensity of the political demands on its conduct and the foreshortening of its timescales. The evaluator's need to 'reconcile research and practical affairs is consequently more urgent and compulsive than it would be in pure research' (1974: 78).

The implications of these distinctions and of the privileged social role I argue for are significant. If evaluation is to test limits of social tolerance it demands a situated political ethic, that is, a stance which shows how it will act in relation to the ethics of power prevailing in the particular field of enquiry. This requires evaluation to be methodologically creative (rather, for example, than dogmatic or faithful to paradigms) so as to respond to the shifting agendas and possibly competing values in the constituencies with which it works. Nor are the requirements as tough as they might be – and often are in the world of research. Evaluation has to be as uncertain of itself as its respondents almost always will be of themselves. Evaluation of programs concerns itself with how people lead their lives and so must live with the ineffability of judging the worth of a life. House (1980: 73) suggests, in the context of an argument that evaluation offers best value when it is imprecise and uncertain,

> evaluation persuades rather than convinces, argues rather than demonstrates, is credible rather than certain, is variably accepted rather than compelling . . . evaluative argument is at once less certain, more particularised, more personalised and more conducive to action than is research information.

But my stance goes further than demanding a political ethic, it also follows MacDonald, House and Weiss in making the case for evaluation as a form of political action. This begins where evaluation exposes political and intellectual authority rather than yields to or reaffirms it. The inversion implied by holding programs to account for realizing the needs and ambitions of participants rather than holding participants to account for their contribution to the realization of policy, this potential challenge to political hierarchy is, itself, interventionist and a form of political action.

The intervention is, of course, methodological and does not assume licence for the evaluator to engage with the aims of the program she is evaluating from a value position. Political action does not mean confronting policy. Evaluation as a form of political action operates at a substratum level where principles of fairness and justice are determined. In arguing for a remedial focus on the individual, that is, perhaps for a further 'reform of program evaluation' (cf. Cronbach et al., 1985), I am arguing for suffusing evaluation with a particular, Rawlsian, view of justice in evaluation (House, 1980). Access to evaluation is a social good, and the distribution of this good should be determined against principles of fairness and in the light of a generally unequal access to the resource by the fiscally and economically wealthy and powerful. This allows us to argue for 'positive discrimination' in favour of the individual voice. Evaluation as political action does not confront society's projects, but it does confront the political infrastructure within which they are designed and operated.

What underpins such views of evaluation is its situatedness – its specificity to context; the existential dimension to evaluation which inevitably smooths out the angular certainties of social science theory and makes it yield to those forms of vernacular judgement that rely on what is reasonable under the circumstances. Cook's (1997) confusion about the global findings of evaluation – which he sees as simultaneously pessimistic and optimistic about social progress (see previous chapter) – are charactersitic of a form of social enquiry which tends to eschew generalization in favour of understanding the particular (Cronbach et al., 1985). To take a specific example, we might contrast program evaluation with policy research. The latter tends to come at programs as singular manifestations of larger policy currents. The policy researcher's concern tends to be with long-term movements in policy development – themselves generalizations – which can be examined by exploring their episodic pauses as ideals and interests coalesce into a program. Programs inform the general case of policy. Meanwhile, evaluation starts inside a program and (if so minded) uses analysis of the policy context as a tool for understanding it – the general informs the particular.

I also draw a distinction between evaluation and other kinds of attenuated evaluative activity – what some call 'evaluative services'. Evaluation, if it aspires to document lives as contexts within which to understand programs and hold their policies to account, must concern itself with all perspectives and aspects of program experience. Nothing can lie beyond the purview of the evaluator in attempting to understand events in their contexts. A pedagogical practice alleged to be either 'poor' or 'exemplary' is based upon observation of the present, but suggests to the program evaluator a trail of data that leads backwards in time into people's life experiences; forward in time into educational outcomes; across the system to colleagues and their organization; down the system to pupils and their families; and up the system to managers and ministers.

Hence, a study of the implementation of a curriculum innovation, say, may be evaluative but is not, in my terms, a program evaluation since it apprehends only a part of a sequence of program events, starting with policy. The appraisal of program participants is also evaluative in that it offers a technology designed to arrive at a judgement of worth of individualized aspects of program process – but cannot stand in for program evaluation since it most likely discounts a range of contexts within which it is ethical (fair) to mediate that judgement – and it also disconnects individuals from their working contexts and policy. Similarly, the measurement of program outcomes (for example, pupil achievement in the case of a curriculum program) is an evaluative act conducted with evaluation instruments but is not sufficient as a base on which to construct judgements about the program. There are too many intervening variables to allow us to work back from the assessment of quality of output to inferences about the quality of (program) processes. In any event, the evaluation of professionals and pupils as a surrogate for program evaluation has the unfair and uneven effect of holding people to account for the failure of policy, organization and curriculum.

Some writers who consider the difference between evaluation and research focus on purpose, and generally on the concept of utility. Whereas social research is concerned with the production of knowledge and the refinement of theory, evaluation has to be concerned with use – 'intended use by intended users' (Patton, 1997); as a service to the policy community (Berk and Rossi, 1990); to determine the merit or worth of a program (Scriven, 1993); to 'help make programs work better' (Weiss, 1998). We can think of evaluation as a broader social service, as an instrument for provoking questions about social justice in particular contexts of action (cf. almost anything written by House) or more broadly, 'to influence social thought and action' (Cronbach et al., 1985).

For me, the principal use of evaluation is to serve this latter principle. Program evaluation creates alternative ways of thinking and talking about society and its purposes, about the relation between people and social institutions. Through a unique combination of an unusual mobility which the evaluator enjoys in moving between stakeholders, the unusual licence to ask questions of purpose and value, a training in or, at least, an unusual exposure to ethical issues, and an unusually privileged position of substantive impartiality, through the unique combination of these as part of the evaluator's warrant she has the opportunity to portray society and its programs from novel, or sometimes just multiple perspectives. Evaluation, at its best, sees programs in ways denied their participants.

I must also say what I mean by social justice and how this relates to my view of program evaluation.

Social justice concerns the form and the consequences of the distribution of social and economic benefits in society – that is, resources including social as well as economic goods (e.g. status, well-being). This has been the historical driving force behind the development of political philosophy – that is, the 'good' society is the 'just' society where what is just is defined by the political formula against which citizens have access to social benefits and opportunities. The one certainty we can bank on in society is that there will always be poor people against whose plight rich people will be able to measure their blessings, and so the quest for social justice tends to focus on relations between advantage and disadvantage, on how people and groups are positioned in terms of the competition for social goods. Mortality is an economically relative experience.

In this respect evaluation is deeply suffused with issues in relation to justice, for two linked reasons: first, that, as I have said, a program under evaluation is a microcosm of society and so exposes prevailing conditions and values in relation to the competition for social goods – we can observe the tussle between the rich and the poor; secondly, that evaluation is an instrument in which that positioning in the competition for resources can be adjusted – for example, the evaluator can privilege the interests and the arguments of one group over others, or take a radical position and choose not to entertain any privileges.

When I talk of social benefits and opportunities, therefore, I imply something more than economic resources and an approach to social justice measured, for example, against the erosion of economic inequalities. A significant social good is the right to those resources (including evaluation) that allow people, as I quoted Peter Berger earlier, to live in a meaningful world. Those resources include discursive opportunities (being heard and becoming informed). This becomes both poignant and controversial in the context of modern technocratic political cultures which, as Berger argues, are characterized by a shift from 'givenness to choice'. Having cast off the constraints of traditional forms of social organization we are free to design our own society, to indulge in degrees of self-determination. We are free to ignore the voices of our ancestors and to decide for ourselves what makes for a meaningful life.

This freedom, of course – the chance to choose – is not distributed homogeneously, and in a society whose political economy is suffused with utilitarian values, the freedom favours the wealthy. Evaluation is a minor instrument in the struggle to achieve meaning, that is, to become sufficiently informed as to discriminate better between life options – and so evaluators face choices about who and how they should serve and who and how they should represent. Sampling, for example, is an ethical issue. This merely restates House's (1980) and Sirotnik's (1990) position on the interwovenness of methodology and justice, but for my purposes it demands a focus on the individual and the imperative of (a) privileging individual voices against, as it were, institutional voices, and (b) privileging the voices of those who are bound to receive program meanings (the relatively powerless) over those who give the meanings of programs (the relatively more powerful). Here, once again, is the basis for seeing evaluation as a form of political action, that is, as interventionist at the level of political procedure.

Another way of stating this concern with social justice is with what we might think of as anti-universality. Simply stated, this is that the interests of authoritarianism tend to be served by universal treatments, by regarding people as homogeneous groups and designing policies that aspire to uniformity – that is, the imposition of state or official meanings.[8] Universality masks individual needs and, therefore, individual demands for social goods. One challenge to authoritarian government is the undeniability of the individual concern – the requirement that policy take into account individual differences and the plurality of meaningfulness.

There is a step beyond freeing people from the imposed meanings of programs and policies, diffusing rights and opportunities to self-determination more widely than the narrow economic frame which currently characterizes opportunity. This is embracing policy and program within the meanings of the citizenry, envisioning the democratic goal of a government whose policies are shaped by citizen experience. This is, of course, the democratic ideal, and as an ideal it must be unrealizable. Nonetheless, there is a procedural principle which mitigates to some extent the failure of democracy in policy. This is the

---

8 Apple (1993) uses the term 'official knowledge' – as he is talking about national or otherwise prescribed curricula.

principle of inverted accountability, in which evaluation is designed not to hold people to account for the success of policy, but to hold policy to account for its success in supporting people to realize their potential and their aspirations.

REDEMPTION SONGS

To reiterate, I am not trying to devise a new evaluation methodology nor to outline a new model of evaluation. I merely offer a stance, a disposition based upon advances made principally in the 1960s and the 1970s towards building evaluation data-bases and strategies from program experiences. In particular, I am not advocating an oppositional stance towards program sponsors and managers – merely an appropriate distancing. Though I do not advocate subverting our evaluation contracts, nor our obligations to those who are responsible for programs, I might sometimes advocate suborning them. Indeed, the realities of evaluation contracting mean that there may often be little available resource to accomplish the personalization of evaluation. In such cases, evaluation fulfils only a part of its promise as a social and political service and we must rest content with continually trying to educate evaluation sponsors and to free evaluation design from their control.

The British advances in case study evaluation were driven by Parlett and Hamilton's and MacDonald's work in, respectively, 'Illuminative' and 'Democratic' evaluation. In both cases a primary value was given as 'service to decision makers'. Program decision making was seen to be defective as a result of poor understanding through having available only partial information on program operations. Better – that is to say more comprehensive – evaluation would redeem educational decision making by providing more insightful and more persuasive data, which would lead to better understanding which, itself, would give rise to more effective decision making. Data on the experience of a program – particularly on the range of views and judgements held about a program – is an essential contribution to being able to make decisions about it. The other area of deficit lay in the paucity of information on programs available to their ultimate sponsors – the tax-paying citizenry. Hence the high value placed on vernacular forms of reporting accessible to general publics.

Experience with implementing these approaches to evaluation suggests that power structures do not yield so readily to comprehensive information, indeed, often resist it – in spite of the belief among case study evaluators that data on how and why people lead their lives is useful. Hence, case study evaluators sometimes do find themselves in confrontation with program sponsors and managers (see Simons, 1987, for an insider account of such a confrontation). This, however, is almost always situational conflict in the sense that it is not given by the logic of how case study relates to power.

I remain committed to this redemption song. Educational evaluation is evaluation *of* educational programs – but it is also an educational instrument in itself. I do not mean to imply a pedagogic, much less an instructional role for the evaluator, but to point to the responsibility of the evaluator to generate diverse data, order it to sustain its·diversity, make it available as a comprehensive resource and create the conditions under which people – all program participants – can appraise that resource independently and arrive at autonomous judgement. Evaluation, that is, creates complex and ethical learning environments. In constructing the resource there are two distributive procedural principles we might keep in mind: (a) to compensate for the marginal voice (usually young people), and (b) to correct biases in data generation which have historically tended to lean towards representing the voices of the powerful. There is a residual obligation on evaluators given what we have learned about the difficulties of translating case study data into utilizable material for making decisions about program improvement and adaptation – and this is to provide analytic guides, to model ways of incorporating such data into practical thinking and problem solving.

None of this compromises the service to decision makers. They are a legitimate audience for evaluation learning, though their needs cannot take priority over others'. Besides, those early case study theorists were clear that decision making structures were not so transparent as to simply be conflated with, for example, those in management roles – that, for example, classroom teachers were decision makers, as were school governors, parents, perhaps even pupils. 'Policy maker' has too broad an embrace to be a useful category. Though evaluation audiences are diverse and may need to be addressed in discrete ways, the ethic of service, at best, is embracing and undifferentiated.

MORTALITY AND THE INDIVIDUAL

Evaluating social programs, then, provides this opportunity to generate alternative, more authentic, ways of reviewing society, its purposes and its options. The ethical dilemmas unleashed by these alternative discourses are good atmospheres for exploring issues in social justice, and it is an inevitability that evaluators will evoke these issues in their work – intentionally or not. The tenor of authenticity – its feel – is given by the degree to which conversations that ensue from evaluation evoke images of society and its boundaries – that is, allow us to look beyond the near horizons of our social fictions to the realities of incompleteness and failure. We will not in any forseeable future – that is, in a lifetime – come close to eradicating poverty (or its reciprocal, unreasonable wealth); we will not discover a society of equal outcomes nor even make a significant dent in the accidental privileges of birth; we will not significantly ease the sufferings of children; we will not crack the problem of freeing the younger generation from the cloying cultural embrace of the older; we will not resolve the tension between schooling and education; we will not reduce the tension between power and democracy. Our mortality condemns us to witnessing relentless failure in these things in spite of the seductive promises of programs and government policies.

This is not to say that evaluators need to advocate a relentlessly pessimistic view of social change, nor that they should be ruthlessly insensitive to shortcoming. Schon (1971), in his existential treatise on social change, argues for a learning role – he calls the role one of 'a learning agent' and much of the role overlaps with what we would now call 'evaluator'. The role of this person is to chart those uncertain territories which lie 'beyond the stable state' – that is, in futures where our actions and decisions cannot necessarily be guided by our pasts. As for that agent:

> His explicit formulations are always inadequate to his grasp of action and response: that is, he is always somewhat in the position of observing his own responses to situations in order to determine what his principles of action are. And he is always subject to surprise . . . He must span the period which includes both the experiences underlying his projective models and the 'next instances' to which those models are brought. (1971: 234–5)

But Schon goes on to remind us that 'projective models' (that is, innovations) do not automatically transfer across contexts in such a way that the learning agent is merely the auditor. 'All projective models are inherently open-ended in . . . that they are susceptible to modification, explosion or abandonment in the face of the here-and-now.' Mutability rules. This is not to say that we cannot witness and contribute to social improvement, but that we need to keep things in proportion, to calibrate our efforts against the scale of the problem. Here is the purpose, or at least the resource that is evaluation. It is in this sense that evaluation is required to confront mortality, and since mortality is an essentially individual experience, it is to the individual that the evaluator must turn in acting politically.

3

Evaluation and a Philosophy
of Individualism

PEOPLE IN PROGRAMS

> ... perhaps the most difficult part of our problem is contained in our failure
> to develop and effectuate a social philosophy that makes men and women
> the end rather than the means to social progress. We have yet to develop an
> adequate philosophy of individualism. (Karier, 1974: 313)

Charles Lindblom (1990) talks of investigation as a condition of living in
society. People are constantly faced with problems which he defines as
situations they need to adapt to. We do not adapt naturally, rather, we
have to develop dispositions, reasons, beliefs which help us to do that. In
order to accomplish this, we, as ordinary people, observe and investigate
life – in his words, we 'probe'.

Although this is a natural activity, it is often usurped by social
scientists. 'Instead of assisting citizens and functionaries in their
enquiries social scientists often propose to take the task of enquiring
away from them, although they of course require lay consent to do so'
(1990: 190). In fact, he reminds us of the obvious: most of the knowledge
we have of life and society springs from lay enquiry – the social sciences
deal with specialized fragments of what we need to know to address our
problems. Think of child-rearing; think of music-making.[1] Stake (1986)
documents in stark terms the way 'common knowledge' and 'social

---

1   ... think of autobiography, points out MacLure (1995). She counterposes what, for her,
is the contrived, ritualized and 'sacred' biography collected by the social science
interviewer with the secular or 'mundane' autobiography which we 'write' in everyday life
through job applications, conversations with friends, diaries, etc. This is not an uncommon
theme in biographical research where, for some, it is expressed as a yearning to return to
authenticity. MacLure makes this more complex, however, by implying that there is no

science knowledge' diverge – the latter pairing reality down to par-simonious and context-free facts and propositions, seeking conclusions that will endure across time (i.e. theories); while, in quotidian life (in fact, in the life of program practitioners) facts are saturated with context and conclusions are valid only insofar as they relate to immediate concerns.

Indeed, the problem Lindblom identifies is exacerbated since the natural process of lay enquiry – simply the way we think about and develop views on the world – is essentially inconclusive, it defers solutions. Lay enquiry is a process of 'muddling through' and leaving the question of who we are open to doubt and renewal. We are not often pressed to make up our minds about fundamental values – a General Election vote is provisional until the next one; we can change our music tastes by buying a new disc. But the social scientist has been seduced by theoretical closure, consensus-building, proof and the twin face of scien-tific authority – rationality and generalization.

And yet, as Lindblom also reminds us, unlike the natural scientists who can reveal to us worlds that are hidden from our perceptions (the quantum world, patterns of biological development, astral phenomena), social scientists are bound to observe things that lay people observe routinely. We are all 'naturalistic' observers. Interpretations remain to be forged, but, for the most part – and excepting obvious cases of enquiry such as at ecological levels and with large data sets – there are no hidden sources of data (in the sense of accessible only through esoteric instru-mentation) on society. This affects significantly the relationship of the citizen to the social researcher in that it at least makes possible some sort of accountability relationship. Remember, at the end of that quote above, Lindblom added 'they [social scientists] of course require lay consent to do so'. ('People own the data on their own lives,' argued the CARE-based case study theorists.)

There are limits to this argument. I have already claimed a privileged role for the evaluator in creating alternative discourses built upon alternative (more authentic) ways of seeing. That citizens 'probe' the social world from day to day does not guarantee their capacity to penetrate the protective fictions in which they live – there is, indeed, a kind of hidden data which requires special training to access. Nonethe-less, Lindblom's argument is significant, especially for evaluators and

---

such thing as an authentic account of a life available to us since all are post-hoc construc-tions – but that we can, as social researchers, locate our constructions more closely in the situations in which people ordinarily do the constructing. As a postmodernist, MacLure has to work hard *not* to convince us that the 'mundane' is the more authentic.

especially in a liberal democracy where claims to knowledge replace the brute coercive power of an authoritarian society – that is, claims to knowledge are appeals to be heard and followed. Stake (1986) warns evaluators:

> Practitioners know that there are many more issues to consider than those the evaluator entertains, but the evaluator is indignant if his/her issues are not considered the prevailing ones. (p. 161)

Here is the source of the requirement that social researchers discover their 'warrant' – their licence for doing what they do, their legitimacy and the limits of their intellectual leadership. The warrant for engaging in social enquiry in a democratic society (at least, publicly financed social enquiry), is an expression of how enquiry is expected to support democratic *procedures* – in Lindblom's terms, how professional enquirers support the processes of lay probing; how, that is, we improve public understanding.[2]

One danger for evaluators, then, is that in our search for solutions to social problems we give ourselves and our (theory-based) ways of seeing higher priority than we afford citizens and their (vernacular) ways of seeing. As I suggested earlier, in matching and interpreting data there is a tendency to assert what, for evaluators, counts for coherence rather than what makes events and ideas coherent in the lives of respondents. One of the means evaluators employ to accomplish this is by asserting the reality of programs – institutional and political artefacts which, when you start to do field research, seem to have the quality of the emperor's clothes – they exist meaningfully only as a construct of the questioning. What we might develop as a counterbalance is what Karier was urging – a practical philosophy of individualism; and as Lindblom suggests, find a way for enquiry to support and promote the reasoning and the investigations of the citizen rather than displacing it.

---

2 Many people engage in evaluation and other forms of social enquiry and do not think at all about warrant – about that democratic relationship. This is because they are either unaware of it as an issue or unconcerned or, just as likely, it is not appropriate. A worker on a music outreach project agrees to take responsibility for writing an evaluation report; an out-of-work school inspector acts as consultant to evaluate a Regional Arts Council project for enough money to pay her family bills for three weeks; a doctoral student struggles to reconcile how she thinks she ought to observe a project within the narrow tolerances of her supervisor. It does not mean that their subsequent work has no appreciable effect on the health of our democracy or of our citizenship. It simply means that the issue has been suppressed by unfavourable circumstances.

To begin to do this I want to illustrate its problems and possibilities and I will do that by conducting some analysis of data. Here, I throw the reader in at the deep end, without context, with no good cognitive framework for treating data as evidence. What I want to do is to begin to introduce the reader to the music education programs that will reappear throughout this book, and to do so from the perspective of some of the people who inhabit them, rather than from official descriptions. The strangeness – the coming-out-of-nowhere-ness – of this data should be thought about by the reader as more than my refusal to put a neat context around it. Here we face one of the most typical experiences of fieldwork. No matter how much the program is 'explained' to us in terms of its formal logistics (resources, politics, staffing, objectives, calendar), data comes at us in the early stages of fieldwork like the babble of voices to the new arrival in a far-flung airport. Here, in its most raw state, is the challenge of discovering what it is that counts for coherence in the lives of those we evaluate. I will start with a portrayal of a young boy in school.

Richard is a slim boy of 10 in a blue-check shirt and slightly faded blue jeans. He has red, fair hair and a thin face with freckles. He has something of a distant look in his eye – a nervous, perhaps wary look. He's quick to break into a smile, but it's tight. He sits on the edge of the group, his hands held at chest height and, suspended from them, Chinese bells, poised one above the other like a two-piece mobile. There are half-a-dozen nine or ten year-old children in the music room with an orchestral player.

Richard concentrates on the bells, his hands still, but not stiff. Sitting on the floor in front of him are four other boys, all playing glockenspiels and xylophones, animatedly looking across at each other – shouting instructions with stern facial gestures – smiling – or else putting on that blank face that belies concentration. One of the four runs his beater up and down his xylophone languidly and in apparent boredom. Richard releases one hand, the higher one, to fall in a precise line allowing one bell to strike against the other. He raises his head – keeping his body and hands in the same position – to look at the rest of the group. He looks back at the bells and repeats the gesture and the sound, and again, and again. One of the group raises a hand, limply, as though it had suddenly become weightless, and everyone stops playing – but momentarily, and they follow the boy who looks bored into the next section of the piece. Richard strikes the bells again. The music continues, and at the urgent signals of Lee the instruments drop out one-by-one, himself included. Then there's just Richard. He sits, almost hunched now, over the bells and, for the end of the piece, strikes them five times, growing quieter each time, until the last one is only barely audible. A flicker of a smile crosses his face as his shoulders drop. The boy sitting on the floor immediately in front of him brings his fist crashing down painfully on Richard's foot and laughs.

At break time the whole primary school is out on the playground in the hot sun. The scene is familiar, has been for years. Ball games, games of tag, huddles, arguments, hints of sexuality, screams and unheard whispers – a hubbub. Richard leans against the wall, his eyes narrowed against the sun. He pushes his hands against the wall and his body jerks forward. He spins round, reaches up, grasps a section of drainpipe and pulls himself up to look into it, his feet scratching for a hold on the brick wall. He lets himself fall, turns again and leans back on the wall, folds his arms, unfolds them and looks down at his feet. He looks across the playground again. Children stand or play in discrete groups like chess-pieces confined to squares.

Richard relates to other boys in his class through a combination of banter and victimization. 'He's a scientist!' his mates laugh tauntingly – like when a child becomes an object of mockery for displaying scholarly detachment.

Now he's standing just inside the door to the playground. As I approach him and start to talk, two of his mates move in closer, bouncing tennis balls off the wall and laughing and chatting, muscling in on the conversation.

'Why are you playing the Chinese bells?'

''Cos I came to the group late and they'd all chosen the instruments.'

But he likes the music – it's their own music, he says. Sure Val comes in from the CBSO but 'she told us when we was playing too high or too low'. 'Yeh,' bursts in John, ricocheting a ball off the wall. 'She says when it's a bad sound!'

'But it's still our music,' says Richard. And the conversation turns more generally to the school.

'Yeh – it's a good school. Better than Blyth,' Richard accuses. 'My sister went there for about two years and she knows nothing. I know more than her and she's four years older than me!'

But John insists that it's not as good a school as one which allows you to come 'when you want to'. Richard agrees, thinks a moment and approves of the notion of a voluntary school.

'Yeh – you should come whenever you want to,' he says.

'Every 5 weeks!' shouts John, catching his ball again, laughing. Richard is not laughing though. John bounces his ball and lurches into Richard exaggeratedly to catch it, and Richard topples for a moment.

'You could come one week', speculates Richard, 'and take the next week off.' But John presses and taunts and continues to knock school. Richard looks at him and laughs and then 'Yeh! Just think! Come in school just for break time!' But he manages to make it clear that he does like school. So it's worth chancing one of those zoological questions that are easier to ask than answer.

'So what's it like to be a pupil?'

Richard kicks an imaginary stone with his foot. 'I don't know. I ain't never been a teacher.'

As an evaluator I was drawn to Richard – perhaps by the intensity with which he played the Chinese bells, but certainly by the combination of that with the treatment he received from his friends and then by his evaluation of schooling. The final comment – reminding me that I, as a more powerful institutional actor knew more about his institutionally constructed identity than he – was the final element in this collection of apparently unrelated facts. He appeared to lie firmly in the orbit of this music program I was evaluating since his playing of the bells was so fine and deliberate and deserved some explanation. And yet the more we read about Richard the less significant looms that program – the more complex our view of him, the greater the tendency to ask questions not about how he fits into the program, but how *it* makes sense in his life and against his emerging values. We will return to Richard shortly.

Some distance away – 100 miles, a couple of years and the yawning divide between childhood and adulthood – Michael, a member of the Royal Opera House chorus, is sitting reflecting on just the kind of activity Richard was involved in – professional musicians working in schools – but from the point of view of the professional. He thinks back to a workshop event with colleagues where they were discussing the role of an Education Department in the Opera House:[3]

'I forget exactly what they were talking about, but they were speaking along the lines of "we desperately need to do educational work to feel that we bring some value into our lives, real job satisfaction" – which most of us in the Education Department feel from what we do in that. But I hit the roof and said to go into it with that motive is really absolutely wrong. If we're not going in for the kids' benefit then

---

3   This fieldwork was conducted by Richard Davies who assisted me on this evaluation.

the whole thing has got upside down and I really refuse to believe that anyone working in the Royal Opera House isn't getting a lot of job satisfaction. We may not be getting a huge amount of money, we've got unsocial hours which wreck marriages etc. - but we've got the opportunity to work with Bernard Haitink etc. and we're terribly lucky.'

Michael reflected more on life in the chorus, praising the appointment of the Chorus Manager who successfully plays a pastoral, supportive role - 'these people are, on the whole, rather vulnerable'. But then he feels that 'people get unreasonable expectations' of what they should expect from their work.

'We all of us feel unhappy. I loathe this production we're doing . . . which I think is very shabby and self-indulgent and old-fashioned - I'm on duty every night and I can't bear the thought of seeing it seven times . . . But musically it is fantastic, and if I've got the privilege of being involved minimally with a music performance of that quality which you couldn't better anywhere in the world - then I'm very lucky.'

Once again, the apparent chaos of values and experiences somehow achieved coherence in Michael's life – in a way that does not make immediately obvious how we might measure the quality or worth of the education program he refers to. Once again, the complexity of the task of discovering the binding logic that allowed the calculus Michael makes, and the stridency of the human voice together, assert themselves over the voice of the program which, itself, becomes wrapped up in this life. Once we have heard Michael we need to understand something about him (and his colleagues, for alone his voice is without social coordinates) before we can return to understand the program – and then we will only understand the program in Michael-like terms.

The program that constituted the work of the Education Department was formally, in organizational terms, distinct from the work of the House artistic companies. It was kept at arm's length so as not to interrupt the artistic endeavour. Artistes, for example, who had been booked for education work could be withdrawn at a moment's notice for rehearsal or performance. But we can see from Michael's comment that such a distinction is not so easily sustained in experience. In the final evaluation report it was noted that the Department was, as it were, the physical manifestation of the contradictions the players live with, and as such represented a developmental resource for the House. Here was an example of the evaluation working from the person to inform organizational and policy debates.

Finally, somehow bridging the gap between the child and the adult, between the school pupil and the professional, we hear Lyn, a Guildhall

Conservatoire student, in training but into something more profound. She, too, is sitting in a discussion, this time reviewing the work of the MPCS innovation.

Lyn sat throughout much of the discussion uncharacteristically trying to join in by raising her hand and trying to interject a question. She barely managed – and she explains now that it required some effort on her part. She is shy and for much of the early part of MPCS she was attentive of workshops but recessive and quiet. Lyn, like Mol, is a flautist. She wears well chosen clothes and has a crisp appearance. Her face is broad and pointed at the chin, she has long straight hair and when she smiles you can see the tiny muscles around her mouth that make her embouchure. She smiles easily.

Lyn's shyness is something she lived with until it was alleged to be jeopardizing her playing.

'My flute teacher said that my main problem is that I haven't got enough "spark", you see, and it comes out in my playing – and it will always do that unless I take a grab hold of myself and go out and – not be shy. Because it can't just come through the music – it has to come through me as a person.

'Somebody said . . . I would never be able to overcome it. My teacher didn't agree with that – she said "no, you can change yourself if you've got the motivation to do it."'

And that is why, she says, MPCS has been so good for her. 'I can't just sit back and listen to people – I've had to take the initiative and be a leader at times.' Lyn has come to believe, with her teacher, that she can change and that this is the route to changing her music. An immediate problem is that the summer vacation is starting and that without the impetus of MPCS she might slip back once more.

'I think I know that I will, because it happened in the Easter holidays. At the end of the term I was so excited about MPCS. Then came the holidays – a whole month passed and the beginning of term came and I – thinking, "my goodness, can I go through another term!", because I'd forgotten about the actual – excitement – you can –'

– then she shakes her head and laughs –

'I hate talking about myself like this! This is just me – there's – thirty other students who aren't the same as me – you're just talking about my – I'm just one person.'

Lyn laughs – there is a paradox built in to the conversation – it has already been established that part of her shyness is due to her belief that talking exposes her to the risk of adverse judgements – that, somehow, her utterances invite a lowering of other people's esteem in her. So, presumably, she finds it hard to fight her shyness like this?

'In a funny sort of way. I hate it and I love it, if you see what I mean. I know it's good for me, therefore I do it.'

Once again we can see, not just the embeddedness of this program in the life of a person, but the continuity between the two. Here, however, we see something of the dynamic of that relationship between person and program and we get a sense of how the struggle between individual and institution waxes and wanes. In the minds of evaluator and program director this innovation endures across time and its many contexts; for Lyn it has a less certain existence – it depends upon its presence.

Here, then, are people united in little, perhaps, other than what it takes to excite the interest of an educational evaluator. They are all somehow or another involved in music education – they are part of programs I was evaluating. But this is barely a distinguishing feature for any of them. They all have a life to be getting on with and a music education program appears across their personal horizons for fleeting encounters, interacts just briefly with their dilemmas – though it does interact. At such moments – and if we suspend disbelief for long enough to extrapolate from these briefest of accounts – we can see that the themes they are playing to in their lives reassert themselves in these fleeting instances – or simply embrace the moments as they come and go. By searching for a sense of coherence in the lives of these people rather than imposing one from an analytic base, we see how the lives of individuals envelope the programs of which they are a part.

So, we might see Richard's participation in the music workshop with the Chinese bells as a replay of his apparently insistent struggle to find an affirmative experience in schooling – somewhat in the face of adversity, and under pressure to be coopted into the strident and dismissive group culture of young boys. Once we hear and see more of Richard – follow him into the playground – it is hard not to see his playing of those bells as something very much more than joining in a music workshop. We begin to get a glimpse of a value system in Richard – less important for what it is than for the fact that we are reminded he has one. With that in mind, and knowing that Richard, for example, seems to be competent to think evaluatively about the educational treatments he receives, it becomes compelling to think of the kind of evaluation Richard might give to the Adopt-a-Player Scheme – how, that is, he would embrace that scheme as part of the way he saw and lived his life.

The final interaction with Richard reminds us, at least, of the vulnerability of young people. I shared this piece with doctoral students in a seminar,[4] asked them how they would interpret it. They all focused on the implication that children (at least in their institutional role) are defined by others and that Richard was ceding control over who he was. At this point their interpretations diverged. One thought that Richard was ceding to the hierarchy of the school; another that this was a general social phenomenon in which we all seek superior authority to legitimate our identity; another, that Richard simply thought it was none of his business and that he had to wait for 'teacher-hood' before dealing with such questions. Although all seminarists agreed about the construction of children by more powerful 'others' they differed in accounting for the means. One, for example, would have children as sensing a lack of 'rights' over their identity; another as merely sensing and obeying social form. But the practical conclusion is that arts workers and evaluators, both, fall into that same category of more powerful people who have the opportunity to define less powerful people.

Of course, this turns back on itself because we have only the utterance of Richard with which to work – he is, in a sense, constructing us constructing him. We are as much trapped by the processes of power-over-identity as he appears to be. If he is saying, for example, that he cedes rights to fix his identity to authoritative adults then this defines a *condition* of evaluative enquiry, and one we cannot escape with the best of intentions. Now, I cannot be sure of how much of this (at one level or another) we can attribute to Richard and this is, in some respects, a difficulty. I will argue later that the problem of interviewing children is less one of whether or not we believe them, but *how* we believe them. But for the purposes of beginning our analysis of the relationship between evaluator, individual and program it serves us well in revealing the complexities we work with.

Michael and Lyn both talk about how music education programs interact with the confusing demands being made by their professional lives. Lyn, bent on a task of almost quixotic proportion – to change her personality – looks to the program as an instrument; the opera musician, struggling with the contradictions of life in a leading opera house, also looks to music education programs as instruments, though for the

---

4   At the University of Málaga, in the Departamento de Educación y Organización Escolar.

betterment of children and, thereby, the enhancement of meaning in his own life. Again, I shared these pieces in that doctoral seminar. There was, again, a difference over how to interpret Michael's data (one that, in the course of evaluative enquiry would normally be resolved by holding further conversations with Michael). One person in that same seminar read the piece as though there were a utilitarian kind of calculation being made by him which was finally resolvable – probably in terms of his accepting that he had a contented life because he could bracket his dissatisfactions with the benefit of being involved in great music. Another argued strongly that there could be no resolution, no matter what the benefits, there were significant costs to cope with – that life could not be resolved by cost–benefit calculations.

It is worth pursuing the implications of these differing views, for they have roots which reach deeply into the sub-soil of evaluation – as with Richard we are looking directly at the tension between the individual and the institution. Here is evidence of the classical sociological battle over agency and structure – do we control the conduct and the destiny of the institutions we work in or do 'they' – pre-existing as we join them – construct us? Who is the creature of whom?[5] The first interpretation, in which a calculation can be made and used to resolve the question of discontentment, speaks of the domestication of the institutional actor, their final submission by accepting the means–end rationality of the enterprise – so long as the rewards are worth it we will put up with the humiliations, as it were.[6] The second interpretation speaks of the continuing struggle and the refusal of the individual to submit to the logic of ends. Perhaps Michael wants everything – to have a meaningful work and home life, *and* to work with Haitink. Anything less offered by the institution spells discontent (– and why not?).

We can begin to see, perhaps, the integrity of the independent concept of 'program' beginning to erode. In these cases, to call these events

---

5   Leaving aside the attempts of sociological revisionists such as Anthony Giddens to ease the problem through synthesizing analysis ('structuration'); or those of the post-structuralists who reduce both institution and individual to the same textual status. In spite of recent scepticism towards bipolar analyses I find helpful the tension between individual and institution, and I find unhelpful the attempt to disguise it.

6   Yossarian, in Joseph Heller's Second World War novel *Catch 22*, is desperate to return home at the end of his prescribed number of bombing missions from northern Italy. Each time he reaches his 'performance indicator' it is raised, requiring him to do more. When he finally persuades the authorities they are best off without him he is allowed to return home. The senior officers impose two conditions – one is that he goes back to the US as a hero; the other that he agrees to 'like them'. *Catch 22* is as good a Weberian analysis of society and its bureaucracies as I have read.

'music education' or 'arts experiences' is to prejudge the issue. There is at least as much personal and social education going on here as there is music. Of course, there is a substantive element of these interactions that involves music and creative art-making, but we have no reason to assume that these dominate the events as the key defining characteristic. Not everyone in the cinema is there just to watch the film.

This presents us with a number of problems, not counting the emotional problem of ceding control over the definition of phenomena. First, we have to be able to work out the range of possible meanings these events might have and know something about the nature of the variation – that is, where the variation comes from. It may be, for example, that there are systematic differences between the ways in which children see these events as compared with teacher–adults and artist–adults. Equally, there might be systematic differences in what these events mean among discrete groups of children – young Muslim girls and young Christian boys, say. Or, it may be that we live in a hopelessly diverse world in which these events mean something different to every participant[7] and no one view is privileged over others.

Knowing and understanding something of the diversity of meanings provoked by educational events is important in curriculum terms and in ways that will be explored later. For now we may note that differences in the ways these events might be viewed are more than mere perspectival variation – a kind of parallax view where you see things this way because of your 'field of social vision', whereas I see things in another way . . . etc. Rather, it creates the possibility that we can *account* for variation in perspective through researching differences in interests, values and experience. The people we have seen in these accounts bring with them certain preoccupations and ways of prioritizing the world, and these are what may account for the variation. If, at the root of diversity, we find plural values then we become aware of an ethical issue in how to respond to the plurality, because we have no right arbitrarily to prioritize one point of view over another. What we might be able to say is that whether these events can be classed as artistic, creative, aesthetic or musical remains problematic (and may not even matter). But they might, on the face of things, have educational potential insofar as uncovering the nature of variation allows learners to explore others' positions so as to better understand their own. Evaluative accounts like these, rooted in people's lives, offer a starting point for an educational as

---

7 This latter position is the constructivist one adopted by Guba and Lincoln (1989) and difficult to distinguish from unbridled relativism.

opposed to a disciplinary approach to music education, and offer an *educational* rationale for evaluation. This is, that is to say, *educational* evaluation.

This is not to rank education and artistic (or any other disciplinary) work, much less to put them into tension. But in the context of school, where we have to discover a public form of legitimacy for arts (as with any other kind of curriculum activity) we need to see artistic and educational justifications as separate. Just because music is a highly valued cultural activity does not of itself make it appropriate for inclusion in the school curriculum. In the context of a curriculum it has to prove not its *artistic* merit, but its *educational* merit.[8]

Let me undertake one further piece of analysis in order to reveal a final element of my argument about challenging our own sense of what is coherent. Here, the substantive field I draw from continues to be music education – but to reiterate, it can be generalized to the substantive aspect of any educational program.

We cannot assume that where the arts come into schools they do so in an unchanging way – that they are once and for all structured by artistic assumptions, priorities and beliefs. Programs are subject to context as their meanings and significance are subsumed within personal lives. Hold this in mind when reading the following observation-based interview taken from my evaluation of the Adopt-a-Player Scheme.

This final group are all girls. They are all, at this moment, grouped around the piano looking inside for the source of a rattling noise as though something is fouling some of the strings. One of the girls is Asian, called Belle, and she says she's about to get a keyboard for her birthday – and a dog.

> *Belle:* And other things.
> *Saville:* What are you going to like best?

---

8   As an aside, Stenhouse (1967: 100) offers a resolution of that tension. 'Just as scientists are creators of cultural innovation, contributing to man's understanding and control over his environment, so artists are creators of culture, enriching man's understanding and interpretation of human experience. In a broad sense, then, the artist is a kind of educator, and if it is necessary to justify him in the eyes of society, one might rest his case on this educational function.' Just in passing, I note without comment Stenhouse's juxtaposition of control (as a social by-product of scientific understanding) and interpretation (as a by-product of artistic understanding). It might be interesting to speculate on how evaluation bridges those two cultural functions.

Belle: I don't know – the dog I expect.

Saville: You're not getting a cymbal?! [Belle plays the cymbal in this piece – this was a weak joke.]

Belle: No, I don't like the cymbal. It's boring. And I don't like the noise – it's too much . . . music. Too loud. I don't like cymbals.

Saville: So why play it?

Belle: I was doing my job and Gina wasn't doing it properly, so she made me do it. I was going to be in a different group. I was doing my job.

Even so, Val [the CBSO musician] keeps her at it – playing the cymbal. She talks to her about it between renditions of the piece – getting her to play it with subtlety, for example, to pause for a fraction longer before giving the cymbal a regal crash after a piece of grandiose playing on the piano.

In this group, too, there are competitions and pecking orders and there are dominant girls. There are two Asian girls on the piano – one is tall, confident and imposing. She has piano lessons. Heather [the girls' teacher] says they are more precocious than appears and they stand somewhat apart from the class, though not aloof. The music is built around them playing a duet on the piano. The others are required to drop out strategically throughout the piece while the two girls play the piano all the time, loudly and with prominent melodies. Val confesses she is irritated by their dominance and by the less than competent playing. Belle taps away relentlessly and faultlessly on her cymbal. She sits half-slumped in her chair, holding a drum stick in one hand and covering her face with the other.

Recognizing value pluralism demands of us that we submit our definitions of what is meaningful to the critical appraisal of – among others – pupils. For we may be wrong or irrelevant or unjust in imposing our single (musical) set of values on the event. To think in terms of what and why we appreciate is manifestly a useful educational goal, but it is of limited utility in helping us analyse the complexities of arts education events. We would miss entirely the important question of what was meant by Belle's seated posture and her holding her hand across her face. Once again, the 'dirtiness' of life has intruded upon the privacy of the arts moment – the 'program' has been embraced and absorbed by the life it touched. Looked at from the perspective of Belle the music aspect of these interactions is a minor sub-set of a larger set of life interactions and cultural experiences with adults and authority.

It remains important to think of Belle in relation to her peers and to the adults around her. She has to resolve the sociological confusions of her presence in this event (perhaps just by hiding?) and so, therefore, do we.

The other Asian girls and Val, the musician, might get by through remaining autonomous and responding only to the event without considering Belle – we cannot. She appears to offer us an alternative perspective on this program.

Faced with a program or event, the evaluator has to make a decision about how far to stray from its 'official' definition as a music education phenomenon. By starting this section with decontextualized accounts of Richard, Lyn and Michael, I strayed as far as I probably could from the official definition. In fact, in the case of the Adopt-a-Player Scheme of which Richard was a part I was asked to write its story (i.e. evaluate it) on the assumption that this was a reasonably successful attempt to promote music values and experiences in schools. What I found was something which achieved some of this, but achieved a great deal more in educational terms. To reveal that, however, meant setting aside that official definition and looking at the program in a wholly different way – in fact, from the point of view of the child, and hence the account of Richard and others. One constraint on this is methodological conservatism, and I will make some comment on this.

PROGRAMS IN PEOPLE: AGAINST BIOGRAPHY

> Investigative practices do much more than order observations of a world that is given – they actually prepare the world that is there to be observed. The observations that are available for ordering may function as raw material within the limited framework of a particular investigation, but they are far from raw in terms of a broader perspective. They are made on human subjects who have been actively selected on certain social criteria, who have entered into particular social relations with the investigators, and whose actions have been carefully circumscribed by the investigative situation. Ordering observations once they have been made is only a small part of investigative practice; the major part involves the construction of special 'forms of life' in which the observations are grounded. (Danziger, 1990: 195)

There is, as I have argued, a bias in evaluation practice and this derives from a persistent focus on the formal characteristics of programs. These are typical of the 'forms of life' which Danziger mentions and which preoccupy evaluators. Evaluators have their own interests – we have our own careers to make and fund. To a large extent these depend upon the existence of programs and programs as particular kinds of evalu-able life forms. For evaluation to be a valued activity we need programs to be cast as laboratory experiments,[9] yielding up measurable indicators of potential or worthlessness; we need them to have impact on the lives of people so that their potential actually matters; we need them to be controversial in that they imply winners and losers in the struggle for scarce resources; and, finally, we need them, ideally, to be balanced carefully so that they are inviting for their radicalism without being too menacing a leap into unknown futures.[10] We also need them to be conceived so as to fit our research methods. Both House (1993, particularly ch. 8) and Stake (1986) point to the potential for methodological choices to generate injustices against programs being evaluated and the people within them, and this implies that we also need to conceive of programs as good vehicles for our view of social justice.

The point – the danger – is that evaluators have an interest in asserting the existence, meaningfulness and value of programs. Not all participants do. Program participants most often measure the meaning of events in terms of personal learnings, not system learnings. Not all, of course, because a few do not, and these tend to be directors, principals, administrators, sponsors – the movers and shakers of systems, those to whom evaluators tend most immediately to relate because we share that same value. We are interested in change and so we are interested in programs as mechanisms of change.

So it is that inhabitants of innovation are cast in programmatic terms. This person is a 'tutor', that person a Course Director, another an animateur and others are 'students' or 'clients' – some in upper case, others in lower case. As actors their script is the program script (for example, in role they are supposedly motivated by program goals), their actions are measured for their value to the program and the scale of their presence and voice depends upon their prominence in the program. They are creatures of our inventions. Berger (1963: 166) reminds us of the dangers of going along with such dissimulation.

> Since society exists as a network of social roles, each one of which can become a chronic or a momentary alibi from taking responsibility for its

---

9   Rossi and Freeman (1989) argue that in the great social programs spawned in the USA from the New Deal on, social scientists saw their opportunity to finally adopt legitimate scientific observation procedures. These housing, education, poverty programs could be regarded as laboratories appropriate for properly controlled experiments and observations.
10   Principally, evaluators need programs and projects to be good vehicles for what they want to say. 'Evaluators', as Barry MacDonald wrote (Kushner and MacDonald, 1987) 'are the storytellers of innovation', and as such we need good material to tell a good story – not necessarily our story or 'the' story, but a good story.

bearer, we can say that deception and self-deception are at the very heart of social reality . . . The deception inherent in social structures is a functional imperative. Society can maintain itself only if its fictions . . . are accorded ontological status by at least some of its members some of the time . . .

In my definition of evaluation the evaluator lives both within and outside this characterization of society. One implication of Berger's existential analysis is that the 'functional imperative' that is systematic deception is also a moral imperative. We are not condemned for seeking alibis from responsibility. We have the obligation to construct comfortable (and comforting) realities – after all, we do have to live with mortality. However, the role of evaluator is based on a different functional and moral imperative – that is, that of supporting judgements of the realities we construct. There is no warrant for evaluators to join in the game of deception. In his utopian essay on social philosophy, Campbell (1999) gave the blueprint for an open society committed to systematic social experimentation ('piecemeal social engineering'). One of its key characteristics was its commitment to honesty which he defined as 'reality testing . . . self-criticism . . . avoiding self-deception'. For him, the issue was one of political cooption into ideologically based rather than descriptive roles – 'the institutionalised, bureaucratic tendency to present only a favourable picture' (p. 13) – reality testing was, therefore, an accountability exercise. While acknowledging this tendency and political necessity I am more concerned here with reality testing as a return, as it were, to pre-judgement, to the moment when deception is entered into so as to understand its nature.

So much for the source of the bias I am concerned with – what is its nature and impact? Its nature is in giving systematic prominence to forms of organization over individual experience; the consequent risk is that we lose, as a result, an important source for estimating the significance programs might have in the lives of citizens (that is, testing the viability of social realities). Reading an evaluation report which consistently asserts the meaningfulness of a program – and in doing so invokes the tacit agreement of individuals within it and touched by it – you leave with the impression that it is an event in those people's lives which stands out, is worthy of comment and which, somehow, matters. All of that may, of course, be misleading. What it might do is reduce our capacity to measure the scale of the archetypal sociological struggle for dominance between the individual and the institution I referred to earlier. As evaluators we too often, perhaps, close down that struggle in favour of the institution.

The alternative is to document something of people's values, their lives, perhaps, and to use this as context within which to read programs – to start the evaluation from where people are rather than from where the program is. So, we seek to understand something about Richard as he fits into his peer group and his views of schooling and to see how the Adopt-a-Player Scheme fits into his life or values – and so with Lyn and others. This is not to say that we simply substitute one exaggerated measure for another – the constructivist or postmodernist might complain that we construct people in just the same way and to the same effect as we construct programs – so this is not an inversion so much as a straight substitution. But the point is not to arrive at an accurate statement of Richard's life and values, as I have already said, but to remind ourselves that there are many worlds of meaning within which to judge the prominence and the worthwhileness of programs in people's lives and that we tend to favour a limited range. To reiterate for a final time, we do not need to have an accurate sense of Richard's life and beliefs, only enough of a sense that he has and holds these things autonomously and that he can use them as a base on which to make his own judgements about our 'program'.

Nor do I want to be misunderstood as merely urging the use of life-history techniques in evaluation, though these clearly have a part to play. It is too simplistic to equate an individualistic perspective with bio-graphical techniques. Debates about case study or naturalistic approaches to evaluation have generally been more comfortable with the term 'portrayal' than with biography, and it is this that I am after. Portrayal has a more contemporary feel to it – it paints a picture of the individual as they are in the here-and-now, as they live and work and reason and enter into social exchange. In existential terms, portrayal allows us to interpret pasts and measure the significance of futures through the lens of the immediate; it allows us to discipline the general with the particular. This may well involve biographical (life-historical) detail but, at least as important as this, it will locate the individual in the recent sociology of their lives – both who and *how* they are. Hence, we can only seek to understand something of Richard by seeing how he relates (or does not) to his schoolmates; similarly with Lyn, Michael and Belle, all of whom measure themselves against those they work with (and against). In fact, the logic of the insight that selves are socially constructed is that they can only be reconstructed for research purposes in the context of society, and this means breaking out of the individual biographical account.

There is, as a final note to this, a version of the issue 'writ-small', so to speak, and it occurs in the interview. I have often advised students who are seeking guidelines as to how to conduct an interview not to ask the question that is at the core of the enquiry – concerned, again, to find the sense of coherence in the experience and views of the respondent rather than risk imposing one through questioning. For example, there came a time towards the close of the Guildhall Conservatoire innovation when I was being asked for summative statements about the course, some sense of how it might have had an impact on students who had passed through it. The obvious thing was to go and ask the students (the least obvious thing was to send a questionnaire – I needed reflective, judgement data).

I took out three months to accomplish an interview program leading to a report, but I was not in the field for very long before I realized that I was achieving an improbably high frequency of comments on the course and its impact. I knew enough of the life and pressures in the Conservatoire to know that I was receiving wildly optimistic accounts of the potential for this program to reach into people's lives and change them. After all, these were music trainees living in a highly opportunistic world – and the course had done little to change the structure of opportunities, much less the external value system against which trainees gauge their musical esteem. What was happening, of course, was that I was receiving answers because I was asking the questions. I developed intimate, high-trust relationships with the students and they were responding to this rather than to the rationality of the interrogation. They were obliging me by theorizing about how the course *might have* changed them – perhaps how they felt it *ought to have* done so. Useful data – but off the mark for this exercise.

I stopped asking the question directly – though the students knew well what I was there for. Interviews became structured in a very different way. I would ask them about what was happening to them, what had happened in the intervening year or so, what lay ahead, what were the live themes for them at the moment. If MPCS had had a major impact I could be reasonably sure that it would surface – this was the structure I infused into these (supposedly 'unstructured') interviews. If nothing of the sort surfaced, it was a reasonable indication that the course had come, perhaps been very meaningful in its moment, and then had gone leaving little trace.

There are special demands made by the particular contexts on evaluation and these have to be reflected in our work, just as there are constraints we, as evaluators, bring to our work and which limit our methodological range. In ways I will explore in the next chapter there is a seamless continuity between ourselves and our methodology; I will consider methodology as a personal construct. In this example it was my (fortunate) capacity to consider how I myself in the context of relationships with these students had a distorting effect on their responses.

In fact, it is useful to think of at least two evaluation programs which share the same space in time. One is the activity made up of evaluative acts – those things which make up our design and which are observable and regulated by our ethical agreements. The other is the reflexive act, the experience of doing it, the struggle to express the self in methodology and to reconcile personal ambitions with the discipline of the job.[11]

REGARDING THE SUBJECT

I was talking to a student about the use of anonymity, trying to persuade him that anonymity was potentially as damaging to people as naming them in our reports (there is an ethical issue in denying identity). He was not so sure, and wanted to ask me how to handle a particular situation. 'If a subject says you can name them . . .'

'. . . if a subject . . .'. I have often thought about the use of that term and the problem of what we call the people who feature in our research reports. Subjects. It is a term, as the student reminded me, that feels more familiar in the discourses of survey research and the psychological experiment. What (how) does it signify?

At the simplest level, monarchs have subjects. The term here defines a relationship of loyalty. A monarch's subjects are those who recognize the legitimacy of the monarchy and who are prepared to play a submissive role in the face of this form of authority. The legitimacy of a monarchy is normally found in tradition and traditional values – it often shares the same mantle as religious authority. But whatever it is, to be a subject means denying yourself the freedom to question the *basis* of the authority.

The 'subject' in English grammar is juxtaposed with an 'object'. Subject – verb – object. The subject is the agent and she or he does something (verb) to the object. This is an interesting inversion. The conventional assumption in research is that 'we' (the researchers) do something to 'them' (the researched). But that makes *us* the subjects of research and

---

11 Albeit in the context of phenomenological enquiry – not evaluation – Bentz and Shapiro (1998: 5) put it thus: 'your research is . . . intimately linked with your awareness of yourself and your world . . . your awareness of and reflection on your world and the intellectual awareness and reflection that are woven into your research affect . . . one another. Good research should contribute to your development as a mindful person, and your development as an aware and reflective individual should be embodied in your research.'

them the objects. Of course, you could turn it around and say that 'they' are subjects because they are *doing* something that we are interested in – they are the agents of actions we want to research (like a teacher is an agent of curriculum). But then they are not *research* subjects – they are professional subjects. Again, the subjects of research – the agents – are us. Confused? I have been.

I want to look at this confusion in a little more depth for this takes us back to our research ancestry – still in pursuit of that inversion by which we come to read programs through the lives of people. I want to look very briefly at the history of the psychological experiment. The psychological experiment has probably been the dominant of the 'life forms' spoken of earlier by Danziger referring to the social organization of educational enquiry.

The success of psychology in this century, says MacDonald (1996: 248) was assured, 'in the context of the development of schooling as a sorting and selection process', but only once it had been detached from its 'original moorings in educational values'. Contemporary revisionists of psychology have made similar arguments, seeking to rescue the discipline from its denial of the individual as a cultural actor (Bruner, 1990), from its denial of the sociology of the individual as meaning-maker (Harré, 1983) and from its denial of the individual as metaphysician (Robinson, 1995).

There has also been a detachment from a more complex methodological history than is often acknowledged.[12] Danziger (1990, see ch. 4 in particular) reviews the history of the psychological construction of the subject, and at one point focuses on the sociology and social psychology of the investigative situation – the research interaction between psychologist and . . . well, subject. He identifies three archetypal approaches to psychological experiments, each of which embodies a different view of the subject (each of which he embeds in a history of the experimenter). Though these deal with experimental relationships they do stand as archetypes – and as progenitors of contemporary relationships, as we will shortly see.

One of the celebrated founders of academic psychology, Wilhelm Wundt, set up his school in Leipzig. His interest lay in the revelation of the inner mind as an accessible field for empirical study – in fact, as the

---

12 Bruner (1979) argues that psychology lost its confidence in 'mentalism' (the study of mind as motivator) early on. Harré (1983) argues similarly, and also argues that psychology drives apart the individual and the collective, confuses causation with morality by smuggling normative assumptions into experimental observations and (Harré, 1989) by systematically ignoring social context.

inner equivalent of the study of the outer, more accessible, parts of the body. He was interested in elements of mental states – apart from personality. In his laboratory, subject and experimenter were interchangeable – in fact, Wundt often featured as the subject of his own experiments. Here was the last major expression of 'introspection' in which the disciplined reflection of the subject was the principal means of observation.[13] Danziger concludes that, given that the task was to reveal inner states, the subject could be a more important figure than the experimenter who merely recorded the emergent data. Intelligent/ intelligible responses were all, and the 'subject' was the interlocutor between mind and experimenter. There was even, records Danziger, a period in which the subject of the experiment was called by psychologists the 'observer' – a clear reference to introspection.

In France a clinical experimental school (focused on hypnosis research) developed under such as Alfred Binet. This school favoured a wholly different form of social organization for the interaction and this was mirrored by the work of such as Stanley Hall and J. McKeen Cattell. Here, the subject was borrowed directly from medical science, a person who presents themselves for a treatment. Investigator/subject roles were less fluid, more segregated (Binet tended to use women as subjects, men as investigators), though they might have drawn from a pool of recognizable subjects. The segregation was partly to do with the aims of investigation. Much of this early work sought to reveal aspects of mind by comparing abnormal phenomena with normal – a comparative exercise. The investigator was cast in the role of expert observer who made comparisons and inferences. Subjects were more passive, though identifiable as individuals.

A third approach – the decisive rejection of the introspective, mentalist tradition – was marked by the work of Francis Galton. In 1884 at the International Health Exhibition Galton set up a laboratory for testing

---

13 The word 'disciplined' is important. Danziger points out that Wundt sought to move from the mere internal reflection on subjective experience to systematic internal enquiry. He sought, that is, to transfer the rigour of external (physiological) experiments to internal processes of perception. The shift is crucial for evaluation for it distinguishes the aims of those evaluators who seek to 'collect' biographical data, for example, from those who aim to engage subjects in the formulation of their own judgement. Hence, for example, Bruner's (1990) critique of cognitive psychology for persistently evading issues of 'mind' – by which he means 'intentionality'. Hence, too, the work of the radical constructivists who argue, as does Glasersfeld (1991: 18), that 'one is obliged to go beyond the mere proclamation that the world we experience is a world we construct. At least one must try to show *how* what we call knowledge . . . could be built up . . .' Again, that 'how' points to disciplined enquiry rather than mere reportage.

the mental faculties of members of the general public. More than 9,000 people passed through. Status differentials were clear – each individual even received the results of their measurements on payment of a fee. Each individual subject (Galton preferred the term 'applicant', says Danziger) was a stranger to the experimenter – but no matter, since the overriding interest was the revelation of patterns and frequencies of mental states and abilities across large populations, in pursuit of his (now infamous) eugenics program.

One significant difference between, in particular, Galton's treatment of the subject and that of Wundt lies in the nature of the collaboration in the experimental act. Experimental roles were fluid in Wundt's laboratory because there was a coincidence of interest between subject and experimenter. This was, in its nature, a collaboration to the point, as we have seen, where the subject might be the higher status person. In Galton's experiment, on the other hand, there were interests for both subject and experimenter, but these were wholly divergent. 'Galton's interests in this research situation were just as practical as those of his subjects, the difference being that while they were interested in their plans for individual advancement he was interested in social planning and its rational foundation' (Danziger, 1990: 56).[14]

What might we draw from this? Well, first it is clear that in seeking to define the 'subject' of research we are faced with a range of options, each of which is appropriate to certain investigative aims – each of which, we might also note, has its own sociology, ethic and, indeed, morality. Educational psychology as a broad disciplinary church has clearly tended towards Galton's 'anthropometric' approach, treating the subject as a person who may or may not be identifiable but who enjoys lower status, presents with certain characteristics that are comparable with those of others, and whose interests in the experiment are divergent with those of the researcher. This is not a consistent picture, of course, and psychiatry/psychoanalysis has had its own influence with the emergence of the psychoanalytic 'case study' – that is, depth analysis of an individual. Even here, however, such cases are interpreted through general theories and again the interests of the individual (to regain

---

14   Campbell (1999: 24–5) cites Janousek as taking the argument further. Janousek argues that the random assignment of citizens to experimental groups is evidence of authoritarianism and of 'treating fellow citizens as "subjects" in the psychologist's and monarchist's sense, as "victims" of the experiment rather than as collegial agents of the experiment'. Janousek argued for a rotation of roles between experimenter and participant and Campbell, though sceptical, supports the notion (cf. J. Janousek 'Comments on Campbell's *Reforms as Experiments*', *American Psychologist*, 25, 2 (1970), pp. 191–3).

normality) and those of the treatment expert (surely to support that – but also to learn more about the character and distribution of psychological ailments) diverge.

Let me return to my theme, to the direct experience of research. We face similar choices as did the psychologists – though we typically, in naturalistic enquiry, find it hard to avoid hierarchical relationships. As we saw earlier with Richard, they are constructed for us. Oddly, choices in subject–enquirer relationships have, however, recently expanded for evaluators whereas they remain limited for psychologist–researchers. The figure of a Wilhelm Wundt subjecting himself to his own experiment is regarded today, perhaps, as naive, dilettantish, speaking of an age of methodological innocence. But the equivalent in naturalistic enquiry in education, the post-positivist researcher who regards themselves as the only viable subject of the research, or at least, who treats their role and that of their subjects as interchangeable (as do some feminist researchers) – is currently regarded as methodological sophistication.[15] Introspection has, in a sense, been rediscovered. History plays some strange tricks.

There have, too, been more recent developments which have extended the sophistication of the Wundt/Leipzig approach, notably by Kurt Lewin (see Danziger, 1990: ch. 10). Lewin worked on psychological aspects of personality and volition. Dissatisfied with conventional approaches, which tended to focus on observable outcomes of psychological states – words and actions, behavioural states – Lewin developed an approach which started with life contexts, to draw the structural and environmental sources for those observable states. To do this he needed (a) to treat the subject as an expert informant, (b) to adopt a highly interactive approach to relationships with the subject, (c) to regard the subject not as a basic unit of observation whose data is to be set alongside many others, but as the unique focus of the observation, and (d) to regard each observation of a behavioural event with a single subject as potentially having a unique set of determinants which distinguish it from others with the same person. Danziger quotes Lewin:

> One ought not to regard the single trial as an isolated formation that is only identical with preceding and succeeding trials of the same kind because that

---

15 There has, for example, been a spate of publications by some leading researchers engaged in self study so as to reveal the hidden mechanisms of researcher constructions of others. See Peshkin (1988) and Popkiewicz (1988) for examples of the researcher treating himself as the (vicarious) subject.

is what is required for purposes of statistical treatment. Rather, one ought to treat each trial essentially non-statistically, as a single, concrete process in its full reality. One will have to take into account the particular position of each trial in the temporal series of trials and partly make the transition to constructing the experimental period as a unitary whole. (1990: 175)

Benne (1990: 140–52) takes Lewin's story a step further into his life in the United States, once he had fled Germany (Benne worked closely with him). Here, he developed his psychological approach by abandoning the controlled experimental environment and moved, instead, to the lived contexts of daily life where he worked with various professional groups, for example, on his program for 're-education'. The experimental situation had outlived its usefulness as Lewin sought to locate psychological knowledge in aspects of group culture and in a context of change. Now the relation between researcher and subject became very complex indeed – more akin to forms we might recognize in action research and evaluation relationships today – and clearly required negotiation to both define and sustain it.

Lewin's psychological studies took place through the 1930s and 1940s. It was 30 years later that Lee Cronbach (1975), one of the United States's leading psychological experimenters in what Danziger would characterize as the Galtonian approach, renounced much of his work, declaring of pedagogical observations that 'the dimensions of the situation and the person enter into complex interactions. This complexity forces us to ask once again, "Should social science aspire to reduce behaviour to laws?"' Cronbach argued that psychological generalizations have a 'short half-life' and decay over time and geography – though they are useful as hypotheses for further reflection. This curriculum might work here and now, but it is increasingly less likely to be replicated in its success the further away you are in geography (another school) and time (with the next cohort of students). He called for more attention to be paid to context. He also argued that the very social organization of psychological enquiry – the fragmentation of research into highly specialized and focused studies – militated against the possibility of generalization and theory-building.

But even by then, Stake (1967) had invented 'Responsive Evaluation', Parlett and Hamilton (1977) 'Illuminative Evaluation' and Barry MacDonald (1987) his 'Democratic Evaluation'. Such insights and others (recently reconstituted as participatory approaches to evaluation) laid much of the basis for interactive and context-sensitive approaches to enquiry – particularly case study approaches. To some extent these were based on the use of case study which, as did Lewin, sought to leave on hold the question of comparative analysis (i.e. with other cases), so as to focus on the idiosyncratic, or the 'intrinsic', as Stake (1995) puts it. They helped to free the researcher from the stranglehold of the independently defined variable, the null hypothesis, controlled conditions – and to concentrate on understanding and explanation situated within the contexts of those being observed. 'To suppress a variation that might not recur', argued Cronbach (1975), 'is bad observing.' Naturalistic enquiry, in particular, but also sociology, anthropology and ethnography have reached for a more sophisticated view of the subject and a correspondingly more restricted view of the research role. Case study evaluation is designed to generate theory out of the contexts in which people live and work – to engage in theory production collaboratively with those being researched. Like Wundt and unlike Galton, naturalistic enquirers get to know their subjects, often very well, and certainly seek to identify them – in personality if not in name. Case study relies for much of its quality (and some of its validity) on the fluency and insight of its respondents whom we ask to take the role of observer of events – a form of introspection, as I have argued. Principally, perhaps, case study evaluation seeks to bring the interests of the evaluator in line with the interests of the subject by sharing the same need to understand local situations. You may note, by now, that the term 'subject' is becoming threadbare and increasingly inappropriate with use.

In case study evaluation we have, too, developed a broader range of enquiry instruments than are available to the experimentalist and, to some extent, these allow us not to climb out of the subject problem, but to render it in more useful ways. Naturalistic, case study approaches no longer resist 'mentalism' (that is, a concern with intentionality) – to the contrary, naturalistic evaluators are dependent on subjective accounts. So far have we travelled in this direction that we are routinely dismissive of the possibility of objectivity.[16]

And, too, we often use direct observation of action which would normally lie outside of the experimental arena. In particular, observation in conjunction with the interview (i.e. observation-based interviewing) allows a range of strategies to break down the hierarchy between researcher and subject, using the observation as a source from which to

---

16 Too dismissive, argue Phillips (1990) and Scriven (1993). Phillips, for example, argues that we need to hold on to objectivity as a procedural device in methodology – not as an assertion of ontological status. Objectivity can, in a sense, be an ever-receding standard which defines the aspiration but denies the achievement. This functions well for those evaluators who may be uninterested in outcomes but concerned with quality of process.

negotiate interpretations and to agree on issues focuses.[17] Observations also persuade us to take a more complex view of the subject since in education we tend to be observing professionals engaging in action at least as sophisticated as research.

In the end psychology became dominated by what Danziger calls the 'myth of the independent individual'. This represents the individual as having only those attributes recognized by and in the experimental situation, which is the only context that is significant. The only links between individuals that are allowed are those where attributes and responses seem to coincide from one experiment to another – such as when people can be grouped together as having reacted to a stimulus in a similar way. Faced with the limited choice between studying the 'concrete individual' in their life context (regarded sceptically as 'unscientific') and the independent, decontextualized individual, psychologists went with the latter. Danziger argues that the bipolarity is too restrictive, however, and psychology might have been better served to have focused on investigative contexts rather than subjects.

This problem is mirrored in some contemporary approaches to the use of life-history in research. There is sometimes a tendency to use biography to place an individual in the context of their own life, effectively sealing them off against sociological links with other individuals. In this biographical nether world individuals hover somewhere in between the concrete individual – that is, made concrete by the particularities of their experience – and the independent individual – that is, made independent by having the reference points which identify them located in the research and not in their lived contexts.[18]

---

17   In fact, triangulation – the technique which uses an observation to stimulate varying accounts from, for example, pupils, a teacher and the researcher – brings the observer into the interpretive frame. Indeed, triangulation was originally conceived as an instrument for action research, designed for the purpose of democratizing the research process.

18   The best example I can think of is one of my own. On a curriculum development evaluation I once wrote a biographical account of the key figure – the Scale 1 (as was) teacher who was in charge of assessment. He told me that he had left school to become a monk; left that to join the army; left that as a sergeant-major (when he was presented with a silver-backed Bible); left that to become a teacher trainer; and finally retired from that to become a teacher who could manage on Scale 1 because of his early retirement money. What made all of this coherent – including his position in the curriculum project? He told me he was fascinated by the combination of authority and anonymity. Case closed, as it were! He lives on in my repertoire of fieldwork tales as this Jesuitical figure. Of course, that was inadequate in all sorts of ways. Principally, I stayed content with a version of that man's life – no doubt a very particular version – because it fitted the notion of coherence in innovation which certainly suited the evaluation. What made this man's story rich and meaningful was the nature of the curriculum project I was evaluating: I needed an odd-shaped peg to fit the

For Harré (1983) the problem is one of a failure to recognize the complexity of the subject represented, for example, in the duality of 'person' and 'self'. 'Person' is the subject as participant in social discourse – a member of the 'social conversation'; 'self' is the introspective individual who integrates 'consciousness, agency and autobiography' – the basis of 'personal being'. One way of thinking about the evaluative act is to think of the interview as moving between the two – which is what I mean when I suggest looking at the individual in the context of their sociology. The task goes beyond the mere representation of diverse selves; it moves on to document transitions between them. This allows for us to explore the nature of solidarity – that is, the process by which we create society and its organizations – but also to gain a sense of coherence in a life.

More up-to-date still, some postmodernists and some constructivists have created mixtures of contemporary methodologies with those three archetypes. There has been a tendency to refute the validity of observational accounts to rely mainly on biographies and documents as data sources, allowing a sharper focus on the relationship of enquirer to subject. One of the more significant contributions of postmodernism is the creation of the unreliable informant at the heart of research – what is sometimes called the 'fragmented self' – that is, we embody different versions of ourselves in response to the different contexts in which we find ourselves.

The danger of informant unreliability is the tendency to reduce data and experience to the status of text[19] – reinforced by the general belief that all reality is perception and so all accounts are constructions – so all can be read in the same way. Once having rendered data into text, the text can be laid out, as it were, in the research office for analysis and interpretation. Although the generation of data may be interactive and relies on the subject to produce vivid accounts, the subsequent processes of analysis and inference may not be. The risk is that the reduction-to-text and the subsequent use of discourse analysis highlights the expert

---

odd-shaped hole I had found at the assessment point. I could see how he fitted neatly into the program. Even so, I failed to contextualize this idiosyncratic view of the man in relationships with his colleagues. I left with no idea as to how his aim to be that rather shadowy but powerful figure was moderated through interaction. I hold this man in my mind as an example of Don DeLillo's observation that 'all plots lead to death'.

19 Stronach (1999: 175) talks of the shift as one from 'representational' critique to 'performative' critique. The former seeks to 'represent a situation in accord with notions of validity, authenticity or some other guarantees of worthwhileness'; the latter is 'more interested in how such guarantees are devised and narrated in discourse, as rhetoric', that is, a shift from action to manner.

status of the researcher against the (relatively) naive status of the subject. Back to Binet.

Guba and Lincoln (1989), for example, in one of the more robust versions of this tendency in evaluation deny any basis for making claims about 'reality' other than through a momentary (and supposedly accidental) consensus among people who all see things differently. There is, for them, little to choose between the perceptions of different individuals (including the evaluator's) and the only hope we have of fixing reference points is by negotiated agreement. Here is another variant of the sociology of the researcher–subject relationship, one that reflects something of the problem of the researcher creating the 'independent individual'. Once again, a subtle hierarchy is created in which individuals – adrift in an undifferentiated, relativistic world – rely on the evaluator to make sense of their relationships with others. All that binds individuals together is the common thread running through the research. The danger, that is to say, is one of stripping the individual out of their sociology.

To return to Danziger, what he offers is a general framework for understanding something of social relations in enquiry. Sociologists, ethnographers, educational evaluators – we are all moving through our own historical development in constructing the subject and, as we do, we form and reform our approach to social justice. The variations spoken of by Danziger are underpinned by values and by transparent beliefs about social justice, and such can be read into contemporary methodological writings. To take one prominent example, Schatzman and Strauss (1973) are quite clear that the purpose of enquiry is to generate theory (science, in fact), which we may imagine would make it difficult to find a coincidence of interest with the subjects; that each individual interview is seen as part of a series of sociological encounters; and that a basic strategy for negotiating access is to guarantee both confidentiality and anonymity. Here are hallmarks of social research freed from some of the more stringent demands on evaluation to elaborate a practical ethic in relationships with the subject. It speaks of a particular kind of ethic in which the anonymity of the subject (for protection) can be contrasted with the inevitable naming of the researcher (partly for display) – it is an ethic of ownership. Compare this with Helen Simons's (1987: ch. 4) account of trying to persuade a school into a participatory relationship with her as the evaluator: 'it was their study, I argued, as much as mine: their perceptions and judgements . . . their construction of meaning' (p. 97). More precisely, she could aspire to shared ownership of the study because the need to generate a situated theory of school change (which is what she was doing) was equally meaningful for the evaluator and the subject – there was the Wundtian conflation of interests.

4

Knowing Me, Knowing You: Evaluation Interviewing

FINDING YOUR VALUES

Naturalistic methodology is a historical construct – more a reflection on what happened than a recipe for action; more the art of the analyst than of the technologist. Naturalistic methodology, that is to say, reflects the conditions of its use – it is, at least partially, defined by the context in which it is applied and experienced. This means that, notwithstanding all those texts which seek to persuade students to 'buy off the shelf' and enter the field 'tooled-up', methodological understanding comes late. Says John Van Maanen (1988: 94) in his monograph on fieldwork:

> I must admit I am far less certain or confident now about the veracity or faithfulness of either my confessional or my realist tales than I ever have been in the past . . . Both, as I know only too well, leave more of my knowledge out of the accounts than they put in. Both close off too early (and too casually) what remain open matters. Fiddlesticks. I am, in short, still very much in the process of coming to understand my materials.

He is talking of studies long since past – and, of course, he is talking of anthropological research, not evaluation. His experience, however, is a general one that preoccupies researchers from time to time and which partially concerns the validity of data that was collected some time ago. But it is more of a concern – it is an issue, for it embodies two fairly obvious conflicting principles. One is that we must allow for under-standings that come late – especially in evaluation where we often work under the kinds of restrictions that limit what we might come to know.

This chapter is derived from an article published in the *Bulletin of the Council for Research in Music Education* (Kushner, 1995).

The other, however, is that time is a significant contextual factor which imposes a particularity on data. Data about people may not grow old with them and it may not be fair to use data which locks people up in past moments and past meanings. The counter argument to this is that where issues endure aged accounts can still be valid as characteristic of interactions that would happen today. The counter argument to *that* is that where respondents are no longer available to negotiate meanings there is an intensification of interpretative authority with the evaluator – if not a free rein.

Van Maanen goes on to put another spin to this issue of understanding outliving the data. He says that what he learned of the talk and action of his respondents is not only incomplete, but it disregards 'the contextual matters that surround my coming together with particular people at particular times'. For instance, the ethnographer's view of the 'inform- ant' has changed over time to one in which he or she is regarded as an 'interlocutor', not merely the passive provider of data on a culture, but something of an interpreter of that culture – a mediator between the culture of the ethnographer and that of the informant. There has, this is to say, been a methodological development in the intervening period, underpinned by a shift in social values. Van Maanen's emerging understandings are being influenced from many sources. No doubt some can no longer be supported by his original data.

There is quite a brew here and it does, I think, have a significance beyond Van Maanen's concerns with how ethnographic accounts get written. My concern is with the personal construction of naturalistic methodology, and I think that part, at least, of that growth in Van Maanen's understanding as well as new understanding of the data and its illumination of issues, is new understanding of the methodology as well. You can't learn 'it' from books or from experts and you certainly cannot take 'it' and apply 'it'. Naturalistic methodology is something you have to discover – it is emergent.[1] You may benefit from reading about

---

1   I am concerned with naturalistic methodology, but it is worth noting that methodology as emergent understanding applies also to quantitative and even experimental approaches – hence Campbell's (1999) account of the development of the quasi-experiment out of the shortcomings of true experiment enquiries. Cronbach (1984: 699) commenting on the recent publication of professional standards for evaluators argued that: '"The approach to case study", we are told, "is as subject to specification as the design of an experimental study." The remark is true in a whimsical sense, because an intelligent field experiment is subject to little pre-specification. In a number of true experiments that started with impartial allocation of subjects to treatments groups, the enquiries paid off primarily because the investigators thought freshly about the data as they came in. Often the experimental manipulation played the role only of increasing the range of a variable . . .'

ways of thinking about methodology and from certain procedural principles involved in its discovery, but in general my advice to research
students increasingly is not to read too much methodology until, at the
very least, practical problems have arisen in fieldwork – until, that is,
there is a personalized *lens* through which methodological reading might
make personal sense. Methodology is, I think, something that is crafted
as a form of expression. It is a personal construct.

This does, of course, make naturalistic enquiry a highly uncertain and
risky activity. It says that there are few guides – until and unless, that is,
you have discovered enough about yourself to know why you are
investigating and what your personal limits are. Until then, the most
common experience of enquiry is of confusion and uncertainty – and
methodological texts rarely teach how to cope with these. For example,
common experiences in field enquiry include such as the following,
which I draw from my own.

- During an evaluation of a careers guidance project I find myself in a
  school assembly being given by a nun. I have so little time here that I
  have to use this observation – in any case nothing else is happening
  in the school – and I feel sure it has something to do with vocational
  education, but I just cannot see how.
- I am sitting alongside a headmaster who opens his diary in front of
  me when I ask for an interview next week. We are both staring at two
  empty pages as he tells me that he is booked solid. We sit in silence
  looking at the diary.
- I was standing in a busy staffroom of a school being ignored by
  everyone there until this teacher came to talk to me. She invited me
  to her class and since I was desperate to do something other than just
  stand about I accepted. Now I am here in her class and it is uninter-
  esting to me and seems to have nothing to do with what I am here
  for. I am increasingly restive and I feel strongly I should be 'somewhere else' – but there are 45 minutes of the lesson left. She wanders
  over to me, bends down and whispers that she'd be interested in
  discussing the class after the bell.
- I am a vain person. I find myself in a school (in the USA) where our
  evaluation is precariously poised, having been excluded from the
  school but just recently rescued. I am here under sufferance. In the
  course of a well-humoured informal meeting a Puerto Rican teacher-
  assistant – one of the most popular members of the school staff –
  offers to cut my hair then and there. Up to now I have been playing it
  'street-wise', trading on my joviality and my ability to speak Spanish.
  She's reaching in her bag and others are laughing.

- I am interviewing a university professor whom I find is boring me, however hard I try to be interested. I lose the train of thought and conversation but realize that he has said something to me which he regards as significant and is waiting for my response. I can't 'busk' one – nor can I even think of a question to ask him. He's looking at me.
- I start evaluating the Conservatoire project and at the first session I attend the students, as a group, consider my position and say that they want me to join in with the music workshops. My own view is strongly that this is not for me to do since it takes all my energies to observe analytically and to maintain my notes, and that the job of an evaluator is to record the experiences of others, not to share those experiences. They insist and turn away to start the workshop.
- There was a controversy in an evaluation following which we agreed (unusually) that we would not publish the final report, and that for anything we did publish about that project we would seek permission first. Some months later I realize that I overlooked the inclusion of part of that report in an article I had submitted to a journal which is about to publish it. I hadn't sought permission. I realize this in a cold flush in the early hours of a sleepless night.

These, I think, are not uncommon experiences and speak to the 'messiness' of fieldwork. Oddly, they rarely surface in this form in accounts of evaluation fieldwork, in particular – 'confessional' accounts generally deal with more dignified (and dignifying) failures. But they imply decisions more characteristic of field enquiry than those of whether to conduct structured or 'semi-structured' interviews or whether to elaborate a sample by adding further variables or which clothes to wear or how to reduce the impact of your presence. In our research courses we rarely teach the skills of dealing with uncertainty, so urgent is it to equip people for fieldwork. Naturalistic enquiry, particularly in its refusal to accept the authority of existing theory in favour of discovering practical theory in the context of action, exposes the researcher to existential dilemmas. These can be invoked by the apparently trivial but, in the living of them, quite massive happenings I have just typified. Says Schon (1971: 231):

> It is taken as given that situations of public action contain more information than we can handle and are inherently unstable. Within them, then, knowledge can have only the validity it is found to have in the here-and-now. The here-and-now provides the test, the source and the limit of knowledge.

The investigator has to have a theory of why she is where she is so as to be able to respond to these instabilities – by which I mean more than simply 'I am here to conduct this investigation'. Consider how you might address the following questions, and how your responses might represent your personal theory of fieldwork (if you are like me you will have at least two sets of responses – one, how you would like to see yourself; the other, a description of what you actually do and are like. It is the second we are after):

- Why are you investigating – on whose behalf?
- How, in general, do you see your status in relation to those you observe – higher, lower, different, more/less privileged? What difference does it make?
- Do you believe what your respondents say to you, in general, and if you do – how and why do you believe them? (For example, do you distinguish the truth value of what people say to you according to their place in the power structure, according to their age, their class, their gender, whether you like them or not?)
- Can you conduct an investigation with people you do not like (that is, and still be fair and rigorous)?
- How do you balance your obligations/loyalties to the institutions involved (including your own) with those towards individuals who live in the institutions implied by your investigation? (For example, if there is a tension between fairness to an individual and protecting the stability of a democratic institution, which are you prepared to sacrifice?)
- Who owns the data you collect? If you, what do you do with it after the enquiry – if not you, what are you doing with it in the first place?

These kinds of questions lead us, in the first instance, at least, to procedural guides as to what posture to adopt – possibly long before methodological resolution has occurred. They are just a sample, of course, and there are different sets of questions that will reach into the heart of personal doubt for others just as these reach into mine. Hamilton et al. (1977: 25) argued that:

> Evaluation entails a view of society. People differ about evaluation because they differ about what society is, what it can be and what it ought to be. Much of the debate about evaluation is ideology disguised as technology.

Personal experience suggests to me that evaluators tend to be more often committed to liberal ideologies and more sceptical of authoritarianism than do our sponsors. Weiss (1987) observes that 'evaluation researchers tend to be liberal, reformist, humanitarian and advocates of the underdog' (p. 62), which Stake (1997), confirms as he confesses to discreet advocacy on behalf of an educational program he was evaluating and towards which he developed a compulsion to protect: 'Ultimately, evaluators must rely on their sense of what is good' (p. 474).

There are rarely debates about the vision of society embedded in evaluation practices, so what are often common practices conceal differences that are too fine to slip through the filter, as it were, of methodology. Those differences might be elaborated through this kind of questioning so as to ease the emergence of methodologies which reflect political and ethical values better. Evaluators need to be aware of their beliefs and limitations so as to make more rational methodological choices.

Addressing these kinds of questions implies an existentialist approach to methodological construction – an approach in response to what Schon talked of as the 'here-and-now'. It expresses a scepticism with 'general cases', particularly with theories that promise the easy transfer of learning from one context to another. We need to treat this as a guide – as does Schon. It may be more useful to think of methodology as a 'tendency in thought' to be realized. The lack of realization in the short term does not necessarily prevent action – we are not stupefied into inactivity by our research naiveté – we merely rely more on intuitive understandings and a memory of previous incidents to guide us. We need, that is, to think of ourselves less as purveyors or *aficionados* of certain methodologies, but as methodologists ourselves.

Our constructions of methodology are wrought of different influences, some of which violate the 'here-and-now-ness' principle, to allow us to recognize and short-cut the analysis of one situation by reflecting on previous experience. Let me explain that briefly. Evaluators (as a community) are experts in thinking about and analysing innovation. But then, like divorce, innovation is a common, virtually universal experience shared by many and yet felt to be unique every time it happens. There is the mixture of the unique and the transferable, the idiosyncratic and the universal which characterizes any case-based approach to enquiry and which requires the enquirer to be both creative in responding to the uniqueness of what she observes while capable of comparing and contrasting with prior events so as to identify the less unique. To reiterate, methodology is to be constructed by the individual given their own biography and the conditions under which they are investigating.

There are, perhaps, two principal ways of thinking about where the constructions might come from if not 'off the shelf' – they may be derived from your values and from your experience. By values-orientated methodology I mean those methodological choices we make long before we enter the field and which reflect our preferred way of seeing the world – actually, the basis for our personal advocacy. Those choices may often be made at the level of paradigm – choices between prediction/replication, portrayal or comparison, depending on the level of social orderliness in the world which we hope to confirm or challenge.[2] You have to know *why* you want to do evaluation before you can know *how* to do it. Such choices have much to do with our values in respect of people and society and, obviously rooted in our epistemological and political leanings, they are also rooted in our parenting and schooling. What differentiates me from, for example, a music evaluator committed to

---

2   This is an essential point and merits a lengthy note – at least for those interested in evaluation theory. Others should stay with the main text.

It may be a curious thing, but the link between methodology and personal values is not one that is often drawn in the literature. Typical of approaches that search for deep structure behind methodological preferences is the one taken by Eisner and Peshkin (1990: 9–10). They start from the assumption that we commence research with a problem and this guides our selection of method. Taking one step back from that they argue that the inverse is more likely the case – that we tend to select problems according to the methods with which we are familiar: 'What we know how to do is what we usually try to do.' This leads them to peel another layer off the onion and reflect on how we are often socialized into certain norms and methods which, themselves, influence our perception of events and problems and lead us to cognitively map out our studies differently – 'those with different maps tend to take different roads'.

Their search continues as they move on to the argument that socialization into methods also means socialization into 'a set of norms that define acceptable scholarship', accounting for quantitative or qualitative recidivism. They conclude at a conventional inner core. 'There are genuine differences. Ultimately these differences bear upon matters of epistemology. What does it mean to know?' Thus, in their scheme of things our personal predilections, the results of our learning through experience, the inheritance of our biographies – these are subordinated to processes of socialization and, eventually, to a philosophical principle. An alternative view is that epistemology (what counts as knowledge) does not lie at the centre at all. It is itself defined by what matters to us – and what matters to us (individually and as groups huddling together for meaningful comfort) is partly socialized into us, no doubt, but is partly what we have decided for ourselves will matter. This is a view of values that allows for voluntarism.

What is curious when it happens is the denial or avoidance of personal values in methodology – or simply the absence of its consideration. Even Stake (1995: 37) closes down his analysis with epistemology. 'A distinction between what knowledge to shoot for fundamentally separates quantitative and qualitative enquiry. Perhaps surprisingly, the distinction is not directly related to the difference between quantitative and qualitative data, but a difference in searching for causes versus searching for happenings. Quantitative researchers have pressed for explanation and control; qualitative researchers have pressed for understanding the complex interrelationships among all that exists.'

The shift to epistemology is, in fact, common, but not as common as the reduction of where methodology springs from to a question of mechanics. Shadish (1987), for example,

comparative, objectives-based approaches to evaluation is nothing more or less than a lifetime. For me to adopt such a methodology is unthinkable (other than as an artifice) – there are limits to my learning.

What this suggests is that there are two aspects to methodological experience, one of which is of consistency across evaluations we conduct, the other of which is of idiosyncrasy within each one. The consistency is given by our emergent values – our views of social and natural justice, for example – while the inconsistent element is given by our willingness to respond to the characteristics of the field in which we find ourselves. It is not merely the case that each evaluation context differs from others, it is that consistency is hard to maintain even within a single context.[3] People change their minds and even themselves in ways that often emerge in the context of a single study as contradictory.

Through an awareness of self (in that sense 'personalizing' evaluation), we can calibrate the balances we strike between seeking coherence and finding inconsistency; between our personal preferences and our obligations to be responsive; between seeking out the strange but yearning for the familiar. Above all, self-restraint is an unavoidable and essential aspect of evaluation experience.

---

in his article on the sources of evaluation practice, cites (1) conditions of the demand for evaluation, (2) that evaluation serves particular purposes, (3) that appropriate evaluation questions are driving the enquiry, and (4) that the methods reflect the best available technology for answering the question. And, too, Maxwell et al. (1987), arguing for mixing experimental and ethnographic techniques, claim that apparent paradigm differences can be resolved where methods *complement* one another. Their concern is with the use of multiple approaches to enhance what they call 'causal validity' – but this merely begs the question raised so passionately by Walcott (1990), who shows how we can achieve validity for a study that is incoherent in its aims and values, that is, we can prove something honest and true which has no coherent reason.

Meanwhile, Feinberg (1983) argues nicely that 'values that are at work in an institutional setting do not belong simply to the subjective preferences of the researcher or to the researcher's subjects. Rather they are embedded in the very practices that constitute the institution that the researcher is investigating. As long as researchers continue to take these values for granted they function, not as neutral external observers, but as important aspects of the institution itself . . .'

3 For example, Radke-Yarrow (quoted in R.B. Cairns, L.R. Bergman and J. Kagan (eds), *Methods and Models for Studying the Individual* (Sage, London, 1998: 2), in her classic revisionist study of social development, argued 'The compelling legend of maternal influences on child behaviour that has evolved does not have its roots in solid data . . . the findings from the preceding analyses of data make it difficult to continue to be complacent about methodology and difficult to continue to regard replication as a luxury. The child's day-to-day experiences contribute significantly to his behaviour and development and are in many respects the essence of developmental theory . . . in attempting to build on this knowledge, each researcher is a methodologist . . .'

LEARNING ABOUT INTERVIEWING

Interview, for example, lies at the heart of what I do not because I planned it that way, but because that's what I found myself doing during successive early fieldwork experiences having been faced with an open choice. First, I think, I enjoyed it; then I found it to be meaningful in my scheme of values which says, broadly, that it is the individual, dissenting voice that is a potent challenge to forms of authority; only later do I come to formalize my experience into a methodological scheme ('behaviour before cognition', some would say).

It takes time and experience to discover your values in your research. I know, after successive fieldwork-based projects, that whenever I enter the field I am likely to devote my principal resources to interview, and that is stable and resistant to change, as are my beliefs. One implication of this is that there can be no such thing as an 'unstructured interview', in that all interviews are necessarily structured by certain predisposi-tions and intents.[4] It is too limiting to characterize the interview as a strategy for asking questions – it has, rather, to be seen as a personalized instrument, an expression of how the interviewer sees the world – how, in fact, an interviewer values people and why. In my own case (which will not be the same as yours) my initial enthusiasm for interviewing *per se* – what Mark Benney and Everett Hughes (1984) talked of as 'the art of sociological sociability' – gave way to a more serious intent. I became more preoccupied with the democratic potential of research, eventually coming to understand that an instrument of authoritarian management and government is 'group-ification', arbitrarily subsuming individual needs under group treatments. A national curriculum is as good an example as any. The interview is a resource for countering authoritar-ianism, for unmasking universal treatments, for generating the dissenting voice. I have my purpose, I have something which will help me slough off the socialization into methods and norms of scholarship which Eisner and Peshkin (see note 2) speak of.

---

4   See Fontana and Fry (1994) for a defence of the notion of an unstructured interview, and Mishler (1986) for an argument that all interviews are necessarily structured, if only by predispositions. Fontana and Fry, in fact, present short clips of field notes from Malinowski and then from Spradley to illustrate unstructured interviewing – by which they appear to mean interviewing which does not conform to a pre-set series of interrogative objectives. But even these short clips themselves show clearly how both anthropologists' relations with their ('native') subjects were intricately structured around cultural theories, personal dispositions, the experience of the day, their responses to the strangeness of the setting – in Spradley's case, the fact that she found a point of contact with a native woman.

All this is not to say that I am left with no methodological choices to make – that my methodology is pre-set or that I have a firm platform on which to design my study. Interviewing is not a method but a method*ology*, which is to say that it is meaningless without situational rationale, that is, a logic of use set in a particular context. It represents a logic of enquiry, not a technique, and there are many logics which justify its use even within my broader political ethic, just as there are many purposes to which it can be put. Choosing among these varying options makes for different kinds of interviews and different configurations of the interview alongside other evaluation activities.

This is where methodology becomes largely defined by the situation in which it is applied, where the methodological construction is derived from direct experience – your own and your colleagues'. We need to make decisions about how and why to use interview and those decisions are grounded in an understanding of the context of application – why interviews make sense in the political, ethical, educational contexts being researched. There is a lot about methodology which really ought to be held in abeyance, pending early fieldwork experiences. This suggests another characteristic of naturalistic methodology which is that it is generative of its own sophistication. This is a reflexive process in which early methodological acts are monitored to see how well they respond to the nature and complexity of the context being evaluated. The result, supposedly, is that successive evaluation projects draw from the same pool of methodological understanding – Van Maanen's methodological reflections, for example, but with different outcomes depending on the particularities of the case.

For me, an understanding of the use of interview developed over a number of enquiries which led, eventually, to the music cases. For example, on a team study of bilingual education in the context of Civil Rights issues in the USA the interview was an essential instrument for legitimating the political voice of individuals and groups,[5] many of them in Latin American communities. Their struggles were represented in the establishment of a bilingual school but then suppressed and supplanted by the plutocrats of curriculum and sociolinguistic research. One interview program (with about 25 people) in this study was used (along with other methods) by one of the evaluation team to construct a story of the emergence of a bilingual political movement in Boston –

---

5   B. MacDonald, C. Adelman, S.I. Kushner and R. Walker (1982) *Bread and Dreams: a Case Study of Bilingual Schooling in the USA*, CARE Occasional Publications No. 12 (CARE, University of East Anglia, Norwich, 1982).

a composite story that no individual could hold. Another interview strategy – this time in the focus bilingual school – was to develop a theory of bilingual teaching derived from the practical and particularized experience of bilingual teachers, rather than from the abstractions and generalizations of researchers. The use of the interview was, in one sense, prospective – to develop analyses and strategies for the improvement and development of bilingual programs. But it was political in that grounding theory in the experience and the practical knowledge of teachers represented a challenge to the hegemony of the (sociolinguist) research community.

The interview also became a crucial legitimating device for the evaluation team in this enquiry in a way that was also unpredictable. A first draft of the school study had been rejected by the teachers as being grounded too firmly in the tradition of sociolinguistics which had repressed their efforts and achievements for so long (and which was seen to be 'white science'). The evaluation's credibility was low enough to persuade the Director of the evaluation to withdraw. What recovered the position was a series of interviews which were aimed, as well as generating evidence, to challenge the sociolinguistic analyses, to demonstrate the evaluation's desire to be guided by the teachers' own theories and analyses. These interviews were conducted as invitations to the school to make a critique of the first draft and its authors – they were a cooptive device.

In another evaluation – of careers guidance and youth unemployment – the task was different again. Here, we used the interview to generate profiles of adolescents as they talked and theorized about their lives, dilemmas and choices.[6] Unemployment and exclusion loomed large. Again, there was an underlying intent to legitimate the voices of those individuals for whom others too often claim to speak and make decisions – but this intent was to recover for those young people some control over the discourse which to some small extent framed their structure of opportunities. The interview was more of a retrospective device – to revise and reconstruct a policy discourse within the world of meaning of adolescents facing a life without work.

In this case, too, the interview was embedded in the moment of that evaluation and helped me to learn something of my own frailties. I was a contract researcher – at that time in the middle of my one-year contract

---

6 S. Kushner and T. Logan (1984) *Made in England: an Evaluation of Curriculum in Transition*, CARE Occasional Publications No. 14 (CARE, University of East Anglia, Norwich, 1984).

and looking ahead with dread at my own unemployment. My reluctance to face my own realities certainly prevented me from asking certain questions of theirs, and there were significant aspects of the psychology of unemployment which were simply and inexcusably lost.

In both of these cases the nature of the evaluation experience demanded the extensive use of the interview – and interviews looked different according to their purpose. Policy-related interviews aimed at constructing the composite story of bilingual education often started with a précis of the construction thus far to both stimulate a particular kind of analytic storytelling and to check the accuracy/plausibility of the developing construction. Interviews aimed at generating a grounded theory of bilingual pedagogy started with direct observations of classroom practice. Interviews aimed at revealing the pedagogical values of teachers started with their lives.

After some years of fieldwork I came to these music education evaluations. These contexts, too, made their particular demands on the interview, as we shall see. Central to these has been the use of the interview as a device to explore – jointly with musicians and students – issues in the construction of identity which lie at the heart of music experience. Of course, there is a sense in which identity is always at issue in the interview, but most often as a procedural matter. We need to know something of the respondent in order to properly understand how to listen to and believe them. In these music evaluations, however, 'knowing' the individual was part of the substantive task of the evaluation, and this thrust the interview to the methodological foreground. I had been prepared in my understanding of this by my experience of the variability of the interview. I came to discover that the interview fits like a glove, in that it finally achieves shape and meaning with the insertion of humanity. At the Guildhall evaluation I spent some six months thinking through and experimenting with the methodological demands of the program I was evaluating – talking, all the while, with colleagues and informants about my data – before settling on a rationale for the interview. Thereafter my evaluation was committed to the centrality of the individual and their struggle for identity.

EVALUATION DESIGNS ARE ALSO EMERGENT

It has not just been the use of interviews which has been guided by the combination of my values and my experience, but also the nature of methodological contingency – the logic and the ways in which different methodological strategies connect. Direct observation is a regular part of my research repertoire, used as a complement to interviews. I use no observation schedules but my observations, once again, are 'structured' by my interest in human interaction, my values and the evaluation issues I carry around with me – I find it hard to think of an 'unstructured' observation. At the very least, observations will be structured by the need for a 'reality check' against claims made in interviews and against my own tendencies, that is, for triangulation. How and when I use observations depends on growing understanding of the case I am working on and 'progressive focusing'[7] (another kind of emergent structure) in which sampling, for example, follows the growth of understanding and the researcher only gradually begins to differentiate what she is seeing.

As I have already mentioned, for example, developing a grounded understanding of bilingual teaching started with classroom observations and inviting a teacher to reflect on what she did. Generating detailed, direct observation data from her classroom was a way of creating an independent platform of evidence from which to generate mutual understandings – independent, that is, from the evidential base of sociolinguistic theory.

One implication of this is that it is not possible to pre-figure the design of a case study evaluation – notwithstanding pressure from sponsors and peer-reviewers to be clear about evaluation 'objectives' as a condition of grant (essentially a control strategy to reduce the potential for unwelcome surprises). There are, of course, aspects of design which have to be predetermined, just as no evaluator can write a proposal, much less start the enquiry, without an inchoate theory of her case. But the notion that an evaluation can be designed at the outset and then pursued relentlessly to its conclusions is to misunderstand the emergent nature of theory. Naturalistic evaluation generally, for example, relies on developmental forms of sampling – a cumulative body of understanding guides the selection of cases, questions and sources – progressive focusing, theoretical sampling, negotiating an issues focus.

This is not to say that the experience of studying cases (i.e. doing evaluations) is not itself cumulative – that patterns and issues do not re-emerge. They do, increasingly so (making for a degree of consistency).

---

7 See Parlett and Hamilton (1977) for the most celebrated source of this concept. The basic principle is that the evaluator needs to be educated into an understanding of the case before arriving at an issues structure, and that this happens through the fieldwork process. In fact, this publication more than any other gives the case for allowing methodology to emerge from the character of the context under investigation. It was, of course, one of the seminal papers in laying down the tradition of naturalistic or case study evaluation.

In a way I find unsettling, and in spite of my claim to myself that naturalistic evaluation should be responsive to contexts of application, I find myself less and less surprised at what I see, increasingly familiar with the issues. Part of the reason is that as I learn from one evaluation enquiry to another I am generating understandings – personal theories – of change and innovation. This is the stock-in-trade knowledge of the evaluator, the shadow the professional evaluator chases through and between each of her enquiries. Into that theory of change coalesce developing personal values and knowledge of the conduct of evaluation, and it is out of this brew that I draw my methodological preferences. But over time, the shadow one chases becomes a clear image, and the greater the familiarity with that image the more one can become beguiled by one's own ability to conceptualize complex matters – to crystallize what others see blurred. What started as a chase turns into a rout and then a crusade, as the evaluator – who may still be responsive and impartial to the substantive nature of a particular case – becomes a covert advocate of certain ways of thinking about innovation and change.

There are obvious advantages to having experienced evaluators in the field – the disadvantages may be less obvious and more seductive. What is suggested by this is that the implied hierarchy of skill between a 'novice researcher' (the term used too readily, for example, by Schatzman and Strauss, 1973) and the veteran or expert researcher is less obvious than might appear at first.

Whatever the case, there is a cumulative body of understanding that travels with me as a 'second record' and it is separating that out from my compulsion to derive formulae that is the task. What, then, have I learned about methodology from my 10–15 years of researching performing musicians working in schools, and what is the nature of that 'second record'? It is to this we now turn.

INTERVIEWING YOUNG CHILDREN

First, interviewing children and students lies at the heart of evaluation in music education – most of all else is evasion. All educational endeavours are hostage to the understanding and collaboration of learners. More importantly, I will try to show how one function of evaluation is to expose the conflict of moralities as children and adults clash during pedagogic moments.

This leads us to a particular problem for educational evaluation. As I expressed it in one evaluation account, there is an issue built into the structure of evaluation which deals with the education of young children. It is that as evaluators we know adults as we know ourselves – but we are, perhaps, condemned to an anthropological view of children. Underpinning interviews with adults – musicians, teachers, administrators – are experiences and understandings about being an institutional actor balancing hope with resources, of being responsible, of the loss of innocence and the inevitability of mutual exploitation. As evaluators working with adults in interview we are more like co-conspirators.

We are, however, curious observers of a child's life. Like the experience of waking from a dream recalling all its salient phenomena but none of the binding logic which made sense of them together, I sometimes find it hard to recognize the nature of contingency which would infuse meaning into a child's perceptions – and young children do not have the conceptual language to help me. There is little opportunity for co-constructing the interview with young children – for 'dispersing the form of authority', in Van Maanen's words. For children, argues Margaret Donaldson (1978), there may be that same connection as for adults between intention and action; the difference is that children cannot regulate the connection as adults do because they cannot reflect on it. Not that this always reduces the confidence with which we speak about children's meanings; all that says is that perhaps we too often borrow systems of contingency from adult contexts to create the illusion that we have some purchase on understanding a child's world. 'What's it like to be a pupil?' I asked Richard, you may recall. 'I don't know – I ain't never been a teacher,' was the reply. We create institutionalized children in our own image, so we too easily assume that we know them at least as well as they do themselves.

In that kind of evaluation which pretends to be collaborative – which seeks to relocate some of the evaluative act in the participant, this is a formidable constraint. We might talk *with* teachers but we generally can only talk *for* children. And yet it is precisely the perspective of the child that we need in order to understand the experience of a child living inside what might well be educational delusions of adults – to generate data with which we might reflect critically on the assumptions we bring to our projects and our evaluations. The ethnographic interviewer's goal to 'stand with each respondent in the latter's relationship to the universe' (Schatzman and Strauss, 1973) is neither an accurate representation of interviewing adults, nor a reasonable aim in interviewing children. When interviewing adults within your own culture the task is more one of breaking *out* of a shared universe of meaning; when interviewing children, the task is simply to break out of your own universe of meaning.

In that same evaluation I spoke with four Muslim children of around eight years old about a music workshop they had just taken part in. The children talked about Salman Rushdie and why they felt he must die, about not liking orchestral music because it is too noisy, and about their schooling. Eventually, they turned to the workshop and to the issues raised by the girls having sung – again, showing how the values and experiences of the children embrace the artistic event within their own meaning.

Girl: In our religion we're not meant to sing because it's a – 'cause you get a – I don't know how to say this because in our language you call it G'nah – it's a bad stuff.
Me: If you sing in English?
Few: Yeh!
Boy: If you play an instrument and things like that.
Girl: No!
Girl: Yes! You are allowed.
Boy: If you sing in English it's not a good thing for Muslim children –
Girl: Yes.
Boy: – and when you did, right, you get punished for it.
Girl: No you don't!
Boy: Yes you do!
Boy: Yes you do!
Boy: It's only that girls shouldn't sing and boys should because Mohamed did sing.
Girl: No!
Girl: If you have more bad doings than good things – something like that – the grave goes really thin and this part goes . . . squeezed . . . and if you do good things, your grave, it gets wider . . .
Girl: They say boys can do anything they want – what about the girls?!
Boy: Stay in the kitchen!
Me: What about playing an instrument – are you allowed to play an instrument?
Few: Yes –
Girl: If the teacher isn't watching us we don't sing sometimes, but if the teacher is watching us we just move our mouths.

I tried to understand that interview in terms of children being trapped between competing orthodoxies – for example, the powerful moral authority of the religious leader against the powerful moral authority of Western music and education which says you have to sing along and appreciate. The levity and the buoyancy of the children's utterances too easily belie the harshness of the words and the concepts being traded about. Running the risk of incurring a narrow grave for eternity makes workshop singing a high-stakes game. Or does it? What would it take to understand (a) what the girl, here, received and understood by the threat of a narrow grave, and (b) how that related to the music workshops – because relate it obviously did.

If we are to have an understanding of educational impact and we want to see projects through the eyes of young people we need to work on the nature of these dilemmas we force children to live through. If, however, we have no full insight into the nature of contingency in a child's world then we have no direct access to understanding what sense they make of our logics – what, for example, connects certain ways of behaving with particular musical outcomes. Here is an example.

In another observation a group of children were collaborating with a performing musician and, on this occasion, were developing a piece of music through improvisation – their teacher was out of the room. They had, in effect, been introduced to a moral system by the professional musician which was suggested by concepts like collaboration, listening to each other and mutual tolerance – offered on the grounds that these were the social glue that held adult groups of music makers together. Quite apart from the inaccuracy of that assumption, what I observed was children making sophisticated (neither 'good' nor 'bad') music through a process which involved a volatile mix of aggression, compassion, competition, loud humour and collaboration. For example:

[Following a rendition of a group improvisation]

- No wonder it's too short – you should let us play for a bit and then come in!
- She told me to come in after them, too!
- I didn't! I couldn't – no!
- You said come in after Wendy –
- She – she –
- Alright – I come in about 10 seconds after Wendy.
- Let Dustin do it, then, and see how stupid it's going to sound!'

Silence

- You're stupid – you just know it's going to go wrong – that's why you just want to show me up.

And they play.

By the end of this session, when the teacher came back in, the children had developed the piece fully – and it had changed its form as a result of what appeared to be this messy process. The children would argue, make fun of each other, shout instructions, countermand and then, at the signal 'Ready!' repeat their prepared piece, but with modification; then stop, relaunch the argument with recriminations over how it was played . . . and repeat the process. The word 'Ready!' was the signal for order, and any of the dominant children could use it.

For an adult, accustomed to being able to *observe* the workings of causality (that is, this relationship cast in this way leads to these inter-actions), this requires considerable interpretation. What makes sense of such a milieu may well be lost to us, though what is clear is that there are different moral standards – competing moral systems – at play. As well as cognitive demands, then, such events also make certain emotional demands on us in that they can challenge our beliefs and our values. Recrimination and argument may well be an effective element of a child's repertoire in developing their music making, but we often find it hard to embrace that in curriculum processes – some find it hard to legitimate it (not, incidentally, these children's teacher who was fully aware of what they got up to when she left them but wanted them to manage their own processes. She was not a music specialist.)

The professional musicians involved in this interaction traded under morally honorific flags of *collaboration*, *tolerance* and *partnership* – but, perhaps more important, the guiding principle – or what locked people into adult universes, was the dependency on logical explanation. Compare the interactions above with the same children talking – shortly afterwards – with the orchestral player with whom they were working. The player sits with the teacher and the children have fallen silent. The player asks a question.

Player: What are you going to play music about?
Child: Puck.
Child: Puck.
Child: Yeh.
Player: Can you tell me something about him?
Child: Well –
Child: – he's a goblin.

And they all start clamouring to have their say.

Player: Can you – wait a minute – one at a time. Can you tell me about him?

Child: Well, he's a mischief worker, and he's a goblin – and he turns Bottom's head into a donkey head.
Player: Really? Anything else?

After some false starts and prompting from the teacher the children became more proactive until they slipped back into their argumentative style. The point with these observations is the shift that happens, the collision of styles. Most obviously, the children's world was one in which relationships were the key to action; the adult world was one in which explanation was the key. We see, here, just a glimpse of the imposition of adult logic on the child's experiences. The effect is to mask and recast rather than reveal and understand the child's world.

The difficulties of researching young children are part of the construction of the methodology – but they are also part of the construction of the account. A portrayal of children through their words and actions does not provide sufficient data for a reader to make sense of it. The interaction with the researcher (and with the research process – rather different) is part of the understanding of the child's world – because that understanding is, itself, process. It is, that is to say, the way we understand children that is important; it may be, in fact, that *what* we understand cannot be disentangled from *how* we understand – and may be the same thing. What this says is that the methodology of portrayal of children has to be transparent in our reports. The account needs to include data on the difficulties the researcher was experiencing in conducting the interview or the observation, or in attempting to relate different kinds of child data – because reading about these difficulties provides another level of data on the children – how they see us, say. For example, here, in another extract from that same evaluation report, I am interviewing four young (about ten or eleven years) girls about their experience of music making. Their teacher is with us – I am already in some difficulty:

Me: Hang on a minute – hang on a minute. Just let me pursue this – that alright? Er – tell me about the kind of music that you – what's music? I know it's a stupid question –

Everyone laughs out loud, this time. I have no idea where this question came from – or where it is supposed to go – it is a bid for freedom. I sit on a chair looming over the girls who all sit facing me on the floor and physically there is no way of righting the situation – so come down a level status-wise. People are still laughing.

Me: Well, these are things that we don't think about normally – you know what I mean – we just say 'oh, music (mumble)' – but you sounded like you were saying that now you play music but before you just made sounds – you know what I mean? . . . do you have to have an instrument to play music?

They all say no.

Girl: Voices – voices –
Me: Right – do you have to be singing to make music?
Girl: No – no –
Teacher: Think about the other two pieces you heard at the concert – especially the Boulez – the first piece.
Girl: Oh – the first piece – it didn't have, like, a harmony and didn't have a tune to it – it was just like they were playing –
Girl: – just sounds –
Girl: – what they wanted to. We thought they were tuning up!
Girl: I know!
[. . .]
Me: Oh – I see! Tuning! Hah hah! What did it sound like to you?
Girl: A mess.
Me: Did it?
Girl: Yes.
Me: Do you not like that sort of –
Girl: No.
Girl: No.
Teacher: Some of the boys liked it, didn't they?
Girl: Gavin did.
Me: So you like things with tunes in –
Girl: Yeh.
Girl: – if it's got good rhythm.
Me: Good rhythm – is that the kind of stuff you play?

The girls are stuck for an answer – not sure whether their music is rhythmic or not. They spontaneously turn to the teacher who confirms that they use rhythm. They turn again to me and answer firmly and together, 'yes'.

Me: Why did you ask the teacher?

They all laugh.

Me: No – why did you ask the teacher?
Girl: I don't know.

In this account it is not possible to disentangle what the girls believe about music from they way they relate to adults – here, a researcher and a teacher. One response could be just to say that what data I was getting here was somehow ingenuous when compared with the conversations about music these girls might have together beyond the gaze of adults. That may or may not be true – but it begs the question of how we understand them and their utterances. We might use devices like leaving them to interview each other on tape, shadow-study them or whatever – but these are obvious artifices which evoke similar issues. The strategy I am arguing for is to reveal the difficulty and the complexity – because, in the end, that *is* an accurate representation of how we know children.

This is, in methodological terms, a little like constructing a Pompidou centre or a Lloyds Building and exposing the working and structural parts as aspects of the architectural image. Methodology can be displayed as it is emerging so as to assist the reader in judging the truth claims of the account – for those claims to truth rest upon certain methodological decisions that were being made.

The problem of understanding children, I think, is akin to how we 'observe' sub-atomic particles which, by definition, are unobservable. We construct artificial environments – bubble-chambers – and create effects from which we can read properties of the particles. We collide atoms and observe the bubbling traces left by their passing but unseen fragments. We are dealing with high-inference data, of course – data that require a significant element of interpretation. Thus, I think, do I act with children. The interview is far from the natural event it might be with adults, more like the artificial environment of the bubble-chamber. A question is less a direct probe than a stimulus, an intervention designed to produce an effect. The effects generated (when the girls, above, turned to their teacher, for example) provide us with data for our interpretation – but second-order data, representational or mimetic data.

Now there is also a sense in which this mimetic data is random – in that it provides us with only random insights into the child's universe. It may be more accurate to say that from the child's perspective our questioning must *look* random since it follows the highly restrictive order of another universe of meaning. To that extent, and to follow the logic of this argument, we are condemned to disembodied glimpses into the child's world – cut off, that is, from the coherent body of routine perceptions and values which make sense of that world. My 'golden rule' that evaluators must displace their own sense of coherence with that of their respondent breaks down in the case of children.

The difficulty is measuring the value of the child's words against the whole series of values held by that child – even before we come to think of the clear possibility of children holding conflicting values simultaneously, as we know we do as adults. So, for example, it is difficult for us to measure the scale – or lack of scale – of despair which results from a young Muslim girl realizing she has contravened a religious orthodoxy. Equally, it is difficult to know how a child balances the priorities of getting the music right against getting their place right in the pecking order of peers. What nails the coffin-lid of possibility firmly closed on us is that if we ask them they will surely tell us. Children speak to adults in a democracy of utterances in which no single utterance stands out against the others – unless we ourselves make it (as I do, for example, by including the Salman Rushdie data and by making such a big thing out of Richard's reply to my question 'what's it like to be a pupil?' – both for crudely obvious reasons).

As a final note on that evaluation, I left the account with a question. In another school children had been rehearsing a dance piece – with some gusto and clear enjoyment. Among them were deaf children. They then moved down into the main hall to perform the piece to adults and there they were clearly embarrassed, their movements more clipped and clumsy, their heads more lowered. I think I remember a child stumbling – I certainly remember children looking rather foolishly on show as I am sure I did as a small child in dance events when asked to 'grow like a tree' or 'wave about like a sunflower'. Some of the adults who were watching cried, and I asked, in the last sentence of that account, 'why?'

The question was not rhetorical – though it was partly, I admit, disingenuous since the crying was merely an expression of sentiment at seeing deaf children playing music and my personal reaction (which had to be suppressed) was to be dismissive of it for the clear implications of emotional predation. But my dismissal was not the story. I was intrigued by the question of how and why adults cry in these situations. I have observed it more than once in music education – on another occasion when equally embarrassed but tolerant black and white children were on stage in a piece of music theatre acting out a chess game where the black and white 'pieces' eventually joined together 'in harmony' to overcome the enforced competition of 'the game'. There, audience and participants were each split between those who responded with admiration for the courage to take on the issue and offer an optimistic conclusion; and those who were annoyed at the simplistic treatment of such a complex issue. But, then, I also recall Maureen, a Conservatoire student leaving a workshop interaction at a hospice with terminally ill patients and feeling disturbed by the fact that she felt no emotion when, as she left the place, she looked back at it.

There are, of course, certain taboos in educational enquiry and perhaps I am pushing up against one of them – part of the attraction of the question. The crying – more generally, perhaps, the emotional response to these events – has more to do with the hopes and insecurities of the adult than with the experience of the child. I have never found in young children evidence of sentimentality of the kind that might produce or justify such upwellings of emotion. Hence, the charge of emotional predation – and hence the taboo.

The particular answer to the question of why people cry is irrelevant, in one sense – perhaps more useful for its resonance than for its explanatory power. But the tolerance of the children subjected to public humiliation and the crying of the adults live with me, a reminder of how invisible public embarrassment can be when necessity calls and how disingenuous sentiment. Such easy exploitation of children has to be countered or at least deconstructed. And the way to deconstruct it is to bring the embarrassment into focus by asking children to talk about it. Thus do we support adults to confront their 'mortal' fears.

INTERVIEWING STUDENTS

We have already come across Lyn, a flautist and Conservatoire trainee. She studied alongside Wendy, who was also a flautist. Wendy was widely thought to have a 'bubbly' personality, she had grown up in a musical family and remembers sitting at her father's orchestral rehearsals. Music had been her life and it came to her apparently as naturally as her smile. Lyn found it harder. She struggled to make sense of her music life. She was an untidy person but with a longing for completeness and order that was represented in the pristine corner of her bedroom amid what she described as a rubble of disorder. She had been told that, unlike Wendy, she would never make it as a soloist because she did not have that personality '*spark*' – she was a shy person and this was the time when music competitions were dominated by the revisionist notion that the best performers would use their personality to reach out and 'communicate' with the audience. Lyn, as we saw, used the Guildhall program to direct her learning towards changing her personality – to develop that spark, to bring an end to her shyness, to thrust herself into leadership roles: 'In a funny sort of way, I hate it and love it . . . I know it's good for me.'

Meanwhile, Wendy's life was emerging, in interview, to be less ordered than might have appeared. She was disturbed by the common assumption in her teachers, family and friends that she was bound for a musical career. Realizing that she had arrived at the Conservatoire on automatic pilot and without thinking of alternatives she found herself asking the question, 'Why does the fact that I want to be in an orchestra represent what is right for me?' She contemplated leaving, realizing that the self represented by her inexorable move into music was neither the comprehensive self she sought, nor was it adequate to cope with the experiences she was encountering and the demands being made upon her.

Then there was Sam, a percussionist at the same Conservatoire, who had already built up something of a reputation. She, too, was thinking seriously of leaving having discovered limits to what she could achieve – limits to her 'musicality'. She was devastated. A geographer, she thought, could just closet herself away in a library for a day and come out a better geographer, but what do you do if the problem is part of who you are? (Geographers, of course, might say the same.)

And so with May, and Joe, and Seb the violinist – and Chloe the oboist . . . 'Going to college killed all my performing desires anyway.' Chloe had bite marks at the end of her oboe. She turned to music therapy, found a child with Down's syndrome who was calmed by putting the end of her oboe in his mouth . . . and Maureen the clarinettist, who left that hospice trying to feel something but not feeling anything. At that hospice interaction Ann, a 'cellist taking advanced solo studies, had listened to two women patients who had written poems which the students were putting to music. Ann had been encountering problems with her instrument for the past six months and she was disturbed by them, losing her confidence. Listening to these two women talking about their terminal illnesses created another per- spective: 'They were so together – better than me, really. It was really upsetting for me.'

During my three years observing this Conservatoire I saw a great deal of levity and exuberance, but also discomfort. Few of the 100 or so students I worked with felt easy about themselves and their music, most episodically rehearsed their reasons for being there and staying there – a constantly burning tension stoked up by competitions, master classes and powerful teachers. The discomfort was educational – critical self- reflection, a searching for and reworking of identity. Insight, perhaps, came harder to these people who had already often spent years struggling with their sense of identity and often, too, struggling against adults to maintain the independence of their vision for themselves. It was, that is to say, clearer. Failures for a music student could, perhaps, be more easily pinpointed as a failure of self.

If I thought that music had any special educational case to plead it would lie in this area of experience. Enough music students to make it interesting have a profound sense of the relationship between the vision and the lived reality, the difference between sentimentality and romanticism, between the fantasy of creative expression and just getting on with the job: 'I'm always faced with failure – just playing the instrument,' said Mol, another flautist. Music, I noted in that Conservatoire evaluation, may be a precious thing to observers, but to musicians it is a costly thing – the cost, that is, to themselves. The relentless vocational drive behind music training belies the education that takes place as students think about themselves and construe their music with their identity – the two go hand-in-hand. Technical mastery is a breeze. Seeing yourself in your music is usually sweat and pain. The point about this is that these may be educational resources for the Conservatoire, though it is not often equipped to use them. But that just makes it the stuff of educational evaluation.

When I first entered the Conservatoire I was told by more than one person that I would get little out of interviewing the students (evidence, perhaps, of the fragility of organizational fictions hinted at by Berger?). The most common theory given to me was a kind of theory of compensation within which the development of expression in the field of music meant a diminution in other forms of expression. This I found to be erroneous. Music students prove to be very articulate people and it is worth reflecting for a moment on just why, for this, too, has implications for evaluation methodology. One of the reasons is that here are people who are accustomed to reflection and critical analysis – albeit often in private. To sustain the level of social isolation and physical effort required to achieve technical mastery – which is the minimal requirement for Conservatoire training – demands the kind of personal commitment which needs constant re-stoking. There is a paradoxical sense in which the more a music student achieves, the closer their relationship with personal failure. Whatever else this does it prepares a person well for conversations with a naturalistic evaluator, because reflections on experience and feeling are generally well rehearsed.

The other reason, I think, is that there is a degree of maturity these people are often thrust into through close interactive relationships with adults, commonly at an early age. The pedagogy of music coaching often reaches less than an educational ideal and often demands of the student that they defend their self-esteem. This, itself, requires a degree of self-knowledge in the student that is rarely provoked elsewhere on a school curriculum. Students, for example, will often talk about struggling with their teachers who may have a different view of what kind of musician (person) they might become.

For all of these reasons music students as 'subjects' of evaluation look much more like the intelligent collaborators in Wundt's laboratory than casual informants. They are not like children in interview, in the sense that they can account for the connection between intention and action (Donaldson, 1978). But nor are they like adults in that the structures of experiences which underpin and prejudice our conversations with adults are still in formation. They cannot yet be assumed as a common base on which to structure the interview. Students can, indeed, be suspicious of the evaluator for their association with the adult world of authority.

I referred, in that Conservatoire evaluation, to a comment made by a prominent observer of arts curricula at a North American conference on the arts that 'our ability to dream goes beyond our ability to explain' (Heussenstamm, 1973) – surely a challenge to educational evaluation. This was offered as an expression of popular sentiment felt by observers of the arts witnessing and admiring the work of artistes. But this, for a methodologist like myself, is defeatist talk. I can think of no aspect of music or music making that the students I spent time with were not able to discuss and provide some insight into – if only through resort to the language of symbol and metaphor. The problem is methodological, that is, how to get at it; it is not epistemological, that is, how to conceive it. In the end, dreams and the capacity to explain them come down to self-knowledge and the capacity to analyse personal experience.

I think there are gradations of difficulty in explaining events in music, but the prize, as it were, for difficulty probably goes to explaining innovations in the music field rather than to explaining music experience itself. Here, the experience and even the vocabulary is far less rehearsed and students need time to develop a perspective. Once conversational norms with Conservatoire students are established – through prolonged interaction – we have access to very different and often confusing views of the innovation which may be the focus for the evaluative enquiry, and this can – should – have a profound effect on the evaluation. Let me introduce this by talking a little about another flautist who was at the Guildhall and part of the MPCS innovation.

She was a high-achieving musician; she had played lead with a national orchestra in her mid-teens, and captured the attention of a world-class flautist. She had struggled with her teacher, who insisted she would be a fine pianist, and she fought to concentrate on the flute. But she admitted to an uncomfortable combination of the kind of self-possessiveness it takes to fight against a teacher at an early age and the kind of dependence on the opinions of others which made her yearn for recognition. By her early twenties she went through periods where it was hard to keep the motivation going – perhaps she had peaked too early, perhaps a life so full of music had been overtaken by now more pressing personal concerns with who and how she was.

We are sitting talking on the balcony of her house in Hackney in a strong early summer sun – well, on the bricked-in top of a bay-window overlooking back alleys. The young woman is talking about Peter Renshaw, Director of the MPCS course. She is reflecting on her encounters with a busy innovator, but the thought having been provoked by an earlier conversation to do with a television debate about Freud she watched the previous night. Watching the debate she was thinking, in particular, about how she was being persuaded one way or the other and discovered that it was more by her emotional response to the protagonists and less by the arguments. She talks about Peter.

'I suppose I find it difficult when I encounter someone who doesn't really believe in anything – or doesn't seem to, but just has endless alternatives . . . and plays games with people and thoughts and ideas . . . But at the same time I cannot bear dogmatic people! Perhaps I feel I'm going to be a bit like him – not on his level. And also – I've said this to you before – he reminds me of my father. I feel, emotionally, sort of, immature.'

Then the conversation turns back on MPCS. How does she think back on the course after two years? 'Well, that's interesting – I see myself as, in a sense, having sold out on all the stuff I appeared to get so excited about . . . at the time . . . It's just remained a thinking process a lot of the time.'

Is that what it is? She laughs. 'Well, no, "What is MPCS?" isn't a prominent question! What it stands for is.' And she confesses that now it is becoming hard – going beyond that to define what it does/did for her. What, then, was she doing when she went along to MPCS events?

'I found it hard – I found it very challenging. It gave me a similar feeling to you coming here to talk to me – a slight sense of anxiety and ambivalence. And, you know, I go to see this psychotherapist – the feeling I have when I go and see her sometimes . . . for me it was very confronting.'

Here we get a sense of someone talking at the limit of their understanding. In these conversations the single event of the MPCS innovation becomes one of a number of elements in a confusion of incoming data for the student. The television debate, herself, me, Peter Renshaw, her music teacher – and then the different analytical levels on which she is operating, such as the distinction between what an innovation *is* and what it *stands for*. Certainly there is a suggestion that the evaluation is part of the context of confusion education creates for students. As evaluator I take my place among the array of adult protagonists and, like the Guildhall program, find myself enveloped in a life. But we begin to be able to theorize at this point about what an innovation and its evaluation mean to an individual, how it gets measured and assimilated against the concerns, the values, the needs and the fears of the individual.

Let me go back a little, now, to revisit my purpose. I said, earlier, that entering into conversation with these music students potentially had a profound impact on evaluation perspectives. Here, we see the genesis of the view I now hold that evaluators need to invert the relationship between people and projects – to use people's views and lives as the lens through which to perceive and help 'measure', if you will, the value of a project – that is, to personalize enquiry. As I spoke to these students over time, and as an individual student's involvement with the MPCS course receded into the recent past, so the routine life and concerns of that individual took over again in the intellectual struggle for personal meaning. May was one of the first cohort of students on the MPCS innovation, was one of the early innovators and featured prominently in early evaluation accounts as an insightful and fluent informant. Two years on, a job in the Royal Opera House chorus under her belt and a grant to continue her music lessons, I met her and talked about these things. I recorded:

May has changed since her year on MPCS – she feels that she has become more adult – 'I'm twenty-four now!' she laughs. She is still, for the next two months, a student. 'But I don't see myself as a student, really.' She has a new year coming up – a grant of £2,000 to continue singing lessons, a settled life with her boyfriend, and now the job in Covent Garden which will earn her around £150 a week (plus overtime). She feels herself experimenting with adulthood. She is, for example, replacing her attraction for older people ('people who I can . . . learn from') with the desire to share a more even friendly relationship from which she might learn at a different level. But she is attracted to experienced people who can enhance her understanding of performance. May has become a performer.

What about MPCS? What does she remember of the course?

'Mmmm. It seems a long time ago . . . I'm not sure that – er – I don't know that – on Peter's course we did a lot on sharing the music and everybody doing it together. I'm not sure I could – I'm not sure I could work on that – I mean – mmmmm.' While she was on the course, she says, her performance skills were not that varied, she had too narrow a range of experiences to build on. 'Sometimes I'll think back to things that might have been said during that course.' But, then, she finds it hard to remember what things they did do on MPCS. 'Did we do relaxation things?'

What has come to concern me more about this kind of data, however, is the necessity to move beyond it. At the time I reported this data there were useful things it could reveal to the music training world about the construction of musical identity and about the personal impact of music training on self and creativity. These, indeed, lay at the heart of the innovation – otherwise they would not have been so prominent in the evaluation. But, in retrospect, they were disembodied from the organizational implications of change. To be sure, I had an institutional focus in the evaluation – eventually I produced a case study of the Conservatoire. Even so, I did not make that connection as fully as I might have and my accounts possibly left some with a sense that there might be a resource for change in the intellectualism and energy of the students but with little sense of how to husband that resource against the adverse conditions created by an inert organizational context.

INTERVIEWING PROFESSIONALS

Finally, there are the players, the professional musicians. The problems that crop up in music education events do not go away for the professionals – they reach no apotheosis and they barely seem to modify other than to reflect the particularities of context. Rather, they suggest educational problems held in aspic, unattended dilemmas, enduring bruises. The struggles may not be with adults or with teachers – more likely with hierarchies and power systems – but they are essentially the same struggles to reconcile the hoped-for individuality of the music experience with the realities of an authoritarianism which is characteristic of orchestral life and work.

There was an occasion on the Guildhall project when staff and students on the MPCS course had 'retreated' to the South Bank Centre for a weekend of improvisation workshops designed to offer the students another way of seeing themselves in their music. In the course of the workshop members of the resident London Symphony Orchestra were invited to join them. One arrived as an improvisation was starting and he was invited to play along with the students – he had, of course, none of the preparation the students had had. During the course of the playing he made a contribution which centred on his extraordinary ability to play more than one tune simultaneously on his brass instrument (using harmonics and the voice as he was playing).

At the end of the piece one student asked him why he had felt the need to make such an impressive display of mastery. A discussion ensued in which the player admitted that he lived in a highly judgemental culture and that it was judicious to stake out your claim to technical mastery in front of other musicians – and especially so in an open-ended and demanding context like an improvisation workshop, where he felt insecure. The students sought to reassure him that this was a group which had eschewed that kind of punitive judgement of an individual's worth and which had found a way of concentrating on judgements of the capacity of the group to discover musical achievements through collaboration. They urged him to relax and to forget technique while he was with them.

This was – or so he said at the time – a significant moment for this musician, who said when he left the workshop later that this was the first time in his career that he found himself playing free of the fear of judgement. He was apologetic of having interrupted the early improvisation with his display. He left the workshop and returned to a rehearsal with the symphony orchestra.

Here, again, the evaluator needs to discover the methodological imperatives that structure the evaluation experience. Here, again, interview plays a central role and, once more, this is to be derived from the particularities of the context. Here we will see the interview exploring the struggle between professionals and the institutions which they inhabit. The tenor of these conversations is different from those of the students. Here, people are in various stages of struggle and reconciliation. Some have felt the reality of the failure to live up to the vision of excellence which drove them to where they are; or, like the brass player above, are still trying to come to terms with their own musicianship and find a way to be confident of their personal worth, no matter what their accomplishments. The interview, here, is a device for revealing and sustaining the experience of living with contradictions which are revealed as enduring – at least into middle age.

One orchestral player with the CBSO, Tim, was on an outreach project working with schoolchildren. For him the 'whole idea of the scheme is to try to highlight the similarities' – the similarities, that is, between his and the children's experience of music making – 'people trying to make music together on different instruments'. He points to the fact that the orchestra, like the schoolroom, has a register of names called at each rehearsal. But the self-denial implied by that is too strong, perhaps, to bear. 'When you compare yourself with them, you do have an innate musicality which has been, perhaps, trampled on all over by your contemporaries at work – but when you're in a classroom full of children, you know a lot more about music than they do, so it's very uplifting.'

Such is the experience of living with contradiction, of balancing uncertain values with conflicting interests – of facing the consequences of having reached your goal. Here is the individual in tension with institutions, and also with institutional roles. There is no obligation on the evaluator to help resolve those tensions – much less to launder them for evaluation audiences – but there is an obligation to explore and confront them. Whether and how this confrontation comes about depends on the balance between ruthlessness and fairness in the evaluator's mind.

Conversations with professional musicians are redolent of the issues raised in Tim's data – they represent the darker side of professional musical experience which is hidden during formal interactions in schools (and concert halls) and which forms little part of the training and in-service training curriculum for the musician. The personal is too easily masked by the ceremonial.

The Royal Opera House, too, has an extensive outreach program with schools, and there, too, the experience of leaving the concert hall and entering the world of school exposes professional experience to self-reflection – schools and schoolchildren often have that effect. But conversations with singers, musicians and dancers ostensibly about their education work inevitably revealed broader questions and experiences to do with their life in the House. Here, for example, is a singer talking:

'When you think of the self-exposure that's going on – people getting up there and performing these things, and living with questions of love and death all day long – and love music. You go in when you're young and you imagine you can handle it all. I feel very strongly that I can't handle it now as well as I used to . . . with music being a very subversive dimension which undermines your nervous system in all sorts of ways – it gets out of control much more quickly . . .'

Here we are looking directly into the relationship between a musician and their music – and at the consequences of entering into that struggle – 'love and death', no less. Here, there is another sense in which music becomes enveloped in the texture and sociology of a person's life. The intrinsic qualities of the music, even the stories it tells, achieve meaning in the context of a person's ageing, feed, perhaps, their nostalgia for youth – certainly play upon growing vulnerabilities. Evaluation works through the individual, again, but illuminates something of music culture and its embeddedness in living. We have, again, that sense of approaching a precipice created by evaluation questioning. We might also be seeing something of the emergence of one of those threads of consistency I spoke of earlier which can link discrete evaluation projects together. It becomes compelling to think of a continuum of experience and issues which starts with the music students and inchoate confusions, and which ultimately matures into the serious existential dilemmas of professionals. There is a sense of the maturation of life issues here – and of a chronological structure to experience.

We can look at a final example – this time of ballet, where ageing is a more serious and corrosive factor. Here is a fieldnote in which we hear two ex-dancers talking of their having left ballet for education work, still in the House. There is more control, here – these dancers made decisions to leave dance behind, to discover meaningful occupation elsewhere, effectively wrapping up dance in those broader contexts of living.

She retired from the Royal Ballet because her 'heart was not really in dancing'. It was a talent she possessed, easily discoverable through the traditional channels of girls doing ballet. She passed successfully through the various stages and to full employment as ballerina: 'I was never a soloist or anything'. Her reasons for leaving the Royal Ballet were the same as the other ex-dancer with whom she is working She says she feels almost ashamed to admit 'it was my talent but I didn't really want it'. Both stress that they find their working lives (i.e. in education) more interesting and fulfilling than they did purely as dancers. When her colleague left she stopped dancing completely – no half measures. If she was not going to accomplish dance at the highest level of her capabilities then she wasn't going to do it at all. For many years her pleasure at watching ballet performances also waned – 'the magic had gone'. Her technical knowledge stood in the way of her capacity just to enjoy the thing.

The experiences and personal sacrifices implied here are also hidden from curriculum view. Presentations and workshops done by professional musicians (and dancers) in schools rarely reveal these realities –

there is a certain taboo on controversy in such interactions. Visitors to school tread carefully, anxious neither to see their name in the next exposé headline in the tabloids nor to jeopardize their precarious and often financially essential foothold with the largest single captive audience in the country. But, then, these professional experiences and understandings are rarely revealed even to the professionals themselves, and often seem to stay subtly influential but cognitively hidden at the intuitive level. In the same way, the paradoxes and questions raised for children through their engagement with adult schemes – the narrowing graves – are hidden from the sight of the musician. The presence of evaluation presents at least the potential for bringing these worlds into contact with each other, once again, through information exchange. This is not to say that evaluators have a pedagogical responsibility – for example, to enhance the learning from these interactions – but that revealing hidden curricula is a strategy for understanding the formal curriculum.

5

To Have and Have Not: Critical Distance and Emotional Proximity

In this chapter I want to start laying down some caveats to what I am saying when I propose the personalization of evaluative enquiry. To do this I will contrast what I advocate with Elliott Eisner's model of connoisseurship and educational criticism. I will describe the model later, first I need to set a context, but we may note now that Eisner's approach is probably the one which celebrates more than any other the individualism of the evaluator. It is certainly one in which the values of the evaluator are written directly into the methodology and in which, above all, the evaluator is expected to discover a personal voice.

THE FAILURE OF DESIRE

I'm not crazy about music. I play a little, listen haphazardly and have little formal knowledge of it. I enjoy listening to music for short periods of time, but even then I can become bored. On the other hand, I think it is the implied failure of desire that has allowed me to spend a lot of the past ten years conducting educational evaluations in various music fields.

I think this is something significant to say because I encounter so many people engaged in evaluating music who do so from a firm basis of uncritical admiration for the stuff. I don't mean admiration for particular forms of music but, rather, an unswerving belief that music is a 'good' or 'inherently uplifting' or 'wholesome' thing. Most people I encounter in music fields are, to some degree or another, 'in love' with music. I am not – I care more about my evaluation. It is healthier for me as a professional

---

This chapter is derived from an article published in the *Bulletin of the Council for Research in Music Education* (Kushner, 1996a).

evaluator to have some emotional and cognitive affinity with the practice of evaluation than with the field being evaluated.

For me this has been somewhat liberating, in that it allows me to harness for other uses the energy I would otherwise have to expend in discovering a position of critical neutrality when music appears in educational contexts. I am not predisposed to judgement. 'Maturity', wrote Peter Berger (1974: 26), 'is the capacity to endure distance from the object of one's passions.' I have the freedom to play the 'immature evaluator' since enduring that distance seems to be small effort for me. More importantly, I present as an unthreatening character to my respondents (in respect of music judgement) since I have little interest in the quality of their music (I have a great interest in *their* judgements of that quality, of course). Hence, in my evaluations I commonly – surely unethically – deny that I even play music.

What practical impact does this have? Well, to take a crude example, as a supposed music innocent I can ask apparently simpleton questions like 'What exactly *is* a symphony?' or 'Couldn't you play that without a conductor?' (Of course, my knowledge of music is a real resource – but more for helping me find good questions to ask than for preempting questions.) Quite apart from the fact that these very questions provoke quite heated discussions since they conceal a range of value positions which would otherwise not easily be uncovered – they are actually controversial – they encourage musicians to radical reflection, which is to say, reflection on taken-for-granted aspects of their world of experience. Once familiar with cocking their head at that angle, so to speak, that person will tend to do it more easily thereafter – sometimes without prompting. People often need to rehearse their relationships with evaluators.

Just as important, my supposed failure of desire allows me a more immediately sceptical stance towards the claims made for music and musicians in educational settings – and so for my relationship with the substance of any program I evaluate. Music in educational contexts is no more or less worthy and flawed than any other social experience or curriculum – for example, with the same obligation to discover and argue for an educational warrant as any other school subject. It is, therefore, an appropriate subject for evaluation and public scrutiny and for generalizing to other fields of action. It is social.

LONG EXPOSURE

As I say, however, I care a great deal about my evaluation practice – perhaps that is my own art. I recently gave over to my students some of the archive of the Guildhall evaluation. The evaluation lasted three years and the six box files, two boxes of tapes and various field note books were part of the archive. I asked the students to find me in the archive and to associate that with my final report, which they had read. One – Ed Bober – gave me an account at the close of the workshop. 'I suppose', he said at the end of five minutes' commentary on my playing the evaluation role, 'what I'm trying to say is that you were in love with the students.' I was genuinely taken aback. This was as close an insight as I had had into that experience, though I think it was even more than that.

The Guildhall evaluation marked a happy period for me in which I discovered 'my voice' as an evaluator. I was able to immerse myself, I achieved a certain intensity of experience. It is rare – these days, at least – for an evaluator to have three years with a project. This allows for all sorts of closures and completions. Over that period, for example, I worked with three cohorts of students on the innovatory course, with each of which I passed through all of the seasons. I was able to watch all kinds of personal and institutional crises brewing, see the turmoil and both observe and reflect on the resolutions. Three years is long enough to ask someone how they are changing; what they are learning. Three years is long enough, also, to capture institutional rhythms as you watch annual rituals being played out. There are, I think, rhythms to curriculum. Outside of a developing curriculum – in the routine world of familiar curriculum practices – changes can be as subtle as the long drawn-out swerves of oil-tankers. But they are there. Early music and jazz were on the up through this period, as was music theatre and the performing polymath. Curriculum seals cannot be wholly hermetic.

These are, in one sense, routine observations, although in the lean-mean world of contemporary research funding they seem to speak of a golden age of longitudinal opulence – I think they do. There is a serious drawback in short-term observations of innovations, for they allow little time for the evaluator to contextualize the momentary enthusiasm of innovation participants in the moments leading up to and some time after their involvement. Here, three years gave me enough time to talk to students, for example, up to two years after they had left the MPCS innovation behind. It is also worth reminding ourselves of some of the subtleties of control and denial to which evaluators are subject as their briefs are drawn more and more tightly – so to speak. I was able to observe music professors adapting their pedagogy; I saw a student gradually overcoming her shyness. These are rare observations – even for a profession as obsessive as ours in its advocacy of personal change. But three years was clearly long enough to become impressed with the students' struggles for emergence – and to achieve a state of emotional engagement which can threaten that critical distance.

The fact that these things were happening, and the fact that I was able to observe them has been unique in my 20 years of evaluation experience and has something to do with the fact that I was working with students of music performance. As we have already seen, identity is even more embedded in the present moment for these people than it is for many post-adolescents. Much of my evaluation was driven by my conversations with the students and some of the principal interpretations were first offered by them. It was easier here than in any other setting I have worked in to realize the naturalistic 'canon' for evaluation judgement 'to take its authority from the subject rather than begin from theory' (Walker, 1991: 113). In any event, in naturalistic music evaluation you are virtually forced to rely on the theorizing of participants since the world of theory in music offers but a meagre resource in understanding the experience of music training and making.

So, to return to my theme, what did it mean to say that I was 'in love with the students', for it felt like, as I say, an accurate observation? I asked Ed to give me evidence of this and he cited without hesitation a piece in my final report which I had written about the singer, May. I was even more intrigued because that piece was written with the intention of confounding the narrative style of the rest of the report, which was itself intended to reveal the intimacy of the relationships I had with the music students. I am careful not to edit out references to me in transcripts, for example, so as, at the very least, to remind the reader of observer/author presence – that is, of the personal qualities of evaluation interactions.

REPRESENTING EVALUATION RELATIONSHIPS

For example, that final report opens with an interview with a student, Chloe, who talks about her music therapy work with disabled children. I quote:

Chloe is learning her intended profession from the ground, reading, talking with others in the field, but mostly observing and trying things out. She is learning 'body awareness songs'. She reaches over to touch her embarrassed evaluator's face with a pointed finger and begins to sing:

On Saville's face he's got a nose,
On Saville's face he's got a nose,
Saville's nose,
Belongs to Saville . . . etc.

And later in the same piece:

- Did the course do anything for your oboe playing?
- Yeah.
(But she sounds uncertain.)
- Yeah! Yes it did. It got rid of a lot of inhibitions, inhibitions about myself, about my playing.
- About 'myself'?
- Yeah – no – about the way I played.
- What's that got to do with 'myself'?
- I said 'myself' as in meaning the way I played.
- So why did you say 'myself'?
- Hell! You're not my analyst, Saville!
- You have an analyst?'

. . . and later again Chloe says . . .

'By rights you [pointing] should vote Tory if you wanted a better life for yourself – you should and I should. It makes sense to vote Tory for us, doesn't it?'

There's a lot happening here. To start with, the location of this interview at the opening of the report is a signal to the reader of my intention to emphasize the students' view – and to demonstrate the kind of relationship I had with them. There is substantive data here, too – obliquely about the course since I was still trying to work out the relationship between the curriculum of the innovatory course and the personal identity-building curriculum of the students. There is data here on the relationship between Chloe and her instrument, society and audience. There is also data on the evaluation process itself in a continuing attempt by me to make the methodology transparent – here, a sense of how I try to use intimacy, playful combat and, especially, detailed supplementary questioning as research instruments. I am also, of course, showing off Chloe. She understood the evaluation process, managed our relationship and always reminded me of my presence – she often talked of 'us'. And, too, there is evidence of my trying to curry favour with the reader, building in a sense of authenticity and immediacy to the account with a hint of self-mockery – even using the power of persuasion to enhance the piece's validity.

To say that I use intimacy as an instrument is not to imply that I intend these relationships to be merely instrumental, although I was occasionally accused of betrayal by students who thought they were talking to me as a confidant/friend and then found their words written into my public accounts. They were right, of course. I was as beguiled as they by the naturalistic process, as confused as the students by the intimacy of the moment – though I, unlike them, had to and was able to slough off that intimacy as I bowed over my portable typewriter late at night. Three years is long enough to recognize such shifts and to develop a certain ruthlessness. It eventually became a style and, I suppose, the betrayal became exaggerated but routine. Far from my increased exposure to evaluation being a journey into a unified and controlled state of ethical behaviour,[1] it has been a discovery of a range of competing ethics and a growing sophistication in my playing one ethic off against another – a journey, in that sense, into ethical confusion (see Chapter 7 for an exploration of that confusion).

Even so, I was 'involved' with these students. As I explain more fully elsewhere, I followed them, in one set of observations I have already mentioned, to a hospice (for terminally ill people) where they worked closely with two women patients and I wrote a case study of the experience. At the close of the study I asked some of the students of their responses. One (as we heard in the opening to this book) had returned to a rehearsal of her quartet but could not play because she was so distraught. Another was disturbed because she could recollect feeling nothing in particular at leaving behind those people in terrible predicaments. I, too, had a confusion of fears and feelings at leaving (I am prey to mortality panics) and they were difficult to disentangle from those of the students. Students and I were, in many senses, the 'us' that Chloe invoked in our interview.

---

1   As represented in music education evaluation, for example, by Liora Bresler (1996).

There were instances like this when I went through experiences *with* the students. This does not at all mean that I abandoned my posture of critical distance. Students always put me under pressure to join in with work-shops and discussions – otherwise how could I understand and, therefore, portray the experience, they argued? My retort was always that it was not my business to describe the 'experience' (events, yes) but to elicit from them what it was like to be on the inside. When they were, for example, preparing that workshop-based performance of a chess game with black and white children playing black and white pieces who eventually 'come together for the sake of the game' I needed, as evaluator, to have a critical distance so as to be able to adequately represent the many sides of what is clearly a complex and controversial event. To be complicit with the performance would engender loss of confidence among my readers.

THE CONNOISSEURSHIP MODEL

I think this is at some distance from Elliot Eisner's position (see, for example, Eisner, 1985). He argues for evaluative observations of educa-tional phenomena to be conducted by what he calls 'connoisseurs' – those with a practised eye and an informed insight. Connoisseurship forms the basis for educational criticism – for the use of the refined judgement of an expert witness to analyse and sum up the phenomenon. In the absence of a single, universally acknowledged criterion for judging the outcomes of evaluation we have a crisis of authority, says House (1980: 61): why believe what evaluators say? One response, says House, is to invoke professional authority, and he says that this characterizes Eisner's approach.

For Eisner, the key to evaluation is the authoritative, learned eye of the evaluator, the capacity for insight which can be mobilized for the 're-education of the perceptions' of others. The aim is not to arrive at definitive versions of reality or truth, but to develop informed insight in others, that is, to spread connoisseurship and to use it as a basis for informed critique. This has something of a pedagogical intent behind it which I have already said forms no part of my view of evaluation roles. This approach to evaluation came, partly, out of a critique at the failure of evaluation to discover rich and evocative ways of portraying events and people, and the subsequent proposal to adapt artistic forms of expression (principally creative writing) and forms of art criticism (particularly literary and dramatic criticism).

Eisner's work also grew out of a movement that gathered some momentary strength in curriculum debates in the USA and which was called the 'Reconceptualist' movement (closely linked, for students of these matters, to the relatively recent rise of phenomenology in the USA).[2] Central to the movement was the (Husserlian) notion of 'return', that is, return to the fundamental lessons of personal experience – to what Pinar and Reynolds (1992: 4) call the 'primordial experiences of childhood', to a state of curriculum innocence. This was to be achieved by recasting the relationship of the 'self' to 'knowing', and who better to model this than the researcher herself and himself.[3] And, since it was the researcher's personal experience – in fact, their autobiography – which was to be the source of new existential knowledge, it was appropriate to write about it in a personal style – personal in the sense of revealing the sources of private deliberation. Hence, the narrative style of Reconceptualist writers purposefully departs from conventional research writing and is heavily ornamented with poetic expression and references to literature, plastic arts and film.

Eisner encouraged his students to use the critic's eye, judgement and expression to observe classrooms afresh. Let me give a flavour of the result, drawn from one of the examples Eisner himself publishes at the end of his book on *The Educational Imagination* (1979: 232). Here a student of Eisner's and of the connoisseurship model, observes a teacher:

> The teacher exhibits a great economy of movement and gesture. It's almost as if [she] were a marionette whose strings are too tight and, hence, her gestures must be tight and close to her body.
>
> There is also economy of voice. [She] parcels out her words sparingly as if inflicted with a chronic case of laryngitis. Instead of speaking she points. If she wants a student to turn on the lights, she points to the student and then to the lights. She says nothing . . .
>
> . . . When the teacher does speak, however, her voice colours all experience within the confines of this classroom, and the colour that is vocally applied is shocking beige. Her voice is the perfect accessory for the tan, plastic drapes which cover the windows and hang, straight without feeling or expression. It's a voice barren of any sort of nuance, as if, somehow the hum of the air-conditioner were reconstituted into words . . .
>
> Although the resemblance is more spiritual than physical, I could not help but see a pedagogical version of that modern American Everyman [*sic*], Mary Hartman, hard at work in the classroom I was observing. As with Mrs

---

2 See Pinar (1992) for its intellectual origins. In fact, many issues of the *Journal of Curriculum Theorizing* (*JCT*), which is the organ of the Reconceptualists, carry some historical account of the movement. The *JCT* remains one of the richer adventures in journal creation.
3 You can read this in the work of Madeleine Grumet, William Pinar, Ted Aoki, Maxine Greene and Jacques Daignault among others.

> Hartman I could sense something beneath [her] expressionless face and
> voice and eyes, something hidden inside the vacuum.
>   There is, of course, and it wasn't hard to find. It doesn't take long, away
> from the classroom, talking over coffee, to discover a warm, sensitive,
> intelligent middle-aged lady interested in music and folk masses and people
> and people's feelings. In the best Jekyll and Hyde tradition, this proselytiser
> of the catechism of productivity is completely transformed when she steps
> beyond the four walls of her classroom, out into the open.

The observer goes on to create a sympathetic picture of a teacher trapped
inside the institutional pathology of schooling, unable to be herself in the
classroom and affected by the dissonance. She speaks in cold tones to a
young boy who is distressed at the failure of the teachers to treat him
kindly, but then breaks down in tears once the boy has left the room.'I
began to think', the observer says, 'about what I might be able to write
that might make life more bearable in this particular classroom . . .'.

Here we see the observer/evaluator using the connoisseur's eye to lay
the groundwork for educational criticism. His informed judgement
identifies key aspects of classroom process – the institutional disassoci-
ation of values from pedagogy; the assumption that the social order must
be replicated in the classroom. Since this is the evaluator's own story, he
is free to share the bases of his theorizing with his readership and he
draws from Feyeraband, Dewey, Helen Keller and others to recommend
to the teacher that she adopt certain pedagogical strategies so as to
'humanize' the classroom.

The piece closes by assuring the reader (and seeking to reassure
the teacher) that it is 'society' that is the villain of the piece, which
dehumanizes this classroom and plays on personal weaknesses.'Any
flaw that might be deeply embedded within [the teacher's] personality
need not be a tragic one' (1979: 239–40).

Eisner's wish to lace science with the rich descriptive and interpretative capabilities of the arts are realized in such pieces as these, which
broaden the range of possibilities in narrative style and allow for the free
play of humanist sentiment. These are rich accounts which carry the
reader into context and which offer informed analyses of educational
events. This observer accomplishes these as surely as he achieves a
ruthlessly honest and almost surgical analysis of an apparently hapless
teacher.

There are questions raised by accounts like these, as there are about all
accounts. This particular account, for example, flirts with stereotyping,
and allows us to raise questions of the rights of the subject to control
inferences made about them. Nor can we disregard the issues raised
when an evaluator makes specific recommendations that tie their

respondents to certain actions. There is, too, an issue about the stability of the concept of 'connoisseur'. We see the piece above shift and change in its focus – from a classroom observation to an analysis of the psychological and moral state of the teacher and to the politics and ethics of classroom practices. Of what is the observer a connoisseur?

For the most part these collapse down to questions of validity and it is here that I need to contrast my approach with connoisseurship. The examples I gave above were intended to show my attempts to make the production of evaluation accounts transparent, that is, to expose the workings of observation-with-judgement in such a way as to reduce the dependence of the reader on my analysis – or at least to extend that 'critical distance' to embrace the reader. It goes without saying that there are limitations to this – that the reader is subjected to much artifice. But the inevitability of artifice makes this a constraint on validity, a condition to be addressed insofar as we can – it does not invalidate the account. Part of the appeal to validity, then, lies in the conjunction of labour between evaluator and audience – somewhat akin to the concept of 'naturalistic generalisation' (Stake, 1995).

My intent is to enhance the reader's confidence in the evaluator as portrayer of events and people; but to correspondingly reduce confidence in her as judge of the significance of those portrayals. Under such an arrangement we can claim a role for the evaluator as a conduit for the views and judgements of others, seeking to drive a wedge between description and judgement. The evaluator describes; there is an interplay of judgement between actor and reader. Of course, the separation of description from judgement is clearly not a viable proposition for an end-state and its critique is now commonplace. It is intended as a procedural principle, a guide to action, a value to be adhered to in spite of its inevitable failure, a methodological *standard*. What is also commonplace is for us to be guided by ideals which we acknowledge are unrealizable. The key point, then, is that the skills and the authority of the evaluator represent a threat to validity, and are, so far as is possible, controlled by building in sufficient critical space for the reader to manoeuvre their judgements. This involves exposing the evaluator in the account.

This makes a contrast with connoisseurship. There, the appeal to validity lies in the justification for the dependence of the reader on the interpretations of the observer. The relationship between actor (in the above account, the teacher) and reader is one that is subordinate to that between actor and observer in the case of both description and judgement. The loss of confidence in the evaluator is the greatest threat to validity. Hence, there is a tendency to make accounts opaque, to hide authorial presence, for the risks of exposure are great. (Best not to think of the bicycle while riding for you might fall off in a confusion of cognitive calculation.)

At stake here are the limits to the justification of the use of subjective experience. Both my position and that of the connoisseur clearly exploit the subjective to a high degree (hence, 'personalizing' refers to the person of the evaluator as much as that of the respondent) and hence appear similar when viewed from a certain angle. However, they differ in that one seeks to position the evaluator methodologically, whereas the other seeks to position the evaluator in a hierarchy of judgement.

THE ISSUE OF AUTHORITY

I think, in any event, there are limitations to the sustainability of 'connoisseurship' in a field setting. People in my experience are suspicious of an evaluator who claims expert status, as I have already suggested. More significantly, what I am recounting from my own evaluations are experiences at the heart of artistic and educational production, and yet the substance of both project and evaluation has a lot less to do with the creative act or product than with the struggle for self-knowledge and the sociology of events. Claiming 'connoisseurship' in these matters is not straightforward.

Indeed, one of the problems at the heart of these Conservatoire observations was precisely that music professors are put up (and sometimes put themselves up) as authoritative figures on the matter of identity construction. This was controversial among students who were struggling to find their intellectual and artistic independence, and I always ran the risk of being tarred with the same brush in their eyes, that is, of having superior judgement to theirs. I want to pause here, for a moment, and look in more detail at this issue, for I think it highlights an issue for my approach as well as for connoisseurship. It is an issue both for the educational practitioner and for the educational evaluator. Here are extracts from an observation of a coaching session with an advanced cello student, Finn, and his personal tutor.

Tutor: . . . there are three ways of playing that.

He shows this by using three different combinations of fingering for the phrase.

Finn: How do I decide which to use?
Tutor: I don't know. But maybe the G.

He plays the phrase himself. Finn follows and replays the phrase.

> *Tutor:* No – no. Don't do the diminuendo too early. What happens when you can't hear something you expect to hear?

He leans forward with one hand cupped over an ear to demonstrate that people listen for resolutions of intervals.

> *Tutor:* They want to hear the A – the audience – but you leave it. Wait!

Finn plays the phrase repeatedly and there is more discussion until . . .

> *Tutor:* Bravo! Good. When you are excited it is too hard to switch off quickly, to make contrast.
> *Finn:* What? In life?
> *Tutor:* In music. In music and in life – it is the same thing.

Here we see something of the generator of student confusions over their identity and personality. The shift so easily made from interpretation of music phrases to a posture on living allows pedagogical authority to bleed across from the former (where it *may* be legitimate to create an intellectual dependence) to the latter (where it clearly is not, in any educational endeavour that aims at autonomy and emancipation). But such switches are familiar to these music students and they seek them out – as did Lyn, the flautist – looking for clues from their teachers as to who they are . . . becoming.

Part of the confusion, here, lies between training and education. Vocational training is concerned with developing skills and dispositions sufficient unto themselves to accomplish certain musical tasks requiring dexterity and interpretation. It does not necessarily imply or demand personal change at any level which implicates a shift of identity. But training can arrive at a point where the student must reach beyond cognitive and motor control into psychological and emotional control, and it is here where the very self is up for grabs.[4] Here is where training ends and education begins.

---

4 Peters (1966: 27) considers what is meant when we say that a man has been 'trained' but not 'educated': 'It is not that he goes through the moves like a mindless robot. For he may be passionately committed to the skill in question and may exercise it with intelligence and determination. It is rather that he has a very limited conception of what he is doing. He does not see its connection with anything else, its place in a coherent pattern of life. It is, for him, an activity which is cognitively adrift.' Conservatoire students often spoke of their inability to talk of routine matters in life, that their music training had put them apart from

The pedagogy of training – in the Conservatoire, a form of apprenticeship – is not appropriate to education, which can only be compromised by creating pedagogy-led dependence. An educational approach demands a more direct address on self and culture – acknowledging the striving for independence and autonomy. This may well rest on forms of authority, but not on that form which demands intellectual submission and dependence. This, we might imagine, was what Lyn was seeking – a new experience of being, making that connection between 'music' and 'life'.

With such a switch pedagogical authority becomes problematic. It may be an essential ingredient in apprenticeship training, where the teacher's experience of having accomplished the skill is a valuable piece of data for the student, who may find model demonstrations useful – dependence is a productive learning strategy. But demonstrations can be falsely beguiling where the nature of the endeavour is to break away from received models of being, where the task is to find autonomous meaning. Here, in any such educational striving, the student must learn to use the teacher as a resource rather than a model (Stenhouse, 1967), perhaps to avoid those terrains which have already been stalked by the teacher. Now the task of the student is to 'kill' (in Zen terms) her teacher, that is, to refute pedagogical authority.

This is where the source of a dilemma lies for the music Conservatoire. It is generally run as a vocational training institution – albeit operating at what are crudely thought of these days as 'higher levels of competence'. The pedagogy (rooted in coaching and the master class) is the pedagogy of training; the curriculum is of a high order of educational aspiration – a personal encounter with excellence. The principal teaching resource in the Conservatoire is that form of pedagogical authority which I have implied and which suggests a prior 'ownership' over the substantive knowledge at stake in the music learning process – knowing how to perform. In Peters's (1966) classic distinction, Conservatoire teachers are often both *in authority* and *an authority* in relation to their students.

I will select just one more example of this confusion and its potentially harmful effect before I look at the implications for evaluators. May left a French song master class having been repeatedly stopped in her rendition of a piece by her tutor. Before her, another young woman had offered a song which had been interrupted very little by this same tutor

---

mainstream currents of social life. There was a General Election during this evaluation (1987) and some students talked of their difficulty of knowing how to vote, for example, of not knowing what was at stake.

who, in fact, had praised her. After the event both spoke to the evaluator. The girl who had sung before May was very positive about herself and the tutor. May was not.

You come out feeling that nothing belongs to you – he's taken everything away from you. Then you just go away and try to put it all back together again. The way he criticizes me, he makes me feel as though I've got no interpretation at all. Whether that's just the way he treats me, or whether I don't fit in. I don't convey anything. I don't know what I'm doing.

Here is the confusion created when 'in' and 'an' authority become combined. This makes for rich but dangerous ground for the evaluator. Rich because the students are, perforce, rehearsing the deep structure of personal struggles and can talk about it as fluently as I hope I am demonstrating. Dangerous because any hint of pedagogical – indeed, professional – authority will associate the evaluator too immediately with the value system of the Conservatoire, which is the source of much of the struggle I am portraying. In such an event the evaluation loses its legitimacy as a neutral, reflective resource – it becomes part of that authority system which cannot be bucked. The evaluator can no longer claim that warrant – much less provide what the students would see as a safe environment for articulating the struggle.

In this sense, the evaluation, though maintaining a critical distance from the object of its observations, is necessarily defined by it. Where pedagogical authority is the substantive issue for student and, therefore, evaluator, that is, where authority is the source of the dilemmas and concerns under investigation, the evaluation must seek a position remote from it – surely, into another form of authority, but one which is neutral to the issue of personal learning. Evaluation can be *educational* in that it offers a *refuge from certain forms of authority*. Insofar as connoisseurship rests for its legitimacy on certain forms of pedagogical authority, this makes it distinct.[5]

---

5 Of course, I cannot argue that evaluators lie outside of all systems of authority – or that they can spontaneously slough off residual pedagogical authority spilling over from 'alike' adults, i.e. teachers. But this is a brief argument. The fuller version would have to address the nature of rules which bind the evaluator's authority and which define the different forms of authority that distinguish teacher from evaluator.

This does not necessarily prejudice Eisner's aim that evaluation may 're-educate the perceptions' of others, though here, too, authority is an issue. Evaluation may be educational – this does not imply the need for it to have an instructional pedagogy. Evaluation may create educational contexts of thought and reflection – persuasion, even; it may provide learning data; it certainly often provides the moment. But, once again, the need for the evaluator to engender respect for evaluation's authority over knowledge of the issue carries risks. It can be damaging to the audience, whose opportunity to arrive at their own autonomous judgement of events (that is, using evaluation data to their own interpretative ends) is eroded, but damaging, too, to the evaluator whose reports become *deniable* – that is, dismissable because associated with a partial view.

SEE-THROUGH VEILS

It is time to come back to May and to that piece of data which Ed felt was redolent of my emotional involvement with the students. It was written purposely to confound the style of the rest of the report, to produce a disjuncture in narrative style. We will see the full piece in the next chapter – for now, here is an extract. The full piece is a descriptive analysis (based on interviews) of what it takes to allow May to sing at this level:

[. . .]

Like all musicians she has, over many hours of work, adapted her body to her instrument. Her diaphragm will be strengthened and her vocal chords strong and differentiated – hopefully without the little polyps that can come with overuse. She has developed those facial muscles which allow her to create the appropriate mouth shape without having to smile and tense the lower jaw. Her posture is contrived to allow the optimum breathing capacity. She has learned breathing as a specialized technique. She has explored all the available space within her head as a sound box for the voice. She has studied how language is produced – how the lips and tongue produce vowels and consonants. Following the early decision, taken by her teacher, to opt for mezzo soprano, she will have worked and will still be working on her tone – on the overall and personal quality of the voice.

[. . .]

The attempt is to be surgical, analytic, purely descriptive. This was written, above all, to be methodologically opaque so as not to distract the reader with thoughts of how it was produced – that is, it was an intended departure from the principles I have just enunciated. With Ed, at least, it had the opposite effect. Perhaps reflecting the paradox I mentioned earlier, and unlike the connoisseurship model, I am left exposed as the evaluation act is personalized. Here was the evidence that I was 'in love' with these music students. Why?

I think for two reasons – one of which Ed gave me. Far from being methodologically opaque, he argued, he could see me sitting with notebook in hand scrutinizing this young woman, somehow engaged in an obsessive act. The detail in the account speaks of the fixation of the observer. Behind this detail lies intense conversation, close questioning and intimate access. Consider, for example, what it takes to elicit this kind of account. In fact, it requires that you push the respondent to certain of the limits of her tolerance. The interviews that derived this data were, in one sense, merely tedious for her since they dealt with trivial detail. The evaluation relationship demands that we can bore our respondents and get away with it. At another level it might have been threatening, for a particular and important reason.

Generating data that speaks of this level of detail is not straightforward. One reason is, I think, that it requires that we ask many supplementary questions – but if you ask enough supplementary questions you are almost bound to touch a raw spot. The evaluator needs a certain ruthlessness to keep on probing. Repeated questioning is not at all natural social behaviour. In normal interaction we look for quick and easy closures – often as a sign of courtesy and respect for the other. We accept implicitly a great deal of what people claim. 'This changed my life' is not often to be met with the response, 'Precisely how and when – can you give me a concrete example?' The implied scepticism is unfair or taboo. The normal desire for self-restraint can easily pervade the evaluation relationship – especially one built on a friendship (albeit an artifice of a friendship).

Anyway, to reiterate, Ed saw through the attempt at narrative fraud to the intimacy within. Of course, one of the obvious implications of this is that there are important aspects of narrative that we simply do not control. We are prey, in our writing, to self-deception and to our own naiveté about our motivations. I say, 'in our writing' for it is proximity to the production process which disables us. In the act itself, there is little protection from self-deception and none from naiveté. Perhaps, too, there is something intrinsically deceptive about the writing process through which we can be prey to a curious example of the 'law of opposite effects'. My students saw me exposed as an intimate in the piece in which I was trying to hide. Interestingly, perhaps, the piece written by Eisner's student, which is written from a purposefully subjective viewpoint, succeeds in hiding the author from view – there is barely a hint of relationship between him and the teacher.

THE FLUIDITY OF EVALUATION ROLES

I think a lot of what lies at the heart of this being-in-love business is to do with holding a more fluid notion of *role* than is conventionally held in evaluation.[6] Evaluation roles are typically spoken of as suits of clothes, as it were, steady states that you can step in and out of. They are changeable in the sense that they provide evidence of multiple evaluation selves – at the very least a duality between evaluator-in-role and evaluator-as-person. But stepping into role does not imply stepping out of 'person'. A more fluid view would see the evaluator juggling with competing identities and attendant feelings and responses in each present moment. I am aware that I am shuddering with fear and loathing as I walk through the hospice, but aware, too, that this is irrelevant to the nature of the hospice as I have to portray it. More relevant are the constructions of those working and living there. Self-restraint is the key to the resolution of these competing inner persuasions.

It also has something to do with a dependency relationship between myself and the students. In an obvious sense I came to rely on the rich accounts they were able to give me – the more so as my evaluation came to generate some interest across a number of audience groups. I was getting 'thick descriptive' data and these students' accounts were proving illuminating to the cultural worlds of music. But dependent in more subtle ways, I think, too. I achieved some sort of heightened experience in this evaluation. I meant by that the rare sense of mastery – sheer ability to do the job – which, for researchers, can evoke a sense of triumph on returning to the office and to conversations with colleagues to tell rich and evocative stories. It was known I was doing interesting work and my stock rose accordingly in the competitive culture of case

---

6   I do not use 'role' here as defined by Scriven (1967) in his seminal distinction between 'roles' and 'goals' of evaluation. He talks of role as 'legitimate activities' engaged in by evaluation and which define the nature of its service. Here, however, I refer to the professional identity the evaluator presents to her informants and which governs her conduct. The two obviously overlap insofar as the scope and nature of activities make certain demands on the stance of the evaluator.

study research. Travelling down to London each week was a 'fix', a reminder to myself that I (too) was in a state of becoming. Hitherto, I would call myself an 'evaluator' – just as musicians sometimes talk of that epiphanous moment when they came to see themselves as 'musician'.

Now my account is beginning to sound as though I was exploitative, and, of course, in a sense, I was. It is often hard to disentangle the evaluator's obligation to publish with her personal yearning for public audience. The Director of the Guildhall innovation (Peter Renshaw) has always disregarded my claims to impartiality and to the purity of the Democratic Evaluation model I was pursuing. He claims that I used the evaluation to promote a 'world view' under the guise of critical detachment. Perhaps he is right – but perhaps what he notices is the subtle self-advertisement that underpins so much of what I did write. To be in love involves, somehow, enlisting the identity of an 'other' to confirm or enhance your own. Again, evidence here of a journey into more rather than less complex ethical dilemmas.

TO SWIM IN THE SAME TREACLE

Eisner, more than any other theorist of evaluation, is concerned to fully exploit emotional proximity. There are no existential dilemmas that persuade him, as they do Peter Berger, to endure 'distance from the object of one's passion'. Maturity, for Eisner, lies in the opposite direction, in close engagement with that very object. Maturity for Eisner (himself an artist) lies in the kind of insight which allows for the trained and skilful use of personal creative faculties – reaffirmation of the self; for me it resides in the kind of insight that might allow for some denial of self.

The evaluator has her own struggle with identity to contend with, her role being constructed by theoretical models, respondents, self – probably family, too. I was never in a that steady state of educational critic, much less a 'connoisseur': I was more often in a state of turmoil, ecstasy, need, confusion, defensiveness. My principal effort went into reconciling critical distance with real personal engagement.

I was also in the process of discovering my professional identity in parallel with the students at the Guildhall, and this involved certain dilemmas of my own in respect of who I was and was becoming. I was (unwittingly) in the business of discovering my own methodological 'voice' in the way I have already explained. This was a complicated business for me because I was doing so within an evaluation rubric which demands from the evaluator a high degree of disengagement so as to remain impartial. Students and evaluator are separate, kept apart by differing obligations, different roles, different values and interests, different opportunities and very different consequences arising from the evaluation. Evaluators may celebrate that separation by striving for critical distance – I do. But somewhere in the heart of the students' struggle to bring visions into alignment with realities the evaluator swims in the same treacle. I suppose I admired these people, maybe for the same reason I try to admire myself. They were taking significant risks against crippling odds – and they *kept going*.

Here, finally, is the complexity in researcher–subject relations I spoke of in Chapter 3. There is close exchange, the subject is known, the subject is expected to be an intelligent informant – but interests do inevitably diverge though they also overlap, and there is an inevitable hierarchy in the relationship. Looked at in certain ways, the distinction between subject and researcher becomes less distinct, and yet intimacy gives the researcher greater degrees of control, over, for example, the interpretation of lives and selves.

There is a great deal of tension between the three essential elements implied here – the need for emotional engagement with the students for the sake of the richness of the accounts; the need to discover a personalized approach to methodology; the need to maintain a distance and an impartiality for the sake of validity. I found no all-purpose solution to how to resolve these tensions – either for me, as I confronted my own confusions, or for the students, as they sought to reconcile the shifting versions of this engaging character who was the evaluator. Much less was there refuge in a role. Rather, the resolutions were entirely situational and in constant flux. Sometimes it made sense to be open about the problems and the manipulations; other times that would have been damaging to me, to the evaluation and to the person concerned, and other disingenuities were fairer.

There was, of course, progress being made all the time, as my motivations and intentions in the evaluation slowly became clearer to me (though never entirely clear). I do not want to suggest that the implied chaos is disabling – it was not to me – but that coherence in evaluation practice does not depend on order, predictability and control. Rather, it depends on being confident at living with uncertainty; being guided more by an unreserved curiosity than by an emerging theory; by believing uncompromisingly what is being said to you, but sceptical about its precision as an expression and about its meaning-in-context; and by worrying less about where you are going and more about journeying well.

The connoisseur is concerned with worlds of knowledge and knowing. Education for the connoisseur is progress to a morally and aesthetically better world – a journey made surer by trained eyes and refined tastes. The connoisseur's implicit question (and you may need to take a moment to think this through) is 'Can you evaluate if you don't know the people you are evaluating and don't like yourself?' Let me repeat that question, for this is central: 'Can you evaluate if you don't *know* the people you are evaluating and don't *like* yourself?'

For me the question is slightly different. It is, 'Can you evaluate if you don't *like* the people you are evaluating and don't *know* yourself (well enough)?' I think not.

6

Essences, Contexts and Transitions: the Individual at the Margins of the Program

ESSENCES

A colleague, Barry MacDonald, was at the point of securing a commission to evaluate the training of racing jockeys (the British Racing School were attracted by his evaluation experience, not his liking for Damon Runyon). As he was planning the enquiry he asked me if I would like to be involved and to write a portrayal of a thoroughbred racehorse. Unfortunately, the money never came in and we didn't do it.

Now any gambling person will tell you that for the regular punter a bet on a horse is as profitable as a spent match – but this does not hinder this billion-pound betting industry. Part, at least, of this has to do with the entrapment of desire or admiration or mythology or something else and at the centre of that is the balletic vision of the brave, sleek, muscled thoroughbred horse. It is – sheer money interests notwithstanding – 'what it is all about'.

Sometimes, in evaluation, we can identify phenomena or events that represent something of the essential quality or complexity of the enquiry – perhaps as the unknown warrior captures something of the intensity of meanings about warfare. Note, however, that the unknown warrior may be an essential image, but its meaning is not constant: for some he represents the apotheosis of courage and dedication; for others, the nadir of collective ambitions. In the case of horse racing it is easy to propose a candidate; in other evaluations it is less easy or simply inappropriate. One research student at my centre (a nurse) was studying an intensive care unit in a hospital and was provoked into thinking about the portrayal of an essential phenomenon by a discussion of what will follow in this chapter. She wrote a detailed observation account of a patient

lying in an intensive care bed. She portrayed a barely glimpsed individual so surrounded by and plugged-into technology that even the
nursing staff found it hard to approach him. The line between an
essential (in the sense of exemplary) observation and the crystallization
of personal advocacy can be perilous to tread.

I wouldn't want to make any great claims for this aspect of evaluation
– some evaluations do not yield such simple reductions, and where they
do they too easily lapse into reductionism, which is not at all where I
want to be. And, too, they have a tendency to violate the principle of
plurality – how can we sustain an argument about multiple perspectives
if we then assert what the evaluator takes to be an essence? But even so,
as an argumentative or analytic device, as an aid to readers to cognitively
elbow their way into an unfamiliar setting, or simply as an attempt by
the evaluator to do that most difficult of all things – to think analytically
about what she is seeing – this artifice has its occasional uses. And, too,
as I will show, it is possible to use 'vignettes' to bump-start organizational analysis. I will also pick up an argument I implied earlier that we
need to think in more complex ways than we customarily do about
context – more complex, that is, than context as a determinant of action;
and than context as an aspect of foreground–background relations.

The account which follows – which you should note was based on a
series of interviews, and which I briefly introduced in the previous
chapter – stands as an analogue, the fusion of thought and experience in
a momentary image. In this analogue I was trying to capture an essential
quality of the Conservatoire, to dilate the vision. The account is of what it
takes for a singer to be able to sing. I reproduce it in full.

THE BODY OF MUSIC

May will not win this one. She stands just alongside the piano on the bare stage. She
sings and her voice carries easily to the very back of this large auditorium. She is
competing for the Conservatoire 'Gold Medal' award. She wears a formal, heavily
patterned dress (short – this is a preliminary round) and she wears make-up. Her
hands hang neatly to her sides and only occasionally does she clasp them together.
The hall is almost empty but with a table in the centre of the auditorium where a
judge sits with head dropped forward and eyes closed, listening. The atmosphere is
tense and the few stragglers sitting here and there are careful to make no sound. She
sings four songs by Fauré, Wolf and Elgar. The songs are challenging in different
ways, requiring her to combine the 'big voice' with gentler, purer forms, and to
demonstrate the full range of her mezzo soprano technique.

Just recently, May has won other competitions – as a result of one win she sang on the radio and represented the Guildhall School in a Barbican concert. Let us consider, for a moment, what is required for May to perform at this level – just what it is that Conservatoire training has to provide.

Clearly, May has to develop her voice. That takes time (at twenty-four her voice is barely mature yet) and supervised work. Like all musicians she has, over many hours of work, adapted her body to her instrument. Her diaphragm will be strengthened and her vocal chords strong and differentiated – hopefully without the little polyps that can come with overuse. She has developed those facial muscles which allow her to create the appropriate mouth shape without having to smile and tense the lower jaw. Her posture is contrived to allow the optimum breathing capacity. She has learned breathing as a specialized technique. She has explored all the available space within her head as a sound box for the voice. She has studied how language is produced – how the lips and tongue produce vowels and consonants. Following the early decision, taken by her teacher, to opt for mezzo soprano, she will have worked and will still be working on her tone – on the overall and personal quality of the voice.

May reads music and has to be able to relate a printed note to a real sound. She can sing in the Early Song style (purer, quieter with little or no vibrato), in the post-Wagnerian style (a bigger voice – to carry over orchestras – with the use of vibrato) and in coloratura (the ornate style with busy runs of notes). She can hold a long, quiet note with the minimum of oscillation, while controlling the note's cutting edge as well as its substance and richness. She can jump large intervals of music from one note to another with precision. She can make theatre with her voice, making it warm or cold, desiring or denying, strident or supplicant.

May has sufficient mental control over her body to be able to relax her torso but to resist reflex temptations, such as to hold the piano. These songs May knows by heart – they are part of her own carefully selected repertoire. She speaks sufficient French, German and Italian to understand what she is singing – she has worked particularly hard on pronunciation in each of these languages. The actual repro-duction of the song is not a serious problem, she is unlikely to lose her place or to sing wrong notes – this is not fragile in that sense. Such problems have, largely, been overcome. But her efforts, at this advanced stage, are to do with interpretation and expression. May looks directly at the audience, using her body as a dramatic artefact to attract and hold people's attention. It is still 11.00 o'clock in the morning – it might well be 9.00 in the evening in a concert hall and May would be able to produce a performance of the same quality.

All of these skills are highly refined in May as in the majority of other students at the Guildhall. They have been developed to the point where they can be accom-plished automatically. Instrumentalists, too, except that more of their struggles are waged with external aids to expression – violins, flutes, drums. They all adapt their bodies appropriately.

But these are merely the basic credentials of the professional music world. Every applicant for a professional music job is assumed to have all of these trained attributes and they are not tested for them. What matters – what gets you noticed – is the allegedly indefinable quality often spoken of as 'musicality', the capacity to put these attributes to the service of expression and interpretation. 'I'll never make it,' said a tuba student. 'I know everything there is to know about the tuba – I can blow every note there is to blow on it with all the different fingerings – but I'm not musical.'

All of this (and more) is accomplished or encouraged through Conservatoire training and, for some, the preparation that took place earlier at school. The Conservatoire exists in order to bring together music students and 'professors' of music for the purpose of producing new performers. That is its historical role and we will shortly see that in operation. Students will frequently choose a Conservatoire in order to have access to a particular teacher. The model that dominates the training curriculum is the orchestral player – the artificer of the music world (not, for example, the soloist virtuoso, who often has never attended Conservatoire). The Conservatoire is a vocational training college teaching very high level job skills.

Here is a piece which purports to reveal something of the essence of what is being evaluated. In fact, in a direct sense, it has little to do with May, everything to do with the institutional culture of which she is a member. When I wrote this I had been evaluating the Conservatoire innovation for more than a year and the methodology of the experience was gradually beginning to emerge. I decided it was the right time to place the innovation in its institutional setting by juxtaposing peda- gogical interactions typical of the innovation with others which were part of the normal fabric of the Conservatoire – to look at the overlaps and discontinuities between the innovation and its host culture. I looked at master classes, coaching sessions, conducting classes, competitions (a central feature of Conservatoire life) and elsewhere. In a seminar, some students, enthusiastic for the iconoclastic aims of the innovation, had been pressed by the Principal to say what they were prepared to forego so as to create more space for innovatory activities. None was prepared to lose anything – not even the almost universally disliked orchestral rehearsals and the often-feared master class. My task, then, was to represent the institutional inertia of the Conservatoire against which any innovation would have to struggle – but to portray that from the point of view of the individual who carries the burden of that struggle.

In this piece, then, we are supposed to be able to see the sheer scale of the effort and commitment that are required to perform *adequately* at this level. Here is the physical, emotional and psychological burden being carried by this one student. Here is the pay-off for the investment May has put into her singing, a place on the platform, the chance – just the chance – to compete for the absurd dream of fame so aggressively marketed by the music training industry. And here, too, is the source of institutional and personal resistance to innovation. What is implicit in the observation is the sheer scale of institutional (pedagogical) support to achieve these minor mutilations of the body. Watching May sing tells you a lot about how the Conservatoire is organized so as to distribute resources for the desired effects. Along with resource distribution goes the distribution of power. What it takes to make May sing eventually confers political favour on some at the expense of others – it certainly defines an imbalanced relationship of power and authority between teacher and student. I say at the expense of others because the required physical attributes of a singer are both disputed and changing and those who share dissenting views of what makes a good singer are weaker players in the scramble for resources.

What is also implicit in this observation is a pedagogical style, since the basic personal attributes required are essentially behavioural – they can be (and are) taught with instructional, rote, repetitive techniques. In these senses, perhaps rather oddly, this observation offers the beginning of an organizational analysis of the Conservatoire – albeit a highly inferential one. We can infer from the skills base of May's singing the kinds of demands on resources the instruction makes and the kind of organization required to support that resource distribution. At higher levels of inference, we can read certain educational and training values into May's preparation and we might imagine (at least at a hypothetical level) the kind of organization which supports and promotes those values. (Instructional pedagogies, for example, demand compliance from students – but also from teachers who are servants of the methodology and subject to the authority of the knowledge base. These can create the conditions for, if not emanate from, command-and-control systems of curriculum management characterized by hierarchy.) Here is one of the special characteristics of the 'essential' or 'exemplary' observation – that it is redolent of institutional culture.

Let me look at some of the institutional characteristics of the Conservatoire. Most spaces in the Guildhall building are related to performances of one type or another – concerts, master classes, coaching sessions and private practice. Reflecting the historical nature of the Conservatoire, which was to do nothing more or less than to bring into contact those who 'profess' music and those who seek 'profession', there are few adequate spaces within which a student–teacher culture might properly develop – seminar rooms, common rooms – the kind of physical spaces which can host conversation. Most music teachers are part-time – reflecting the priority given to using people with practical professional experience, but also tending to reinforce the instructional pedagogy centred on models of 'mastery'. Department heads and administrators tend to be full-time posts (most of their work involves staffing/rooming logistics, assessment and student counselling). This itself both reduces the power of music professors (who are, in teaching terms, a casualized force) and hinders the emergence of a shared professional culture. There can only be, for example, fragmented and infrequent discussion at best of pedagogical practices and in-service professional development.

Neither space, therefore, nor employment conditions encourage educational discussion. Pedagogical practices are 'privatized' – taken to be the province and the responsibility of the individual – and comparisons between individual professors can only really be made by the people least able to voice an opinion – the students. There is common talk in the Conservatoire about the personal insecurity of music teachers and one of the most often cited pieces of evidence for this is the virtual absence of in-house concerts given by them. This contrasts with the fervour with which competitions are promoted to the students, requiring them to perform regularly to the teachers under very demanding conditions.

What we can do with modest beginnings like this is to conceive an evaluative picture of an organization that serves to promote specific kinds of learning – an *educational* organization. For example, if we try to think of the Conservatoire in terms of the priorities represented by its organizational form we would quickly notice that development (curriculum, personal professional, management) was less of a consideration than continuity. As the name implies, the Conservatoire serves to conserve. We would also notice that the Conservatoire as a learning organization seemed to achieve more in terms of personal learning than was easily accounted for in its formal recognition of what counted as curriculum. The Conservatoire is more than the sum of its parts.

May, at this very time, was one of the most passionate advocates of the innovation and featured prominently in my accounts. This piece, then, was also illuminative of something personal about May – something of the essence of her personal struggle. She was committed to an innovation that was openly questioning of Conservatoire traditions, pedagogies and relationships; and yet she was sufficiently committed to those very traditions and relationships that she was one of those who floundered for an answer to the Principal when he asked what these innovation advocates would give up in their curriculum to make way for more innovation. She made it through the Conservatoire and achieved a coveted place in a leading opera chorus; she made it through the innovatory course as one of its principal (student) innovators. As it happened, she also made it through the evaluation, since I was often at her side seeking her views. She was to write to me shortly after this piece:

> I'm not sure, I expect you've met 'hostile' evaluated people before. But I think that it might have something to do with the nature of this (innovatory) course. The course demands that you look at yourself honestly as a potential performer/communicator and then to assess your worth in society. As you know, I've been thrown about from wanting to be a 'star' to 'social worker' . . . sometimes you get happy, sometimes depressed. Sometimes you get lost but I think recently I've been feeling quite settled and so I don't want you asking me questions and screwing up my peace of mind. I think also, while you're trying to find your feet it's not always helpful to be reminded of why you fell over in the first place.

Again, there are important insights here into organization, especially if we juxtapose this letter with the earlier observation. One reading of this suggests that there was, indeed, a fracture in the Conservatoire culture created by the innovatory course. The fracture is felt by this individual – as House (1974), in his thesis on the morality of innovation, argued, the real costs of innovation are driven down the system to be carried by the most vulnerable and those who can pass it on no further. Here, too, is evidence of the capacity for innovation to reveal something about the conventional – and, of course, of the complexity of the evaluation role in documenting this.

This piece, then, claims to capture an essential or exemplary quality of Conservatoire life – but it also stands as something exemplary of naturalistic evaluation, too – so long, that is, as it is read alongside May's letter. The presence of the evaluation, its urgent probing and insistence on analysing events and feelings that would otherwise be left to unspoken routine, often place enormous pressure on people. It is the person being evaluated who carries much of the cost of public understanding. Personalizing evaluation has its price.

CASE STUDY AND CONTEXT

Embedded in this analysis is an aspect of case study which it is worth pointing to at this moment. Conventionally, case study implies population. Whether treated as a 'sample of one',[1] an 'instance in action',[2] or as one of a comparative series,[3] the general purpose of case study is to illuminate something of the relationship between single instances and general populations of which they are a part. This school tells us something about all schools, say.[4] Case study as a *sampling procedure* allows the evaluator to measure and to balance idiosyncratic, unique characteristics of a case with characteristics that are shared across the population of cases.

But the principle operates at different levels and can be applied to the internal properties of a case study so that single instances within the case can illuminate something of the holism or the culture of the case (especially, as in the evaluations I am recounting here, where the boundaries of the case supposedly coincide with the boundaries of the institution or program). I usually think of this working something like a hologram. A piece of glass holds a three-dimensional image. Shatter it and imagine a single shard taken from, say, the top right-hand corner. Looked at face on, you will see whatever part of the two-dimensional image corresponds to the top right-hand corner. But tilt the shard slightly and you will glimpse the whole image – but *from the angle of view of the top right-hand corner*, looking down and in at the image, as it were. Equally, a shard taken from the middle-bottom of the picture when tilted will give you the view of the whole image looking, this time, up and into it.

Think, then, of the essential observation as such a shard. The one above, looked at directly, is about a singing competition and May. Tilt it slightly, look down and in at the Conservatoire from the perspective of this fragment and you will see where that tiny part of the image is connected to the whole. You will get a view – albeit this situated view, distorted by its localization – of the whole. You remember that the competition is taking place in a concert room inside the Conservatoire and that the doors are closed against the bustle and noise outside; that similar competitions happen here all the time for singers and instrumentalists; that in the audience are other singers jostling for a place in the pecking order – among their friends, one of whom will win, and they will meet up for a drink together later; think that May will finish this

---

1 L. Stenhouse, 'Case study and case records: towards a contemporary history of education', *British Educational Research Journal*, 4, 2 (1978), pp. 21–39.

2 Walker (1974).

3 R.K. Yin, *Case Study Research: Design and Methods*, 2nd edn (London, Sage, 1994).

4 Barry MacDonald (in Simons, 1987: 63–6) gives a nice account of how he discovered the use of case study by being slowly drawn in to the particularities of single schools to the point where he had to sample the 36 schools hosting the project he was evaluating.

competition and rush off to a coaching class with a professional singer who comes here fleetingly for six hours each week; recall all of this while reading this piece, and it becomes evocative of institutional life.

Accounts like this are useful for raising questions (for example, Who is the judge in this competition? Where do his or her criteria come from? What do competitions do to student relations?). These, conventionally, drive an evaluation forwards through progressive focusing, developmental sampling and the like, and they are essential for that. But the questions themselves are, in an important sense, data about the organization in that revealing the *kind of* question that can be asked is some sort of measure of the place.

The capacity for single, small-scale observations to raise larger questions about programs, institutions and cultures is probably insufficiently exploited. It does, too, have something of a destabilizing effect on one of the canons of naturalistic evaluation – the notion of 'context'. The failure of social science – psychology and economics, in particular – to acknowledge the impact of social environment (what Parlett and Hamilton, 1977, called *'milieu'*) gave great impulse to the emergence of case study-based evaluation. The need to understand the promise and the shortfall of innovation had not been met by outcome studies and eventually, for a short period, at least, yielded to the necessity to study the performance of programs and the conditions under which they operated. Context was all.

At least three notions of context came into popular usage – as embedding, as signifier and as determinant. In the first of these there is the image of 'foreground' and 'background', where events that were the focus for evaluation needed a setting in which to be placed. Typically, for example, studies of a curriculum set in a school might begin with descriptions of the school, its community, history, population, policies, etc. There may be no immediate link made with 'foreground' (the curriculum innovation, say, under study) but the 'context' at least prevents the sociological isolation of the events being portrayed – there is, at least, a sense of embeddedness for the reader, and a sense of 'particularity'.

The second – context as signifier – takes the portrayal of context a stage further. Here, the school context, for example, does not necessarily help us to understand the case any better, but allows us to measure the significance of what we read in 'foreground' events. Hence, for example, the study of a curriculum innovation set in a school that we have heard is a historically innovative school gives us a measure of significance which might not go so far as to say that the curriculum innovation came about *because* this is such a school. Here, the use of context serves as a sensitizer for the reader, alerting them to the possibility of certain contingencies.

The third – context as determinant – gives a more assertive role to portrayals of background. Here, context is not the immediate focus for the evaluation but helps to explain the nature of contingency, that is, what links foreground and background in a weak or strong causal relationship. Hence, the fact that the school is an innovative school helps us to understand *why* and perhaps *how* this curriculum innovation emerged in this school. In this case we might be persuaded to look more into context, which then assumes more of a prominent place in understanding the case.

In each of these there is a discontinuity between context and focus – that is, there is a discrete notion of context. Perhaps what the observation of May does is to fuse the two, to smooth over that discontinuity. Her observation is saturated with context; the context is revealed as made up of many such observations – is itself the observation. It is hard to know whether and when we are looking at foreground or background – perhaps so hard that it barely matters. Hence, the curriculum innovation that was MPCS was redolent of the Conservatoire culture that was its host, but in many ways *was* that same culture – in the sense that it embodied its promises, constraints and dilemmas and failed fully to break out of its cycle of beliefs and rituals.

Finally, I want to look a little closer at institutional contexts and to expand a little on the capacity of such pieces to 'bump-start' institutional analysis. I argued earlier that methodology grows partially out of the values of the researcher and also out of those of the researched (as methodology responds to the nature of the enquiry field). This is not to say that all authentic methodology is advocacy – or that everything is seen through the lens of personal expression. There is too much at stake in understanding institutional conditions to leave research to those tender mercies. Feinberg (1983), a theorist of cultural reproduction, reminds us in his critique of empiricism that there are institutional values to which we are subjected, which may suffuse our professional and research practices. He argues that educational institutions serve 'intergenerational continuity', and as such embody – represent – those forms of consciousness, including values, which endure across contexts of time and, being part of the social order, are independent of the individuals within. Values cannot simply 'be turned on and off at will' because they are part of, as it were, the biography of the very institution.

> . . . the values that are at work in an institutional setting do not belong simply to the subjective preferences of the researcher or to the researcher's subjects.

> Rather they are embedded in the very practices that constitute the institution that the researcher is investigating. As long as researchers continue to take these values for granted, they function, not as neutral external observers, but as important aspects of the institution itself . . . (1983: 45)

With hindsight – I understand this piece very differently now from at the time – this is part of what is being expressed in this observation. To say that we have the beginnings, here, of an organizational analysis is to suggest that what seeps out of the account are the institutional values, the vision and the tradition into which May has bought. We can even measure the dissonance between her personal values and those of the institution she ends up defending by sensing the strength of the contradictions she lives with. In one conversation she asked with truly impassioned indignation why the Conservatoire system relied on such consistently high levels of failure. Shortly after that, she secured that coveted place in the chorus of a leading national opera company.

I am, within limits, with Feinberg. I am prepared to live with a degree of reification to argue that institutions have biographies, that social – perhaps especially educational – institutions are 'frozen institutions' (House, 1974) – frozen, that is, by the chill ambient effect of the existing social order. They freeze for long enough, at least, to sustain certain values from one generation to the next. In this sense, every evaluation – insofar as it takes the persistence of institutional values into account – is a reappraisal of our own culture. It must be so because every project and program is a child of our institutions, which themselves stand as the architectural expressions of cultural values – they are, empirically, microcosms of (current and historical) society with their power systems, their sociologies, their rituals and their inequalities. All programs, even supposedly radical ones, are borne in our own image – they are, as I argued earlier, an extension and affirmation rather than a denial of personal histories. Innovations at least as often as not express more our inability to break free of our cultural bonding – our 'intergenerational continuities' – than they do our ability to realize our dreams. Structure matters.

In the end, we cannot reify the concept of institution. All institutions operate through the agency of their actors and we are responsible for them. We could, of course, control our institutions – why, otherwise, do we aspire to educate rather than merely socialize our youth? So here, once again, surfaces the rationale of personalizing evaluation, for rendering it an interactive and collaborative search for meaning and control.

To understand the Conservatoire we need to do more than what I did in my case study – to write a portrayal of the institution as it functions

today, rooted in the values of its actors, exhibiting a range of characteristics and functions, observable, apprehendable, variegated. This is
most but not enough of what it takes to explain what this complex
institution is and stands for. For to understand the Conservatoire we
need to know something (more than I know even now) of the historical
sociology and politics of the opera and the orchestra in whose image it is
cast; the tension last century between the different operatic forms; the
impact of the Wagnerian voice on the constitution of the orchestra; the
political economy of the orchestra which diminishes the individual
player and so disproportionately elevates the conductor and soloist; the
power structures of sponsorship which for so long repressed Early
Music, favoured opera and emphasized the fragmentation between
composing and performing music; and, of course, between the various
disciplines of music. We need, in program evaluation, to document
historical context more, perhaps, than we do – for people live inside
these histories. Their experiences are not so much explained by history as
they are part of historical context.

I do not want to argue that all evaluators are anthropologists 'at home',
much less that culture is something that can be directly observed. I am
not arguing that we could ever do adequate justice to the claim that we
are enquiring into our own culture. Nor am I even arguing that culture is
a reasonable end-point of enquiry – or that we should forsake our contracts and become mere ethnographers of program culture. Rather, I am
arguing that the programs and institutions we evaluate do not exist apart
from the cultures we inhabit and with which we struggle; nor do their
participants experience them in ahistorical or non-cultural ways. The
chorus at the Royal Opera House is inextricably linked to the ideological
struggles over the operatic form; the singing students had their own
seating bench in the foyer of the Guildhall Conservatoire, unique among
the music students there; the trombonist with the CBSO came from the
British working class brass band culture. If institutions have histories
and values these are felt (and carried) by individuals – May, in every
immediate sense, lives the history of the Conservatoire. More than that,
she (as others) has to resolve for herself the contradictions created by the
clash of history and contemporary change. Institutional tensions
typically have a trickle-down effect – they are those at the bottom of
the pyramid who feel the weight of the superstructure.

By now you will probably be aware that in these few pages I have
travelled a long way on rather a small data vehicle – though that is
precisely the point of this rare animal, the essential observation. You are
the judge of whether it works or not – whether my extended analysis
appears to balance precariously or securely on this little pinnacle. I

remain sure that this 'vignette', as Stake (1995) would call it, serves the function of an exemplary observation, crystallizes something of the essence of the institution and of how the institution represents culture. In the preparatory interviews I made plain to May what my task was – to represent the scale of effort required to fulfil the basic objectives of the Conservatoire – and so I believe I achieved some of that particular aspect of validity which is dependent upon shared perspectives between researcher and researched. Even so, we need to take Stake's (1995: 130) caution seriously:

> Persuasive vignettes are often emotionally tinged and unrepresentative, logically troublesome, so that Charles Brauner (1974) author of 'The First Probe' worried lest we commit 'narrative fraud'. Any overfocus on a rare and vivid moment mostly because it happened to coincide with the researcher's predilections needs to be challenged.

The difference between my 'predilections' and an evaluator's insight is so moot that it calls for the spectacular displays of those philosophical birds that inhabit the exotic territory of the 'thin line' – the deconstructionists, the critical and post-critical theorists, the constructivists and fellow travellers.

TRANSITIONS

Musicians and students on these outreach programs had a 'crazy' view of community – crazy in the sense of crazy-paving. Outside of the routine and fairly ordered life of the Conservatoire and the opera house they lurched from hospice to prison to special school to black-ghetto youth club. They met patients, prisoners pupils and pensioners, often struggling to find people among them. Among the most *musically* challenging contexts were those of special education. One young violinist was brought to tears of frustration because she had failed to notice the insistent pattern of descending fourths (a difficult interval to recognize if you are not expecting it) being played to her by a young man with cerebral palsy in an improvisation workshop.

The paraphernalia they carried with them was a 'powerful' arsenal – expensive instruments in professional-looking cases, sound equipment, bags and boxes, bicycles, coats and scarves, watches and, of course, plans. They dominated other people's spaces. But there was one special school they visited preparing a music performance through workshops with young mentally handicapped children where Michael turned the tables. He was a child of eight or nine years who achieved some renown for his capacity to hold a rock-steady rhythm with claves. The Guildhall students would enter an empty room set aside for them and typically stand in its centre awaiting the children. When the children arrived Michael would systematically approach each visitor, shake hands with them, grin broadly and welcome them in animated fashion – easing them (intentionally or otherwise) out of the centre of the space into the edges. Once at the edge he would release the hand and move to the next person, until all were at the edge with children in the middle having, as it were, recaptured their territory. This happened almost without fail and was much noticed.

I would not underestimate this, though I made little of it at the time. It speaks of institutional transitions, struggles over meaning at the boundaries. What is interesting about them is that they reveal something of the boundary-crossers and of similarities and differences of life on each side of the boundary. Caught alone leaving an airport in a strange country we review who we are and the resources we have for enduring the challenge to follow. If we could, some of us would occasionally turn back and re-board the plane. If we press on the strangeness that we do encounter, of course, makes us think back at what is familiar. This is prime territory for an evaluator. Transition moments are moments when aspects of normality are laid bare, when the pretence of theatre slips and we see the intentions behind the mime. They are also places where we see something of the illusion in which we entrap individuals within projects and programs. As evaluators we are accustomed to observing the program and its internal characteristics directly, but rarer are observations of how the program slips into and out of routine institutional and personal lives, that is, how it creates and crosses borders.

Here is an extract from the report of the CBSO scheme based on conversations with some of the players. Once again, we look through personal accounts at images of innovation and continuity – this time by talking to people as they cross and re-cross boundaries, and of the confusions this creates as familiar rhetorics are made clumsy by the unfamiliarity of new contexts. Here, we see how moving between distinct contexts helps to expose contradictions people live with.

School has many faces, and noticing them – interpreting school – is one of the things that preoccupies players. Ken, a brass player, was startled. 'The school is the kids' school – not the teachers' school! Everything about it is what the kids have done . . . it's all their stuff!' He remembers going to school as a child, and feeling 'I was going into the teachers' environment.' Ken, too, speaks of the isolation of the children ('they've got illusions') and shifts, as he speaks, to talk of the isolation he feels himself. 'It's the same with us,' he says, 'we walk on the platform and we play – then we walk off the platform and we go home.' Though Ken is a fully committed performer. He went only briefly to Conservatoire before taking a year off to accept an orchestral post overseas. He couldn't go back to college, and took up free-lance work. And those who stayed at college? 'Well, certain people are qualified,' he admits, 'but they really can't play. It's an ability – you can either play or you can't.' He can.

When an orchestral player walks into a school, then, who are the children seeing – how much of the person who stands before them? Ken gave a presentation to the children in the school hall along with Nell. They talked about the orchestra and life in it and tried to paint a less than glamorous picture of it – but trying, too, not to undersell its mystique. Children listened attentively until concentration was sapped and they began to fidget. Questioning was a matter of cajoling and was more subdued and perfunctory than naturally inquisitive. Indeed, the presentation itself was a subdued account, talking of the sections of the orchestra, what it was like to tour, rehearsals. Nothing, that is, of the isolation or of the more controversial issues in orchestral living. Ken and Nell had to stand 'at the front' to talk while the children sat on the floor with their teachers watching over and their voices echoing across parquet flooring and bouncing off egg-shell painted walls.

Visitors to schools walk around in a bubble of identity not of their own choosing. They are generally visiting for esoteric professional reasons in order to do something to children . . . In what sense do children encounter, in such interactions, performing artistes who are people with 'real' stories to tell, as opposed to professionals with professional stories? We heard in a previous chapter of Tim, another CBSO player. I reproduce that piece here more fully to further explore the issue of the contradictions he faced in his working life. Tim is very committed to the educational thrust of the Scheme . . . The 'whole idea of the scheme', he explains, 'is to try and highlight the similarities'. In the classroom making music is the same essential activity that the orchestra is engaged in – 'people trying to make music together on different instruments'. He points to the orchestra manager sitting in the rehearsal attended by the children ostentatiously taking the orchestra register – 'it's just the same as them – we try to relate it to their normal lives.'

But there is another side to the coin, Tim says, and that, too, must be explained. It is that not just anybody can do the work of an orchestral player. It's the difference between the person who plays cricket at weekends and the professional cricket player. 'What we can do which they can't actually do on their instruments – just to show a difference in standard.' He has been playing violin since he was six. 'When you compare yourself with them, you do have an innate musicality which has been, perhaps, trampled on all over by your contemporaries at work – but when you're in a classroom full of children – you know a lot more about music than they do, so it's very uplifting for the player.'

Tim struggles to make sense, not just of the new context of school and what it demands of him, but also, as we saw earlier, of the contradiction he so clearly lives with – his ambivalent relationship to his music and to his colleagues. Now, however, we see more closely how that contradiction plays against the changing contexts in which he finds himself. Berger (1963: 75) talks of this effect as 'alternation'. Trapped inside a dominant, enduring world of meaning – our continuing professional life, for example – 'we stumble like drunkards over the sprawling canvas of our self-conception . . . we might accept the existentialist notion that we create ourselves if we add the observation that most of this creation occurs haphazardly and at best in self awareness'. However, if we move into a world of unfamiliar meanings our reinterpretation of our pasts can become part of 'a deliberate, fully conscious and intellectually integrated activity'.

Now Tim's words sound more like evidence of an educational process – a 'working-things-out' rather than merely confusion. The presence of evaluation emphasizes the possibility of a dynamic, allows us to witness the possibility of change. Berger reminds us that the individual is a more fluid entity than is often represented in evaluation reports. The self, says Berger (p. 124) in similar terms to those commonly voiced today by postmodernist writers, is 'a process, continuously created and re-created in each social situation that one enters,' but he adds, 'held together by the slender thread of memory', the thread we see running through the accounts above.

I do not want to join the advocacy for 'fragmented selves' or for abandoning notions of authenticity and coherence in subjective experience. I, too, want to hold on to that 'thread of memory' which links competing versions of self. If we are to proceed with aspirations to social justice, coherence is essential. There has to be some inter-contextual stability in, for example, concepts of fairness and self-learning. We need a notion of the judgemental actor who can sustain a sense of value and judgement across diverse contexts and during the chameleon-changes we make as we move across boundaries. Indeed, it is what happens as we move from one context to another that ought to preoccupy evaluators more than the fact of our occasionally settling on different states, different versions of the self. After all, evaluators are theorists of change and here is a complex version of it.

What we see in Tim is not a fragmented self – contradiction does not imply loss of consistency. Here is a self which struggles to find consistency, but whose struggle itself constitutes a sense of coherence. No matter that his confusions are, at this moment, unresolved, he can use his different notional contexts of the (elite) concert hall and the (democratic) school to help explain each other.[5] Movement *between* contexts prompts inconsistent thoughts which are addressed in a coherent way – that is, through a combination of reflection and experience. What gives a sense of authenticity is the commitment to the struggle to find meaning. It seems to *matter* – both to Tim and, we may imagine, to the educational mission. There are important consequences in life – for him, his colleagues and the pupils he works with – of his elite/democratic confusion being addressed, if not resolved.

So life at the boundary, moments of transition as we pass from one context to another, tend to be moments when individuals are in self-reflective mode, rehearsing analyses of who they are and where they come from – and, too, people are sharp-eyed observers of the new worlds they move about in. Treated with appropriate speed and dexterity an evaluator can complement observations of the context of the school or the hospice or the prison with observations of these newly conscious, 'alternating' boundary-crossers.

There is another sense in which transitions make for rich evaluation territory and this has to do with the possibility of exploring central ideas. Again, thinking back to the Guildhall project, a concept at the centre of the project was that of 'community', a notoriously difficult one to come to terms with. I had already noted that both project and its collaborating institutions were meeting in that same no-man's-land where all were under sanction to renew their links with community in search of a new

---

5   This is a view drawn from philosophical *coherentism* which is (Everitt and Fisher, 1995, for example) contrasted with *foundationalism*. The question is how we justify our beliefs and, crudely, the foundational position would have it that we do so by reference to some basic, authoritative source of belief and wihout a process of inference – there is a hierarchy of belief in which some justify others but not vice-versa. The coherentist position, on the other hand, is that beliefs can be justified by inference one against the other. There are no hierarchies and no authoritative beliefs – our relative beliefs justify each other so long as they form an acceptable, coherent set with which we are comfortable. The fact that we are one person with our families and another with our friends does not represent incoherence in our subjectivity (fragmentation of the self) but rather, each helps us to understand the other. The difference between our*selves* in each context is self-affirming.

legitimation. The project visited a school in South London where the students worked with children – again, in search of the link between music and community. Interested in transitions I arrived at the school before the students came, and stayed once they had left. I wanted to see how adjustments were made, whether 'make-up' was applied and removed for the public encounter.

In order to explore this issue I will take you through a mini-case study that featured in an evaluation account. This will be a lengthy encounter with this project, but it will illuminate well the experience of observing projects at their many boundaries. This mini-case study provides another instance of the embeddedness of a program in the common social and educational world, and reminds us of the difficulty of calibrating the end of foreground and the beginning of background, that is, of the seamless connection between action and context. Here, the concept which integrates all perspectives is 'community'.

On this occasion the students had had a difficult morning, unable to animate or control the children. They had already discovered that they had to work to find a common language – just to make contact with the children across the boundaries of class, age, institution, interest, culture. For example, in one workshop:

They needed ideas and to generate them they lapsed into the Project convention of asking the children for ideas.

'What sort of music is right for a Queen?'
'Yes, what does it sound like? Loud, soft?'
'Fast, slow?'

The children go quiet and one or two put their heads down. The students press them.

'Think of a Queen – all grand –'
'– would the music be loud, do you think?'
'Or soft?'

Still no response.

'Fast – or slow?'

'Fast and slow,' says Graham, staring at the cymbal in front of him. Finn sits next to him and is caught in a moment of indecision – the logic of the situation telling him that Graham had probably just said the first thing to come into his head and, probably, something meaningless. But he checks himself, visibly.

'Fast *and* slow you say? How? Show me.'

Graham abstractedly taps the cymbal with the brush in his left hand to a slow, regular beat; then adds the right hand at double tempo. Success makes him more purposeful.

'You see?' he says, as though demonstrating a strategy he'd been working on all morning.

'Perhaps we should have some loud chords from the guitar representing the bodyguards,' suggests Finn, 'like a massive G7.' Smiling at Bob, who sits there in his gym shorts with his guitar on his knee. 'Wham!'

'Wham!' echoes Graham, in instant recognition of the pop group. Finn looks round at him.

'Wham – they're breaking up soon.'

This is typical of pedagogical exchanges within an arts innovation, probing possibilities of language, looking for avenues for expression which make sense to both parties – these are negotiations across a boundary. One of the students, Finn, a 'cellist, had spent a lot of time observing the children, playing games of their choosing – even playing Beethoven to them to test out the supposed calming effect of music (the children ignored it). By the early afternoon the students had left the school to return to the Conservatoire and the children were being eased back into their classroom routine. Read on.

On the rooftop, the school has settled back into its after-lunch routine. Sara is preparing to take the class that was working with MPCS this morning to visit the Railway Arch – but first she has to re-establish the order that was beginning to disappear as the children became increasingly excited during their contact with the students – and 'they're all hot – hot and bothered'. She hesitates. 'I'm going to go in and read them the riot act – I'd rather do it privately – I'm less inhibited that way,' she admits with a smile. Minutes later, the children are sitting as quietly as they have done all day, completing a handwriting exercise. They are learning cursive writing, copying from the blackboard. Fifteen minutes of that and they are back in their classroom attitude. Some wander from table-to-table chatting quietly, comparing notes, checking the eel in the fish tank.

Sara gets them to line up at the door ready to walk down to 'the Arch'. For a few moments there is more excitement and disorder – more disciplinary standing behind desks, lining up without saying anything – and then they are off. Not in any special order, but relatively decorously, trooping down the staircase animatedly, alternately laughing and snapping at each other . . . There is an alley running between arches and derelict buildings across from them. Underfoot, the ground is a mixture of caked earth and oil . . . The children walk past men, bared to the waist on this hot day . . . All of the men, whose eyes follow the children as they pass, are covered in oil. At the very end – about 25 yards from the place where the alley gives onto the High Street – one of the arches has a massive, pillar-box red sliding door. As the children approach it they are locked in a competition.

'I tax that one!' Pointing at a car. 'Tax that one – and that one – and that!' – 'You can't – it's already done!' – 'Terry taxed that one!'

Sara unlocks the door and slides it back. The children are bunched around in anticipation – now they are quiet. She heaves on the door, which is heavy, and it gives all the way. Inside, as the children pour in, is a miniature railway museum. Around the wall are photographs of trains, maps of railway systems. There are displays of guards uniforms and lanterns, leather bags, books, a tape-recorder ready to speak railway stories . . . The children sit at the tables in the centre of the area. Jan sits with them, Sara addresses them standing. One of the class walked here with a pedometer and measured the distance. None can guess what it was until one receives a tip and announces 365 metres. '365 metres,' confesses Sara. 'What other thing can we count that comes to 365?' Eventually one of the children suggests 'a year' and Sara prepares to tell them what they can do here.

[. . .]

The sun is still strong . . . Jan sits in the entrance on one of the miniature schoolroom chairs as a member of a semi-circle the rest of which is made up with children. They are playing musical instruments – the same used that morning with the Guildhall students. Xylophones, 'bokkers', triangle, kabassa. The music is soft but sure. Two girls play arpeggios on xylophones, while the others tap and scrape. In one corner of the arch a group of four sit listening to a tape. One boy listlessly rests in the crook of Sara's arm saying he doesn't know what to do. The semi-circle sits quietly, concentrating on the music. Under their chairs, the ground is thick with bird-droppings.

Lisa, playing a xylophone, misses the rhythm and drops out for a few moments. Jan listens and carries on tapping her own percussion instrument. 'Actually, that's quite effective when you stop playing, isn't it?' They play on. Improvising. They've been playing, now, for about twenty minutes. '. . . alright . . .' ting – ting – ting – tap – tap – ting, 'we'll drop out next when you come back in.' She gently orchestrates.

The children continue, casually disciplined – engaged but nonchalant. A policeman walks past. He is heavily built, dressed in shirt-sleeves. He flickers a half-look towards the ensemble, but otherwise walks on with his gaze directed ahead. The music plays on. A black man walks past and smiles as he goes, nodding his head.

Then the alley is empty again, but in the distance cars continue to be broken, mended, disassembled, painted. Figures emerge from arches and half disappear again, bent over deep into motor engines. A Mini drives past having turned in from the High Street. As it passes, the driver twists round smiles and starts tapping the steering wheel as his other hand waves rhythmically out of the window. He careers up the alley.

The music stops for a few moments as there is some negotiation between the children who want to play each other's instruments. There is some 'argy-bargy'. Another black man walks up. He is dressed in rough though clean working clothes. He has a beaming smile and has an ambiguous appearance. He points to one of the girls. 'I'll tell Mrs Williams I've seen you,' as though accusingly, but with a laugh. The group are momentarily confused but assume that he knows someone among them. He carries on with his well-meaning joke, caught in a hiatus of misunderstanding, poised to move on, which he eventually does with a jaunty bounce and backward smiles. The music restarts. The faces on the children have barely changed. They look – 'cool'.

'tap – tap – ting – ting – ting – tap -' The next to pass are three black adolescents on BMX bikes.

'Yeh, man!' one of the black kids shouts out. They look back with the urban frown of city youths. 'I know him – and him!' – 'Terence,' concedes one to acknowledge that at least one of the children is known.

The music plays on. Next comes a woman – in her mid-thirties, perhaps, well-dressed and leading a toddler. As they pass, the toddler is attracted to the music and drags on his mother's hand. She pauses and the child stands with his hand pressed to his mouth listening. After a few moments Jan notices and without pausing in her playing asks if the toddler wants to join in. He shies away from an instrument that is handed out and the woman takes the opportunity to begin to pull him away.

'I've got to take him back for a drink, actually,' she says, but the child resists and they stand there for a while longer. The children playing the music, suddenly look older. They barely show that they notice the little child watching them. But as the woman pulls him away finally, Simone reaches out at the last minute and strokes the child's arm, looks deeply into the child's face. 'Look miss,' says Lisa, pointing across the way at two men who have just emerged from somewhere opposite, one with a camera. 'He's the one who took the picture of us last week, Miss.'

'You get all the street life – it's great round here,' says Jan.

It is time to go. Everyone mills around waiting for Sara to close the door – an operation she is trying to do with Darren and with some difficulty. A fly lands on one of the party as the children are looking around for something to do in the dying moments of this out-of-school afternoon.

'Look at the colour – red!' – 'It's one of those blood-sucking things – that's why it's red.' – 'Eergghh – ' – 'I don't think so – is it?'

The fly is knocked off and lands on the floor. One of the girls has the pedometer that measured the distance here. She aims it at the fly and starts wheeling it.

'No – no – don't kill it!'

Karl stands next to her with a look of anticipation on his face.

'Why not?!' – 'Yeh – go on,' encourages Karl, surrounded by others. The pedometer hovers. – 'You got to kill them: I don't like them.' – 'No, don't do it – leave it be.'

The girl reaches out her foot and half-steps on the insect, drawing her foot back as she does. The insect emerges, half-crumpled up, moving and obviously broken. Karl steps forward quickly and grinds it into the pavement.

'Well, I had to kill it – it was hurt, wasn't it?'

This account was appended to the final report of the evaluation. The intention was to juxtapose the naturalistic way in which music and community met ('underneath the arches') with the necessarily artificial, planned way in which students arrived at a school for an encounter with community. Again, the data serves many functions but it shows the multiple contexts in which educational events are embedded – pupil culture, local community, school, ethnicity etc. There are many boundaries being created here, though the Conservatoire program (the students) worked across just two – that with the school (as they struggled with issues of control and teacher authority) and that with the pupils (as they struggled to find a common language).

We can contrast the students' struggle to find a common form of expression with the naturalness and ease with which the children express themselves in their own environment. The almost 'Camberwick Green' feel to the observation (of course, carefully constructed by me in the narrative – but actually a surprise to me on re-reading it after some years' gap) gives 'Underneath the Arches' a historical feel to it; it seems to speak of traditional relationships, embeddedness in the kind of continuity and stability that allows people to recognize each other, not to be surprised at what they see. As a contrast, we have observations of the students' interactions. Does this suggest that the success of the innovation would be to find itself merged in stable, traditional, unchanging community life?

This kind of analysis and questioning is opened up by studies of transition. Again, the evaluator travels far and wide on small amounts of data – and again, that is both the point and the problem of such vignettes and we need, still, to keep Stake's caveat in mind. But Berger is still there, reminding us that every act of social enquiry is an exploration of our own culture and of society itself. We can ignore the scale of our undertakings, imagine that we are moving only from here to the near horizon which is where we will write a report and be off – but the larger journey is always implied. Any social enquiry – whatever its scale – is always a light vehicle in that sense.

Nor should we be too easily beguiled by the argument that because this account and others like it are based on observations of personal experience – routines, at that – that they are somehow lacking in indications for policy or for decisions prefiguring educational action. Individual action, the argument implies, is not a solid base for collective resolve. However, this is to misunderstand the function of such accounts as this. The function of such pieces as this – of the vignette, either mini- or extended – is to speak in Stake's (1995) intrinsic case study tongue. There is no attempt to characterize a population of cases and nor is there any appeal to representativeness in the data. Rather, the appeal is to typicality. If we are interested in learning about such things as music in the community or about interfaces between programs and people then here is a case. Not all other cases will be like this, but perhaps this one will reduce the impact of surprise in others, may prepare something of the ground of issues and might even suggest something of the categories of information you might encounter in other cases. At the very least you will know what it means to base observations of phenomena on accounts of individual experience. At best, this case might awaken some analytic insight into the case you are interested in through recognition.

7

Ethical Space, Mortality and the Conduct of Evaluation

PREAMBLE

Evaluation does something odd to the 'stable state' which, on a day-to-day basis people carry with them. Evaluation displaces everyday ethics and insists upon a new – albeit provisional – set of ethics; provisional, that is, upon their testing for effectiveness and tolerance in the rarified atmosphere of an evaluation. Though evaluators can always be ejected from a setting one way or another, with ease or otherwise, and bearing this in mind, we frequently seek to impose a moral and ethical order on the field of our enquiry. We set the rules.

In doing so, evaluation creates an ethical space[1] – that is, a space defined by a temporary suspension of normal ethical assumptions. We will assume in this space a vacuum of intentions, a sense of anticipation, that its boundaries are given by abutting edges of varying expectations and perspectives. If all stakeholders shared a consensus view on how to relate to the evaluation there would be no such space – for there would be no suspension of assumptions. This is a space in which some people are invited to make novel judgements about the work of others, and in which the nature of those novel judgements can be regulated and scrutinized. It is in making relatively transparent the basis of judgement, that is, providing the data which people can interpret in different ways, that we add the ethical dimension. Ethical space invites regulation, the re-imposition of ethical order, and this often happens in operational

---

1 The term comes from Roger Poole's (1972) *Towards Deep Subjectivity*, in which he argues that subjectivity is a relationship, and that exploring subjectivity involves analysing the 'ethical space' which is created when people with varying intentionalities come together and which leads to a sense of anticipation of novel relationships.

terms, through agreement on principles and procedures governing the conduct of the evaluation, ruling on participant rights and the obligations of the evaluation in respect of them. What is less noticeable, perhaps, is that when we mount an evaluation and secure agreement on rules governing its conduct, role and obligations, we establish a moral order to which participants are expected to conform. For some – for many responsive, naturalistic or democratic evaluators – this is a most critical aspect of evaluation. The moral order I tend to operate in – as a practitioner of democratic evaluation – is one in which there are mutual obligations to openness, to reflection and information sharing. We might think of this – not entirely frivolously – as a redemptionist morality which rests on an assumption that we might regain a state of political 'grace' through better understanding, greater tolerance of diversity and the neutralization of pathological power structures.

The creation of that ethical space is not neutral and nor can it be impartial with respect to particular stakeholders: we can never be fair to all. This is because, as we will see, ethical principles are mutually bracketed and, therefore, potentially confusing. But there is a root unfairness, here, which is the very imposition of this ethical space and its displacement of quotidian ethics. For example, the data I will draw from in this chapter comes from a case study I wrote of the Guildhall students working in a hospice (outside London) for the terminally ill.[2] As a normal working environment, the hospice could foreclose on the many moral issues it obviously faced, or treat them according to its tolerances, decide which dilemmas to address and which to set aside – but in line with its own judgement. With an evaluation around, the hospice lost control of what to and what not to consider, for many of its options became relocated – at least exposed – in the public, ethical space. The curtain of illusion was inexorably drawn back and a regime of authenticity imposed where, beforehand, a regime of organizational artifice was sufficient to get by.

So we enter this arena of highly volatile meanings and relationships through a portal which is, itself, somewhat distorted. Our attempts at being fair are potentially frustrated at the very outset. What I will explore in this chapter is what happens thereafter – how people move about in and negotiate that ethical space.

---

2 For confidentiality the names of the hospice and associated people have been anonymized.

ETHICAL CONFUSIONS

An old lady sits on her bed explaining what the doctor has told her, that she will not get any stronger. She feels fine, she says, if a little weak – but the evaluator knows she is dying. The Mother Superior talks openly but hesitantly of her own fears of mortality. Music students assemble in the middle of a ward to recite and play music to Keats's 'Ode To A Nightingale'. All the while the priest keeps a precise tally in his notebook of the names with dates of those who come in and those who leave – noting that the average stay is about 2 weeks. This is a hospice for the terminally ill – the atmosphere light, positive, apparently relaxed. The evaluator takes notes, interviews, barely suppresses his own fears of mortality, but unsuspectingly reads Conrad's *Heart of Darkness* at night. At a workshop with those students one woman resident recites a poem to life while another recites hers, which explains dying – they argue ideology as student heads turn this way, then that. One student leaves without a thought while another stands outside in tears and yet another just gets angry. A case study is written, rejected, redrafted, rejected again, fought over and published against opposition.

The problem is not that there are no ethical guides to the conduct of evaluation – but that there are too many. More common than an evaluator searching for an elusive ethical principle that will arbitrate in the midst of a dilemma is the evaluator struggling with two competing ethical impulses – each one exclusive of the other, both reasonable. Ethical principles bracket each other reciprocally; they don't exist in hierarchical relationship. Another problem is that the social world is constructed in such a way as to lay multiple ethical traps for the evaluator. Existential dilemmas in life demand that we accommodate ourselves to our fears at least as often as we confront them. And so we draw curtains of role, institutional rituals and diversionary actions behind which we shelter. Evaluators do not share that luxury. If they cannot assume a search for more authentic states they are, at least, driven by a sense of the inauthentic – otherwise why employ us?

Suggesting that the evaluator should expose the accommodations social actors make to assuage fears and insecurities is likely to provoke ethical controversies and that is what this chapter is about. The very nature and success of these accommodations – roles, rituals, power systems, organizations – lies in the suspension of disbelief. They erode under scrutiny.[3] The warrant to go about disturbing people's sense of

---

3 'In Western philosophy', say Wax and Cassell (1981: 227), 'self-knowledge is a desideratum, but when it comes unsolicited, it is often not appreciated.'

equilibrium comes at a price, and that price is sustaining an acceptable public ethic. This becomes a complicated business in those situations where ethics offer themselves as options. Where a decision on action has to be made, any decision involves damage of some sort, but any of the available options can none the less be justified with appeal to a good ethical principle. This is not an uncommon state of affairs in evaluation. Says House (1993: 168):

> Ethical principles are abstract and it is not always obvious how they should be applied in given situations. . . . Some of the most intractable ethical problems arise from conflicts among principles and the necessity of trading off one against another. The balancing of such principles in concrete situations is the ultimate ethical act.

The Guildhall students visited a hospice over a period of weeks. The central idea of the hospice project was for the students, during collaborative workshops, to put to music poems written by two women residents – Kathryn and Diana. The hospice was experimenting with the use of interactions like this to advance their mission of helping people 'to live until they die' – the intimacy and profundity of this particular interaction was a significant learning opportunity for both Guildhall and hospice.

Diana had written a poem as a celebration of life, set in a rural idyll. Kathryn's poem was an analysis of the self-learning required to cope with terminal cancer. The tension between the two – one arguing that there was no need to dwell on tragedy, the other that improving knowledge of these things by direct reference to them was all-important – was an unexpected and dramatic curriculum for the students. Ann, a 'cellist, said:

> It was so absorbing – but I was going through some strange personal thing at the time anyway – to do with my music. Kathryn and Diana, they'd got things together so well – they were so together. Better than me, really. It was really upsetting for me. And people looked more ill in the hospice than I'd ever seen before when I visited other hospices. But that's probably me more than them – the mood I was in – the way I was looking at them.

Artistically this was enormously demanding of the students, too. Maureen had elected to play a solo taken from a Stravinsky piece during the reading of the poem about cancer:

> You normally try to understand what the composer was trying to say, and then interpret it. But here, I had to make it fit in with the cancer theme and someone dying. That was something Stravinsky didn't think about.

She, too, had been monitoring her reactions, unsettled by what she found:

> we sat on the bus quietly and went back to the Guildhall . . . I think we got a taxi . . . and someone was really upset and crying. I remember contrasting that someone had real feelings and I didn't feel anything. Well – I was – what was I? It was like feeling totally isolated.

Maureen, too, had been watching the two women closely. Unlike Ann, she responded by discovering an absorption in the artistic challenge:

> I didn't think to imagine how Kathryn really felt when she found out she'd got cancer. It's like I was being incredibly objective about it all. Maybe I was protecting myself. Kathryn was such a wonderful and vivacious lady – I was so inspired by her.

And then there was Hillary, who also felt unsettled by the hospice collaboration, and again from the artistic point of view:

> I don't feel I'm even a person until I'm secure in my musical foundations. I didn't get past that phase in the hospice.

These are difficult views to represent to a hospice and came to prove controversial to people who, just because they had elected to work there did not mean that they were exempt from feelings of insecurity and uncertainty. The ethical space created by the project interaction and its evaluation was complex and demanding – more so, in some respects, than that the hospice created for itself. And remember that there was a discrete ethical relationship between project and hospice – which became problematic. Over and above that came an evaluation with an entirely 'other' set of ethical issues – for example, dealing with publication of the experience.

This was, then, bound to be an ethical minefield for the evaluation. As Wax and Cassell (1981) remind us, ethical concerns in research literature tend to centre on the possibility of *harm* done by enquiry, but that we need also to consider the possibility of committing a *wrong* that may well do no harm, that is, we cannot assume a neat boundary between ethics and morality. We cannot plead innocence on the basis of an act that is ethically suspect but results in no noticeable damage to persons or institutions. (An ethical 'wrong' does do a kind of harm, that is, to the social capital that is our sense of collective morality – one of society's foundations slips fractionally.)

Consider, for example, the question of intimate conversation within earshot of an evaluator. The procedural principles to which I customarily work say that in the context of evaluation fieldwork nothing is 'off the record', though everything may be confidential until negotiated. Even conversations overheard accidentally are potential sources of data. Stake (1995: 59) records a student of his talking of a conversation he had overheard. Stake recounts the event and his own reaction to it:

> Upon returning from observing these activities Benny said, 'I was standing near a family listening to what they were saying when I realized that I shouldn't be hearing this; this was a family matter.' Benny surprised me. I had come to suppose that this is not ethically problematic to overhear intimate facts about people. I had thought our ethical obligation was a matter of avoiding improper use of what we learn. But Benny had a point.

I don't think he did.[4] For me, the question is one of use of the data, not its generation. But no matter; this is my personal judgement, and yours may well be different. Here is a case where the evaluator might justifiably yield the very fact of evaluation, that is, for the duration of this moment, if there is no data there is no evaluation. Which ethical/moral ditch we choose to die in is a highly personal decision for the evaluator. In the end, recourse can only be made to personal values and beliefs and the rest of the world makes its own decision about the evaluator it has been landed with.

At the time I was writing the case I was – I like to think, by chance – reading a book (*Into That Darkness* by Gita Sereny) based on a series of interviews with the ex-commandant of a Nazi death camp. The parallels (*not the comparison*) were as obvious as they were horrific as they were unfair. But whatever else, they were influential in terms of the intellectual lenses through which I generated and conceptualized my data. Should I include that openly in my account? I did not, in fact, refer to the book, knowing that it would be too threatening – and far, far too insulting to the work of hospice professionals, which I came to admire. In the event, the book did prove to be influential – I still maintain it was a valid theoretical resource – and my first case study draft was suffused with an indignant pessimism which, nonetheless, had no direct expression in the words I used. The people at the hospice felt my hostility as they read

---

4   Nothing prevents an evaluator 'being there' and overhearing just as any citizen might – after all, its confidentiality can be measured by the pains taken to make the utterances out of all, some or no earshot.

the draft but could not properly attack it because they couldn't pinpoint it. It was too deeply embedded – hidden behind the narrative – the evaluator's dark secret. This did, of course, handicap them in subsequent negotiations, as we will see.

I was there not to evaluate the hospice, I constantly sought to reassure them, but the Conservatoire project. This was (planned as) a key experience both for project and students alike and I was obliged to document it. I was committed to publishing case studies of project interactions in community institutions and it seemed obvious to write one about these events. I used this argument to persuade the hospice that I was not aiming to write a case study of *them* but of the project – though, clearly, this would have to involve a *portrayal* of the hospice. The truth of the matter was that the case study of the project was so contingent on the portrayal of the hospice that it would be difficult to tell them apart. In any event, in other contexts I am a strong advocate of the view that case study is partly a process of discovering the case boundaries – that it makes no sense to announce that this is or is not a case study of . . . whatever we theorize about the case in its end-stages of enquiry. At the personal level which constantly surges, the intrinsic complexity of any interaction in a hospice environment was compelling in itself for the opportunity to portray what were likely to be heightened states of sensibility. I always *thought* of this as an opportunity to portray a hospice, though my primary interest throughout was to illuminate the Guildhall program. One strategy for doing that was to immerse the evaluation in the specific contexts in which it worked.

I was reasonably secure in my ethical base with students and staff at the Conservatoire since there were long-standing and good relationships on which to base negotiations. I had no concerns about sharing 'risky' drafts with them. In any event, they had bought into the relationship with the evaluation by volunteering for the course. But the hospice was a different matter. Of course, I could – and would eventually – claim that the hospice was bound by the evaluation contract which they had from the beginning, but they were essentially third parties – not, in legal contractual terms, 'privy' to the evaluation agreement with the Guildhall project and having no interest in the evaluation.[5] To

5 House (1980) draws off Norman Care, 'Participation and policy', *Ethics*, 88 (1978), pp. 316–37 to enunciate 12 principles underpinning the fairness of an evaluation agreement – including such as non-coercion, rationality, joint agreement, disinterestedness and equal and full information. Two important elements are left out, however, which can be drawn from English contract law. Both are significant here. One is the principle of 'privity of contract', which is to say that you can only be bound by a contract to which you were a

maintain an evaluation position there, to be free to document enough of the hospice context to understand the complexity of the Guildhall interaction, it was essential to downplay the prominence given to the hospice. This had the inevitable effect of implying that their complaints about the case study were unwarranted obstacles to the expression of others.

The music students had their own ethical issues to deal with. They had, for example, to make decisions about their music programming – what to sing and play. This was a sensitive issue. The previous year another student had raised controversy by singing 'The Way We Were' (the song that starts *'me-mories* . . . of the love we left behind . . .') in a prison. 'We're trying to get them to *forget* their outside life,' complained an Assistant Prison Governor. 'Love we have lost – it was the only thing we might have had in common,' said the female singer. Now, at the hospice, one student decided to recite Keats's 'Ode To A Nightingale', with the first line:

Thou was not born for death immortal bird

They agonized over its inclusion, listened with trepidation as it was read on a crowded ward. It was the subject of fevered discussions among the students and served, for a moment, as a focal point for how they were reacting to the whole experience.

But this was merely a precursor to the controversy that was to ensue over the performance. The poems written by the women finally were read and played in performance to residents at the hospice, many of whom were engaged in the desperate struggle to sustain their personal fictions against their impending mortality. Not only did they have to sit in front of a didactic performance, but every effort was being made to ensure that they did not lose the pathos and the meaning of the poems. For some, there was, quite literally, no escape.

---

knowledgeable and acknowledged party. An agreement struck between two parties (e.g. the Guildhall project and the evaluation) has no meaning in law for another party (e.g. the hospice) – unless that contract is recreated with them – which, by definition, it could not be. The other principle is known as 'consideration' and signifies that for a contractual agreement to be reasonable and valid all parties to it have to be able to draw significant benefit from it, that is, the contract has to offer due consideration to each party. In this case, it was clear that both evaluation and project stood to gain from the enquiry, but the hospice (were they to be thought of as party to the agreement to mount the case study) was far less clearly a beneficiary. (See Cheshire and Fifoot (1964) for the legal principles involved.)

The relationship between students and hospice switched from one of mutual tolerance and exchange tinged with the excitement everyone felt at charting new territory, to one of tension, regret and an urgency (felt by the hospice, not the students) to forget. How should the evaluation respond? At one stage in ensuing negotiations over publication of the evaluation case study the hospice implored me to stop the process. We will see shortly, and in some detail, how those negotiations proceeded. But I was constantly faced with questions of what to include and what not, seeking to balance adequate portrayal of the events with the need to guarantee the survival of the evaluation for long enough to publish. The students, in their own ethical searching, discussed important educational and social issues and they wanted these aired in my reports. The hospice was, however, becoming more and more nervous about the can of worms that had been opened up and increasingly sensitive to a probing evaluation. To complicate matters, the hostility being generated by the evaluation was spilling over onto the project as the hospice found it hard to distinguish both *de jure* and *de facto* between the two.

There were signs that the evaluation might be asked to withdraw altogether from the case study. Student views in particular (and my presentation of them) were creating confusion and dismay among people who, unlike the Guildhall project, were simply not accustomed to such ruthless public theorizing. My strategy was to argue that student views were *complex* and not merely *negative*.

We need to pause for a moment to take into account the personal aspirations of the evaluator. I was facing my personal demon (mortality), and I was anxious to emerge with a well-crafted account of life at the edge of social and mortal existence. My reading had moved on by now and I had read Conrad's *Heart of Darkness* – another powerful treatise on death which by now seemed to be asserting itself as a momentary theme of my life. My personal philosophy – I believe strongly in serendipity – persuades me to be responsive to such accidental themes and to allow them to play out. As the agent of much of the unfolding unrest, I was myself prey to forces of self-persuasion that could easily de-stabilize the ethical position of the evaluation.

We can already see here the many levels and types of ethical imperative, each jostling to bracket the others. Most end positions could be justified by appealing to some ethical principle or another.[6]

---

6 Michael Quinn Patton (1997: 363–5) gives a frank account of a debate he had with Ernest House on the matter of ethics. House condemned as 'immoral' the utilization-focused approach for placing evaluation at the bidding of the privileged few who could commission it; Patton replied with an appeal to an alternative ethic – that of service.

Almost 10 years later I was to find myself at a Qualitative Studies in Music Education conference at the University of Illinois, listening to a presentation by a good friend, Liora Bresler. She was recounting, among other things, how her developing experience in case study research brought her to a resolution and a growing understanding of ethical issues. I said to her afterwards, thinking of the events I am describing, that my own experience has been of a journey into ethical disarray – a disarray caused, I now think, by the fact that my developed skills and my dexterity in negotiation allowed me to juggle with competing ethics – employing artistry in the complexity of what House earlier called 'the ultimate ethical act'. There is a certain confusion that arises from a heightened awareness of ethical dilemmas coinciding with a heightened capacity to deal with them. At no time, during the events that will unfold, was I acting unethically, in the sense that there was always a reasonable ethic to which I could appeal to justify my actions. But that by no means implies foreclosure or resolution of ethical issues.

One of the difficulties, here, relates back to the principal theme of this book – the search for the theory of coherence in the lives of our respondents. The problem in relation to the ethics of evaluative enquiry is that as evaluators we travel with a more rehearsed sense of what constitutes ethical coherence. I know why I am in the field at any one time – I have a theory of being there and part of that theory is an increasingly well articulated sense of ethical mission. My evaluation is largely motivated by some sort of concern with social justice. People I talk to, however, whether because their jobs neither demand nor admit of an ethical mission, do not have such a rehearsed sense of what constitutes ethical coherence. More than that, however, as we shall shortly see, my job has demanded of me the development of refined skills in ethical *process* – and that is an advantage. In the context of enquiry ethics, the evaluator's game is often the only one in town.

What will shortly follow is a series of letters and memos which passed between myself as evaluator, the Director of the evaluation, my colleague Barry MacDonald, and the hospice. I advise careful reading of these letters because they contain far more than appears at first sight. I will add narrative comments from time to time to explain the moves that are being made. I should point out, in a way that is not intended to mitigate the critique of my own actions, that I have no question that my eventual publication of the case study of this hospice interaction was justified. I tried to act reasonably – even though I may not have been as competent as the hospice would have wished – but there is an almost unavoidable unreasonableness that is forced by situations like this.

NEGOTIATING POWER

Before proceeding with this I need to resurrect a short article that has been largely overlooked in the consideration of ethical procedures in evaluation. This will help put a frame around much of what I am about to reveal. David Jenkins (1986) published an insider's critique of demo-cratic procedures in evaluation – 'insider', because he was one of those involved in the early development of Democratic Evaluation working with Barry MacDonald. Jenkins's basic claim was that evaluators exploit their position as rule-maker and experienced negotiator to manipulate the negotiation process to their own ends, and those ends are always to promote publication (that is, pursuing the democratic ethic of making knowledge public). They achieve this in the following way. First, they separate out two distinct negotiation processes – one for access to data; the other for release of data. Each appeals to a different ethic. Ethics concerning access to data promise to deal with the rights of the subject (the 'right to confidentiality', that is, the ground position is privacy); those to do with the release of data appeal to the rights of the public ('the right to know', that is, the ground position is exposure). These are obviously in tension, form a central paradox of evaluation case study and account for much of evaluation resources in seeking to balance the two.

The first set of negotiations – for access – creates expectations of high degrees of control over data on behalf of the subject. Here, the evaluator is concerned to display her credentials as a trustworthy person whose conduct is regulated by the 'ethics of human relations'. The evaluator typically concedes much and promises more. For example, here is one of my first letters to the hospice, who have already agreed to let me observe and write about the music interactions there. To the extent that I had explained the procedures and purposes and discussed the likely consequences of having evaluators around and here send to the hospice the formal evaluation 'contract', there was what might be deemed to be 'informed consent'.[7]

---

7 It counted for little, though for some, in spite of such difficulties, informed consent is a *sine qua non* for evaluation studies (e.g. see Howe and Dougherty, 1993).

University of East Anglia
Centre for Applied Research in Education
School of Education
University of East Anglia
Norwich NR4 7TJ

Dr Leslie Goode
Firgrove Hospice

Dear Dr Goode,

You may remember my coming to Firgrove with Peter Renshaw's course – I am the evaluator. We spoke briefly at the end of the MPCS Project's last visit and I promised to send you anything else I wrote regarding the hospice. I have written a draft report which features Firgrove prominently at the end and I am enclosing a draft for you to read and comment on. I am also sending you a copy of the principles and procedures to which I work in generating and publishing my data. You'll find them a little legalistic – but the thrust of them is to say that, since my concern is to report things as other people see them, my reports are open to correction, improvement, deletion. In fact, it always proves helpful to me when people do offer critical comments – often my understanding has been improved.

You will see, in this case, that the account and the analysis which permeates it are still in a crude stage. This will go through at least one more draft before it is ready for any kind of publication. I am trying to portray some of the complexity behind the kind of institutional interventions made, not just by MPCS, but by many Arts groups these days. There are a number of threads to the draft as it stands – perhaps the crucial one lies in the notion that the MPCS/Firgrove one, as different institutions engaged in similarly-minded innovations meet and help solidify each other's resolve. I don't want that to sound abstract, it is a real welfare issue given the current political climate of government centrism allied to a forced devolution of welfare responsibilities to voluntary organizations and the family. It is, of course, also central to Peter's claims that projects like MPCS have a role to play in the 'regeneration of society', as he puts it.

Well, please let me know if you have any comments. Let me know, more importantly, if I have written anything in the draft which is in any way injudicious in the light of the work and discussions at Firgrove and, of course, your own position. I am not in the game of exposure or 'investigative research'. I just want to get it right.

[. . .]

With best wishes,
Yours sincerely,

Saville

Here I am preparing the ground for launching a full case study – I need access in the form of agreement to negotiate drafts. Says Jenkins (1986: 224) of this stage:

> The researcher makes it harder for the subject to find adequate models of refusal at the first gate. Why fight in this ditch when the next one is so impregnable?

Indeed, I am invoking, in this letter, a moral imperative underpinning the evaluation such that it might be thought an immoral act not to go along – the appeal to complexity, solidarity with innovators facing great adversity, implicit dismay at putative attacks on the welfare state. As Jenkins implies, the Principles and Procedures (I note, in passing, that I did not emphasize them in the letter with capitals as I do here) do, in fact, offer high degrees of control over release of data for publication and so promise that second 'ditch' to fight in.

Some months later I had made the decision to afford full case study status to the hospice interaction. The evaluation proposal had promised case studies of interactions between project and community, and this would be one.[8] I sent the draft and in the accompanying

---

8   What goes into the selection of cases? Stake (1995: 4) considers factors such as their representativeness of issues with which we are concerned; their promise of yield (i.e. the researcher's favoured crop of understanding); that they are 'easy to get to'; and that they are 'hospitable to our enquiry'. Although it is often maintained that case study is not a sampling approach, none the less, certain loose sampling criteria such as these are often invoked. Indeed, they formed part of my decision. But selecting case studies *within* a project you are observing offers a broader range of possibility because you probably know something of the context before you make the selection. Your sampling frame, therefore, is full of personal judgement data, some of which can influence your ethical stance. Certain contexts appeal for their excitement, personal comfort or interest, challenge or convenience. (The older I get the more I am influenced in the selection of cases by their geographical proximity to far-flung family.) In this case I was attracted by the human drama of the hospice – by the possibility that interactions at the edge of social experience might create powerful effects on individuals and generate enhanced data.

letter further added to the pressure to go along with the negotiations. I said:

> Firgrove Hospice is, for me, an obvious choice for a case study since there has been such a high level of contact and such a strong commitment to exploring the issues and dilemmas raised. It may well be that we can help to improve our understanding of the interaction between community institutions like a Hospice and a Conservatoire.

We are still in the embrace of Jenkins's 'human relations' ethic and I am still appealing to reasonableness and agreement as a basis to proceed. I have had discussions with Dr Goode and he has told me that he is fascinated with but sceptical of the case study approach. He seems to be a good collaborator. But events are working against me. The music performance has created waves at the hospice and minds are beginning to change as the whole interaction is generating anxiety. The hospice is nervous, already vulnerable to professional and public judgement as were all hospices at this time before the movement took a firm hold. My first draft was suffused, as I explained earlier, with negative reactions I had myself experienced and which no doubt influenced my selection of data. I insinuated a critique of authority, of the lugubriousness of the hospice mission, even of the predatory nature with which society treats its weak and dying. This was unfair and was partially a product of my having to work through my own difficulties in controlling my emotional reactions in such close proximity to mortality.

The hospice response was to reject the case study – but not me. I was still in the game. I was invited back to Firgrove to get a better look, to see the positive aspects I had missed on other visits. I went, tried hard to develop a positive view and wrote a substantially different draft. I sent the second draft of the case study to the hospice, and continued to provoke hostility – quite possibly as a spill-over of frustration at not being able properly to attack the first draft. But by now I was more than a casual observer since I had focused my observations and interviews, and my growing sophistication shows through in my second draft which looked more closely at policy and publications of hospice personnel. Says Jenkins:

> The way is now open for the cultivation of rapport . . . The researcher cannot only argue that he can be entrusted with secrets because release of data is off the current agenda. He can also implicitly present himself as the knowledgeable quasi-insider, increasingly unlikely to be fobbed off with just any old account. The wagon gathers pace . . .

I wrote the following letter to the head of nursing:

University of East Anglia
Centre for Applied Research in Education
School of Education
University of East Anglia
Norwich NR4 7TJ

Dear Sister Maureen,

We spoke on the telephone the other day, when you told me that you and Dr Graham still had reservations about the case study. I should have mentioned to you, then, that I will be away for a week or so, returning on December 1st. I will contact you then.

I am not surprised there are still reservations. I think I said to you in an earlier letter that these things can take more than one or two attempts. Both you and Dr Goode have said to me on different occasions that I am dealing with very difficult human matters in writing this study. I never disbelieved you – but it is made more and more obvious to me as I go on. I hope this second attempt, in spite of its failings, shows at least some response to what I learned from the first set of comments I collected. One of the skills I do have is one of learning fast, and if you continue to feed me comments on what I write I hope to learn enough to write a study you can support. I confess, this is taking some time, but that is due, as you have reminded me, to the fact that the hospice needs a very special kind of understanding.

There are many things written about the health and caring services, most of them, I think, from the point of view of people from the outside. I could write a study like that, but it would suffer the same problem most of those other studies have. It would fail to express what it is like from the inside, if I may use that expression. The result would be more misunderstandings of what, in this case the hospice and the music college, are about. In the end, the humanity can only come from the people directly involved, and, ideally, I am just a vehicle for that humanity. That is why your comments and your support are so crucial. Without them, this study and the way it might be used would be much more of a flimsy exercise than it ought to be.
[. . .]

Yours sincerely,

Saville

By now I am in the serious business of protecting my report and responding to the ethics of disclosure. I felt by this stage that I had managed to displace my personal reaction to the hospice experience so as to present a reasonable, humanistic account which dealt with the difficulties and psychological complexities of caring as much as of suffering. Some of this shows through, I think, in this letter, where I feel confident enough to engage the hospice professionals in discussion on their own ground. I feel, at best, that my case study might have a contribution to make to the hospice movement and so am becoming an advocate of my own work. The implicit message of this letter is that the hospice would be doing a disservice to itself and its partners by restricting my publishing aspirations.

Besides, I had put too much resource into the case to dispense with it now. So I play a little politics and seek to coopt a powerful figure from the hospice itself – the priest. I had interviewed him and used some of the data in the second draft, a copy of which I sent him. The hospice capitalized on the opportunity and asked him to respond to me which he did with a list of critical comments – these went along with even more critical comments from a relative of a hospice resident who had been shown the draft (by the hospice). I had not known of this but I was pleased to hear it. My own Principles and Procedures did not allow me to share drafts with third parties, but it was obviously desirable to recover as wide a range of critical comments as possible.

One telling comment suggested that 'an eventual reader could feel like asking himself what was the difference in experience for the students between a visit to Firgrove and to a place, like say Madame Tussaud's or some other non-usual location'. My evaluation career to this time had taught me that such responses were almost always both useful and positive – evidence that people were prepared to enter negotiations; warnings as to failings in my reports; certainly moral levers to be used to justify publication. I would respond to all the comments in a further draft and henceforth argue that I had consistently met any objections offered to me and thereby earned the right to publish.

To be sure of my ground I make another political move. In this next letter I implicitly invoke my relationships with the students, who are less easy to dismiss than is an evaluator.

University of East Anglia
Centre for Applied Research in Education
School of Education
University of East Anglia
Norwich NR4 7TJ

Dear Dr Goode,

I just wanted to drop you a line to say where I think I am with the case study. Please excuse me for taking up more of your time.

As I understand it, Sister Maureen and Dr Graham still have reservations about the piece. I have written to Sister Nell to say that the 'rules of the game' still require me to be responsive – that it is crucial for me to receive and understand those comments, and to use them to improve the account . . . The more clearly I see what you try to tell me and what I am shown, the better I can represent you – rather than my own shortcomings, as you quite rightly alleged on another occasion.

I spoke to Peter [Renshaw] and he told me of a conversation he had had with you. He was concerned, I think, that the comments of the students I had used were suggestive of a wholly negative experience. I confess, I was surprised. The one question I purposely refrained from asking was, 'what did you get from the hospice collaboration?' – it would have invited a courteous and bland confirmation of what they would think I wanted to hear. Instead I asked them, effectively, what the experience meant. The result, I feel, is a complex, some-times painful for the reader, uncomfortable account of an educative experience. I have rarely been so impressed by a bunch of students responding to such an intense learning situation. What I wanted to do with the conclusion was to juxtapose the sophistication of the thinking that goes on well after the event, with the raw enthusiasm that seems to be characteristic of going in to these situations.

Well all that is an exposure of how I see the very study that I am attempting to write. Please tell me that I have it wrong that I am still being insensitive and, even, too idealistic. I have my own learning to do. But such comments can only be helpful to me.

[. . .] I very much look forward to talking to you again. I hope we can find a time when it will be convenient for me to come down there. I have a virtually open diary – again, I promised that to Sister Nell. I'm even happy to meet in the evening, though that is usually sacrosanct to people other than researchers!

With best wishes,
Yours sincerely,

Saville

Jenkins lists (1986: 225) the various tactics used by evaluators to ensure that the negotiation process goes their way. These include manipulation of time-scales (offering open diaries and threatening evening meetings, for example); what he calls the 'cynical employment of a cosmetic red-herring by which the task can be represented to the subject as "improving" the account . . . deflecting attention from the **fact** of release to its **form**, and inviting bogus co-authorship'; the use of personalized accounts which in their nature discourage people from taking exception; playing one audience off against another; management of negotiations kept in the hand of the evaluator. Each of these, to some degree or another, can be seen in my letters and in my strategies – though I would not describe myself in these interactions as 'cynical', I obviously admit to what we might think of as 'ethical manipulation'.

By now, however, the hospice had had enough and decided to exercise their option to pull out. I received a letter: 'There is a lot of improvement in the piece that you wrote but still the impression which it conveys is not one which I feel would be helpful to us for you to publish, however interesting.' The letter reminded me that the music interaction had been a source of controversy in the hospice and that its continuing recapitulation through my drafts was damaging the arts program which was still in its early and fragile stages. There was no hint of capriciousness in the letter, nor of resentment nor of struggle – just a simple expression of preference, well within the margins of expectations I had allowed to build up. 'You said to me in the past that we could call a halt to this when ever we felt it appropriate and I have recommended . . . that we should now call a halt to this whole procedure.' The letter ended by offering me 'best wishes' and regretting what I had lost by way of effort to produce this case. Another letter confirming this and from another of the hospice managers was more robust, and complained about the account, using words such as 'empty', 'cynical', 'bleak' and 'worldly-wise'. This second letter attacked me just where I had carefully erected defences – the detached tone of the account; my inability to grasp the 'spirit' of the place; the immaturity of student responses.

'It is at this point', says Jenkins (1986: 225) of the evaluator faced with opposition, 'that he pulls out the second trick in his bag. The ethics of consensus are surreptitiously replaced by the ethics of power.' The full power of the evaluator can now be revealed, power which derives from being in control of the ethical procedures and of data which comes from different sources in the power system. The following is the full version of my response to the rejection. Note that I could not argue with the claim that I had promised they could pull out whenever they chose – this was said in a loose moment, an unguarded promise made by an over-enthusiastic suitor. This had to be worked around. I start by demoting their 'decision' to opt out to the status of a 'position'. Note, too, my copying the letter to 'Guildhall Students' – indeed, expanding the evaluation constituency along Democratic Evaluation lines and rejecting the notion of privileged audiences, but also deepening the moral dilemma of those who might wish to suppress the report for their own concerns.

University of East Anglia
Centre for Applied Research in Education
School of Education
University of East Anglia
Norwich NR4 7TJ

Dr Leslie Goode
Firgrove Hospice

cc. Sister Maureen, Dr Graham (Medical Director, Firgrove), Peter Renshaw, Professor Barry MacDonald (Director, CARE), Guildhall Students

Dear Dr Goode,

I am responding to your two letters regarding the case study of the Guildhall/Firgrove interaction. I note the position you lay out – that this is taking up too much of your time and that your confidence in my capacity to adequately represent the hospice continues to be shaky. I am also aware that I am asking you to collaborate at a time when you are already spending time on a continuing and demanding interaction with the Guildhall.

I am afraid you may be feeling that I am getting hard to shake off, and I am afraid also that that is true. I have assured you that I will not publish this case study until and unless you find it reasonable, but, at the same time, I will only abandon the exercise with the greatest reluctance. As I have said before, I regard the prospect of a jointly agreed case study as something of considerable importance in terms of public knowledge of the issues raised by these Guildhall activities. My responsibilities are to respect the privacy of individuals and of professional groups whilst pursuing the role I am paid to carry out, of helping the public to understand the complexity of such situations. I would be failing in my job if I fell short on either of these counts. In this letter, then, I will urge you and Dr Graham to read a third and final draft which I intend to write in the new year – but I will also outline how I will fulfil my duties in the event of our difficulties overwhelming our efforts to arrive at an agreement. I think the situation is a tricky one, because if I am not able to publish a case study I still have to account for that. But let me come to that in a moment, after I have laid out the situation as I see it to date.

First, I think it is important to remind you that I am not seeking to evaluate Firgrove. I am evaluating the Guildhall Project. We have collaborated in the production of two drafts of an account – the first, seriously flawed. After reading that first account, you suggested to me that I should learn more about the hospice and talk more with the students – both of which I did. The current draft includes both hospice data and student data. It incorporates comments received from a range of people including Peter Renshaw and the Guildhall students, Dr Graham, Sister Maureen, yourself, and the relatives of a hospice patient to whom Sister Nell showed my first account. I have been sent further detailed comments from Father Thomas. My own view is that I can now move to a third and, hopefully, final draft on the basis of Father Thomas's comments and your own comments in your recent letters.

But what happens in the event of this exercise coming to an end before we arrive at a mutually agreed account? As I have said, I still have to report to my sponsor, to my Director, to the Guildhall Project and to their sponsors, explaining the kinds of difficulties we have had and why a full evaluation of this MPCS activity has been problematic. I also, of course, have to report the students' perspectives of the work they undertook at the hospice. Let me outline what that will look like.

First, I will use that part of this case study which is made up of the student views. That has been negotiated with the students and represents an important moment in their experience of the MPCS Project. Now that raises a paradox which I am sure does not escape you. I know that some of your disquiet about the case study arises from the student perspectives – that you feel they are somehow incomplete and, to use one of your words, 'worldly-wise'. Publishing student views without a contribution from the hospice will result in an imbalanced account. In fact the only representation of the hospice will be that offered by the students. I will of course make that absolutely clear in my report and I will advise the reader that they have to read the students' comments in that light.

The second element of my report will be an account of the negotiation process we have been (and are still) going through. For that I will revert to my usual principles and procedures which I sent you earlier on and which I enclose again. I will give you every opportunity to comment upon my report and to amend it under the principles of fairness, relevance and accuracy. The aim will not be to highlight a failure on anyone's part to produce a collaborative case study. As I have said, I am not in the business of evaluating the hospice. It will be an honest attempt to portray the difficulties of conducting evaluations in such sensitive areas and with such high aspirations.

Well, there is the full position as I see it. It is not one I feel wholly comfortable with – of course. I cannot shake the feeling that had I written a more sensitive first draft, then your confidence in me would have been rather greater. I am also aware that the kind of evaluation I do can feel uncomfortable, and that you would not necessarily have volunteered to collaborate in this evaluation of the Guildhall Project. But I have been conscious of that all along and I have tried to respond by changing my normal working rules to try and make them fit this particular, sensitive situation. I have departed from my usual principles and procedures and I am virtually flying by the seat of my pants. The consequence of this is that we all have a considerable amount of discretion over matters which cover important social issues. What is at risk, and what I trust will not happen, is that we end up suppressing all trace of events which would improve public understanding in an area which – as you have so often reminded me – could do with more than a little improvement.

Let me make one final comment which is absolutely crucial. Let me remind you – and I do so for Peter Renshaw's sake – that my evaluation and the Guildhall Project are entirely independent. I am sponsored independently (by a different body) and I am accountable in a wholly different way. Of course, errors and intrusions of any evaluation spill over into the project being evaluated – that is unreasonable, but inevitable. But so far as you are able, you should not make judgements and assumptions about the Guildhall Project based in any way on your experience with me and with my evaluation. I came in with the Guildhall Project, and they may, and do, have a continuing interest in my reports – but I work independently of them. Peter Renshaw cannot control my work any more than he can always like what I write about him and his work.

Well, let me leave it there, give you my best wishes for the festive season, and promise to contact you in the new year.

Cordially yours,

Saville

There were further exchanges as the hospice sought to reconcile themselves unsuccessfully to the new shift and as I briefed my Director. As Jenkins notes (1986: 225), 'the tokens of esteem (the only coinage of the first negotiation) have a low exchange value in the second'. The hospice wrote to my Director asking him to call me off. Here is another subtle source of inequality. The very nature of the evaluation relationship almost certainly means that whereas the evaluator has a knowledge of the workings of the institution with which she is negotiating, including its politics, there is no reciprocal knowledge by the institution of the evaluator's home terrain. Here, the hospice could not know that the term

'Director' concealed a collegial relationship based on mutual support and shared values which contrasted with the hierarchical relationships typical of the medical professions and, I think, at the hospice. Barry MacDonald wrote – and I reproduce in full once again:

cc. Saville

University of East Anglia
Centre for Applied Research in Education
School of Education
University of East Anglia
Norwich NR4 7TJ

Dear Dr Goode,

I am writing in response to your letter of the 30 December, in which you ask me to intervene in the hospice-related work of Dr Kushner, the evaluator of the Guildhall innovation. The delay in responding is due to the time I have taken to reconsider the history and sequence of events and products that concern the hospice as a project site.

Let me begin by summarizing briefly our responsibilities and obligations. We were invited to assist the development of MPCS by undertaking an independent evaluation of its work over three years. Funds for the evaluation were provided by the Leverhulme Trust on the basis of a proposal outlining the aims and methods we would employ. I attach a copy of the proposal, in which you will see that a major question for the evaluation was, as it remains, how effective is MPCS in providing services to the community, and that we intended to feature case studies of the institutions and audiences at the receiving end. I think that you will agree that, with respect to the case study of MPCS in the context of Firgrove, we are simply carrying out an anticipated, pre-planned and important element in our total program of evaluation. I want to make that quite clear before going on to comment on the present impasse.

The central issue is the adequacy of the portrayal of Firgrove in relation to its interaction with the innovation. Not an easy task for anyone, even for an evaluator of Dr Kushner's long experience, which is why he has invested so much time and effort (as indeed you have) in an effort to ensure that it is both fair to those represented and illuminating with regard to important issues at the core of the project's aspirations. In my view he has done well on both counts; in yours he has failed, at least on the first. He is willing to make further alterations or additions to meet your reservations but you, apparently, wish to withdraw collaboration and eliminate from the published account any data deriving from your collaboration. Dr Kushner has pointed out to you one consequence of such a decision – an unbalanced public account of the MPCS experience in the hospice. This is anything but a threat. We are obliged to report on that experience as best we can in order to fulfil our contract.

Let me clarify, in the hope that it may prove helpful, that it is not our task nor our intention, to evaluate the hospice. Our focus is MPCS, our interest in portraying the hospice is to characterize one of its contexts. Our audiences are interested in music education, and we try to help them to visualize and think about the innovation in the range of community settings which comprise its constituency of action. In a modestly resourced enquiry like ours we cannot hope to give more than a glimpse or a feel for those settings, but we know that people find such data helpful in assessing the value and claims of the innovators. We are not in the business of doing definitive studies. We go to some lengths to disclaim such a goal and of course, as you know, we give every opportunity to those like yourself to ensure that we do the best we can within limited resources to present such settings in ways which minimize misrepresentation.

Does that help? Do you really feel that the study as it stands seriously misrepresents the views of those who carry the major responsibility for the hospice, or the life within it? As an outsider (and therefore perhaps typical of those who may read the evaluation report), I must say that I do not share your view of the second draft, despite the fact that I shared your reaction to the first. Surely there is a way forward. What would you say to a limited circulation of the case study, in order to obtain some third party judgements? Surely there can't be any harm in that – say, six people, three of your choosing and three of ours, asked in confidentiality to make comments on the fairness and adequacy of the study within the context of the innovation and its evaluation?

Yours sincerely,

Barry MacDonald
Professor of Education
Director of Centre for
Applied Research in Education

A final hidden source of power is embedded in paragraph 3 of this letter where MacDonald ends talking of our 'contractual obligation' to publish. Here, what is at stake for us was what we thought of as 'suppression' – a term as loaded in its psychological mind-set as in its semantic meaning. The rules of the game are still being staked out – more by the evaluators than by the hospice.

The last letter from the hospice accepted the inevitable and judiciously refused to call the bluff. It was unlikely that we would have published an incomplete account – that would have been too punitive and there were, in reality, no ethical brackets we could have deployed to justify such an act. The hospice took exception with some of the claims we were making – that the case study was pre-planned, for example, or that there had been a 'contract'. Damningly, it claimed that the evaluation had taken up more time and had a more profound effect than had the project that was supposed to be the focal point. The evaluation was likened to a camel putting its head into the tent to shelter from the sandstorm and eventually clambering in entirely to displace the residents. The word 'nightmare' was used. Finally, they said that they never intended to stop publication, merely to state their dissatisfaction and disagreement with the account. They asked that their refusal to accept the account be prominently advertised in any publication – of course we complied, and here it is reiterated.

I hope I had no cynical intent, here, though I am sure that I had *concealed* intent – although perhaps the two amount to the same thing in the eye of those at the receiving end. I certainly recall being motivated and strengthened by feelings and thoughts which would have been regarded as threatening to the hospice and which, as I have said, emanated from my inability to suppress my own fears of mortality. But even now it is hard to be sure what to reveal and how to reveal it. Recall what John Van Maanen admitted about his 'confessional tales' which – 'leave more of my knowledge out of the accounts than they put in'. And, too, I return to the issue of the age of this data and the concomitant fact that I have played and rehearsed these events in seminars to the point where there is what Van Maanen (quoting Ricoeur) calls a 'textualisation', in which my analysis no longer is driven by the events themselves but by the increasingly detached form of representation that is the data. Van Maanen, in the end, discounts fieldwork confessions for having created a kind of spectator sport disengaged from the direct experience of culture. Ethnography had saturated the possibilities of confession, to the point where 'fieldwork is presented as a moral trial having anguish and ambivalence as the felt result' (1988: 97) – the anguish of the researcher at least as much as of the ethnographic subjects.[9]

---

9 An example – and I offer this as an instance and not for judgement – might be Fine and Weiss (1996): 'we are still a couple of White women, a well-paid Thelma and Louise with laptops, out to see the world through poor and working-class eyes . . . we toil on, looking for friends, writing for outrage . . .'.

This, however, is not ethnography. This is evaluation. Self-critique – of which there is possibly too little in the evaluation literature – has more of a function than mere methodological quality control or of generating a second-order theory of culture by analysing the distorting lens of its analyst. Confessional tales for evaluators are not redemption songs. Evaluation is itself as much the subject of democratic enquiry as is the substantive area it is observing – if, that is, we are serious enough to take the means of achieving democratic enquiry as part of the problem of creating and maintaining a democratic state. Much of the validity of an evaluation is to do with its conduct and with the way the evaluators conceive the relationship of means to ends (methodology to product). Ericson (1990) describes as 'incomplete' any evaluation that does not purposefully deal with social justice, and, as House (1990) shows, methodology itself is often a source of injustice in society. An evaluation cannot – validly – achieve a democratic solution with non-democratic procedures.

There is an ethical sting in the end of this tale, one that I have not drawn even some years later. It concerns one of the women poets at the hospice. She was Kathryn, the one whose poems were about the real experience of cancer. She was in the final stages of her illness during the music collaboration – a woman who came to be much admired by the Guildhall students. I wanted her to see a copy of the draft case study – partly because it was her right and my obligation since she featured in it; partly because I genuinely wanted to know her opinion since she had strong educational views; and partly because I was sure she would sympathize with the idea of publishing the case. I received a message via a third party that she wanted to receive a copy of the draft. I asked at the hospice for a copy to be passed to her and I was told that this was not medically advisable. I was sceptical of that (I had no reason to doubt it) but I chose not to question it.

My reason for not challenging the decision was that doing so would have challenged medical authority. I might have been happy to do this, but not at a time when it might have jeopardized sensitive negotiations over the case study. I was prepared to challenge all sorts of authority, but not the professional authority which reigned in the area under scrutiny (question it, yes, of course – but not challenge it). That would have been a breach of evaluation impartiality and of the principle that the evaluation broadly accepts the values underpinning the professional culture under investigation. Again, there may be times when I might feel free or justified in risking this, but not when the price is losing a case study.

The chief protagonist arrived to play his part. The woman died without seeing a draft.

HOW WE INHABIT OUR EVALUATIONS

How do we begin to make sense of all this? We recall House saying that day-to-day ethical matters cannot be too closely regulated since abstract principles are not good guides to concrete action. Newman and Brown (1996) urge evaluators not to be conclusive about ethics. They argue that being ethical is not about making ethical choices in response to particular situations, but more about engaging in a process in which you seek to express something about yourself – a life-style issue, as it were. Ethics are about how we inhabit our evaluations. In an important sense they are about the balance we strike between our personal values in respect of justice and morality and the public values we have to acknowledge in our role. This is part of the construction of methodology I spoke of earlier, which can only be accomplished in the context of action.

And yet evaluation 'contracts' – attempts to regulate evaluation ethics in a pre-specified, legalistic sense – are now virtually *de rigueur*, in the form of undertakings towards confidentiality, access, release, management of conflict etc. The hospice interactions did, you will also recall, fall within the terms of such a contract. There are, too, proponents of greater ethical regulation of qualitative research which has, hitherto, not attracted the kind of close tribunal-based regulation applied as a matter of course to more conventional studies (see Howe and Dougherty, 1993) – most typical in Britain in relation to medical research, but no doubt on its way in other areas, too.

One problem, as we have seen, is that contracts rest upon agreements, and, as House (1980: 161) argues, 'an evaluation agreement might be reached that is not fair to the parties concerned, no matter how fully articulated or specified' and for House fairness underpins validity. But we have to stay aware that the mix of ethical issues at play in any educational context reaches far beyond the preoccupations of the evaluator. We have seen throughout this account evidence of students, for example, wrestling with personal moral dilemmas which, when translated into actions, become ethical issues. Evaluation may well intervene in the subsequent ethical tensions – if only indirectly – but may have little warrant to regulate them. Evaluation creates the ethical space within which such tensions can be played out, but they can neither control nor resolve the whole of the ethical discourse which fill that space. Evaluators need to be prepared to yield as well as wield ethical principles – others may have ones better suited to their ethical agendas.

Indeed, evaluators need to be ready to yield up the evaluation itself – more ready, that is, to lose data than we customarily are. A difficulty is that evaluators have to be the judge of these matters when they are, at the same time, interested players. An evaluator's commitment to an account can be heightened by resistance to its publication by participants. Each such expression of resistance can reaffirm, in the mind of the evaluator, the value and the 'rightness' of the struggle. The harder the hospice tried to prevent my publication of the case study the more my resolve strengthened. Should I have abandoned the study? This is the question that haunts many 'confessional tales' with rarely a resolution. Researchers who worry about the ethical basis of white people researching black people, middle-class researching the poor, the innocent researching the guilty, for example, rarely conclude that they shouldn't be doing it and that there are times when they should retire from the field. Nor is my conviction shaken that my own case of a well man researching the dying was anything other than legitimate.

Another key problem is that there is no necessary relation between absolutist ethical principles and the ethical decisions we face day by day – something which many students of evaluation find challenging. There may be no absolute ethical value at all. For example, 'honesty' is clearly a *sine qua non* in evaluative enquiry – as a general disposition. But what if honesty finds itself posed against fairness or justice: think, for example, of my decision not to reveal my theoretical sources to the hospice? Think, too, of my refusal to admit to people in the context of my music evaluations that I play music – lest I provoke a feeling in them of being judged by an informed eye. Honesty is an ethic that has to be situationally defined along with all others. To declare an intention to be honest at the outset of an evaluation is to do nothing more (or less) than to signal a willingness to enter into subsequent negotiation over its situational meaning.[10]

---

10 In the English law of contract there is a prior position to agreement which is called the 'invitation to treat' which has the status of an invitation to consider entering into a contract. For example, in a restaurant when you order a plate of food this is not considered by the courts to constitute a formal offer. If this were so, the restaurant would, by accepting your order, bind you into a contract and you would have to pay for the plate by force of law. To the contrary, your ordering the plate is the invitation to treat; the restaurant displaying (serving you with) the dish is the formal offer and it is up to you whether or not to accept. The point is that evaluators often confuse formal moves with invitations – and then confuse who is in charge of making the first formal move. Agreement over ethical stage 1 is more like an invitation to treat. Indeed, the presentation of ethical principles and procedures is

There is, too, a merging of ethics and morality at the level of the day-to-day conduct of an evaluation, and this is important to recognize in the attempt to regulate the fairness and the justice of an evaluation.

Some philosophers go further than this. Lindblom (1990: 21) quotes Rorty[11] saying we 'are making rather than finding, creating morality rather than discovering it' a typical constructivist position. Lindblom argues that values and interests are not discoverable, in the sense of building a bedrock against which to arbitrate matters of social change and preference. We should not talk of fixed, apprehendable judgements (or, by implication, values) but of 'volitions', tendencies to thought and action – expressions of will – a 'commitment' to tests of reality. He develops this by arguing that our wants do not lead to our decisions; rather, they derive from our decisions. 'Alternatively, one's hypothetical informed and thoughtful decision on what to pursue does not derive from his interests; his decision creates his interests' (p. 22). We have to understand, he says, that people 'write rather than read the human scenario'. This approach takes away the possibility of any *pre hoc* regulation of evaluation ethics, but emphasizes the need to work with robust procedures. As always in (progressive) educational discourse, it matters little where we are going, so long as we journey well.

These are thoughts on the margins of what evaluation can reasonably stand. We do not need the fixed and unswerving security of a bedrock against which to measure the justness and fairness of our actions, but we do need something more secure than volitions – and so, more so, do our respondents. In the hospice negotiations all parties were clearly, desperately trying to read the other person, to understand enough of them to be able to predict responses to strategic moves. Even so, we cannot ignore the implications of Lindblom's position that people act as a way of testing possibilities, and out of the consequences of their decisions work out where their values and interests lie. Evaluators usually work the other way around. We start with an expression of values – rather, we ask others to start with that in our interviews – and then we seek to create a moral system out of the alleged coincidence with our own values and finally use that moral system to justify our future actions. We leave little room for people to test out their decisions, for example, to join an evaluation – and to work out at leisure whether an evaluation is in their interests.

---

probably best thought of as such an invitation. The response of those to be evaluated can be thought of as the formal offer which the evaluation accepts or rejects. The shift in responsibility is subtle, but changes the sense of the relationship.

11   R. Rorty, 'Method and morality', in Norma Hann et al. (eds), *Social Science as Moral Enquiry* (Columbia University Press, New York, 1983).

Let me give a very brief argument as to why we might. Social programs in contemporary society assume a status beyond experimentation (Campbell, 1999). At their mildest they are legitimator-pilots – harbingers of what the politicians and economists have already decided we should eventually have the full dose of. At their most ruthless they are coercive instruments for rounding up the citizenry and persuading them to conform to an immutable policy. Somewhere in between they may simply be adjustments to the management of decline camouflaged with the ticker-tape and frills that accompany expansionist adventures into brave new worlds. In the contemporary Western world of education, innovatory programs have developed the ruthlessness that is borne of the political conviction that policy is 'right', that is, that there are no issues to do with policy sources, merely with their implementation. Requirements for compliance have displaced tolerance for understanding.

None of this is to say that individuals as program participants share program aims. We are often conscripts to social and educational programs and once in one we act through subterfuge, compromise, creative compliance or whatever – we accommodate ourselves to the instrument while staying reflective about its objectives. This implies two things: first, people should not be held accountable for their loyalty to program goals. They may well value the program for reasons other than its declared intentions, or they may have no choice but to go along with it. Secondly, people clearly need an opportunity to suck-it-and-see – to test out their participation so as to see whether they can, in fact, accommodate themselves. This may take a long time, during which they pass a point of no return. I think there are cases where people have a right not to be evaluated – unless the evaluation can legitimately, fairly give voice to their predicament.

I want, now, to define three stages in striving to be ethical which evaluators need to keep in mind. These concern:

1   the ethics of role;
2   the ethics of evaluation agreements;
3   the ethics of conduct.

Each of these is a separate ethical area, which is to say that they may call upon wholly different principles and values to resolve issues. An example of such a separation is given by Jenkins (above), who argued that the ethics of access to data derive from one set of values (reasonableness, individual right of privacy, human relations) while the ethics of data release call upon a different set of values altogether (public right to know, justified coercion, power). Now these distinctions do not solve problems – as I have said, ethical principles *bracket each other reciprocally* and do not exist in a hierarchy. But it may be useful procedurally to know which sub-set of ethical space we are in at any one moment. In broad terms, these three ethical areas cover, respectively:

1 **The ethics of role**: concerns the warrant of the evaluation and its public legitimacy as a form of/reason for enquiry, that is, securing agreement over the existence of the evaluation in this program. Here, for example, we confront the existential dilemmas created by the presence of an evaluation which forces us to question comfortable assumptions and fictions (cf. Berger). By what right do evaluators visit this obligation on others? This also concerns questions of how we bring to bear our values and views of justice in evaluation.
2 **The ethics of evaluation agreements**: concerns the nature of the consensus under which the evaluation proceeds – in accordance with a given (perhaps negotiated) design *in this place, at this particular time.* Here we confront questions of the political role of evaluation and how we receive and relate to our contracts. Here, too, is where we negotiate a provisional design against ethical criteria governing, for example, sampling issues – that is, who gets heard, whose agenda?
3 **The ethics of conduct**: concerns agreements that are reached on an hour-by-hour basis on what is legitimate for an evaluation to do and witness and including publication of accounts. This would include agreements enshrined in principles and procedures governing confidentiality, for example. Here is where questions of methodology are mediated through experience and responsiveness.

The crucial point about these three areas and their separation is that agreement or resolution in one cannot be assumed to extend automatically to cover questions and dilemmas in others. For example, the hospice was put under pressure to reach agreement with the evaluation over publication of the case study because they had agreed to treat with the evaluation at the outset and were therefore assumed to be bound in – they had accepted the role of the evaluation *vis-à-vis* the Guildhall project and their own engagement with it. Their acceptance of the usefulness of critical scrutiny was translated into tacit acceptance of the publication of a case. Under this arrangement this would be considered an illegitimate move. This is not to say that the evaluator has to re-negotiate the basis of the evaluation at every step because people who agreed at stage 1 and then again at stage 2 can opt out under a subsequent set of ethical negotiations. Each evaluation of a public program has to be assumed to be a valuable social resource as a matter of democratic principle and, as such, has to be able to call upon a degree of obligation on behalf of those whose work and lives it observes – and obligations need to endure a little while in the course of an enquiry. But it comes close to arguing for an opt-out. Let me illustrate.

Many of the conflicts that arise in evaluation practice do so within the ambit of the evaluation 'contract' – the principles and procedures which are often given to people at some stage of the enquiry (preferably, more than once). Frequently, this contract serves as a bridge between ethical stages 1 and 3 above, that is, they derive their authority from the evaluation warrant and use that to regulate how the evaluation is to be received. This contract may be negotiated before fieldwork commences and is generally invoked after – or in the later stages of – the fieldwork. With experience and hindsight those being evaluated finally come to understand the principles of negotiation and what is at stake – and sometimes realize that what they agreed to was fine at the start but did not match their worries here and now. This was certainly the case at the hospice. The basic agreement was that we would negotiate the draft – and when it came to it the hospice realized that what this entailed put them at a disadvantage and did not appear to serve their interests.

Such contracts fall under the ethics of agreements – the second on my list. They might set out broad guidelines, some starting points for negotiation – but they cannot be assumed to cover the actualities of the evaluation seeking access to and release of data, or, more accurately, they should not be invoked to coerce someone into agreement under stage 3. Nor should people be persuaded to go along with an agreement simply because they might have agreed that an evaluation would be a legitimate and even a good thing to do.

Finally, just to reiterate, there can be no hard and fast rules under the ethics of conduct. This is a cat-and-mouse game we play with ourselves and whose rules need to be discovered as the game proceeds. It operates at a high level of subtlety and sophistication and cannot, generally, be managed by an evaluator working alone. Nonetheless, although there may not be rules governing conduct at these levels of detail there may well be procedural principles to guide the selection of actions and to help prioritize options. These do not determine action – they merely assist in conceiving of action. Here are some contenders:

1 **Keep talking**, that is, with those being evaluated. And not just about the substance of negotiation (can I use this piece of data, can I observe your workshop), but about the evaluation itself and how you are thinking about it. Listen to Louis Smith (1990: 272–3):

I keep the enquiry goals not only in my own mind but also in front of all research participants. As the goals elaborate and differentiate into sub-goals and new goals, I keep talking about those changes. I try to listen to the ideas and sentiments of the various groups and individuals in the setting and reach agreements on how to incorporate these ideas into what I do. Further, as I invent ways of garnering information about these elaborations I keep talking to individuals about the reasonableness of those goals and the reasonableness of the strategies and tactics for reaching them. Concerns and hesitations from all parties become opportunities for creative, mutual problem-solving.

Now I don't imagine everyone can accomplish this – besides being a very personalized strategy, mutuality is more demanding than it sounds. After all, we all mediate our moral positions through strategic promotion of our interests. But the point is that Smith relies on conversation to create the kind of ethical space I am talking about in which specific decisions about the use of data, say, do not come as a surprise – because they are embedded in relationships which, themselves, are embedded in a shared understanding of the evaluation problematic.

2   **Develop an elaborate sense of what fairness means to you, but don't confuse personal morality with public ethics**, that is, rather than rely on the help of a protocol. House (1980: 173) says that 'fairness is an idea that pervades evaluation, almost always at the intuitive level of consciousness . . . a fair agreement is binding unless it is in conflict with our natural duties, or, more important moral principles such as those of justice'. The condition 'unless it is in conflict' is the natural condition of evaluation practice and the 'elaborate sense of fairness' I am talking about is the capacity for independent judgement on when to invoke the exception. In one sense it does not matter what decision you finally make, so long as the process of arriving at the decision has been a personal ethical one – that is, with fairness receiving due consideration and self-discipline exercised to constrain the impulse towards self-interest. This is closely related to the principle Smith advocates of 'committed relativism', which suggests that you stick to a personal principle to the point where you find you cannot – and then you change it. You recognize that no principle will govern all situations – commitment is a procedural matter, a moral state. However, recall the dilemma I cast myself into through my private readings while researching the hospice – how I transferred my personal reaction to 'people-processing' to the case. My own moral sense of what may or may not be right might not be a good guide to the world others have to live in.

3   **Assume no symmetry in evaluation relationships**. Many ethical procedures advocated in the evaluation literature assume what legal

contract theorists call 'parity' – that is, a symmetrical relationship in which no party to the contract has a strategic advantage over another. This can never be so in evaluation. So long as we have external evaluators operating under a degree of independence or else representing either their own or others' interests, so we will have an imbalance of power. As my correspondence shows, the powers assumed by even (I like to think) benign evaluators who are concerned with issues of justice and fairness are formidable. This was no low-stakes game being played with the hospice. They were, I think, in genuine torment over political difficulties being created, the possibility of loss of public esteem, the exposure of private fears and weaknesses, the straining of internal relationships over what was being revealed. It was no mean feat to persuade them to acquiesce.

Related to this is a principle invoked by Yvonna Lincoln (1990) in responding to the Smith paper just cited. She interprets a Kantian principle as invoking a 'categorical imperative' (and presents a forceful argument in support of imperatives that are categorical, that is, irrefutable). This she gives as 'act in such a way that you would not be distressed to discover that the principles under-girding your own action were now a law that could be enacted by others upon you' (p. 291). There are two problems with this – both rather obvious. One is that we are trying, here, to deal with (not uncommon) situations in which there are mutually exclusive but both justifiable ethics at play. For example, not giving that woman patient the case study draft was an unwelcome act, but so would have been seeking to undermine medical authority. Here was a common situation in which we would want both mutually exclusive acts to be committed on us and we would, at the same time, want them not to be visited upon us. Like all social imperatives this one withers at the first falsification attempt. The other problem with Lincoln's categorical imperative is that these things will *not* be visited on the evaluator because the ethical dilemmas often stem precisely from the problem of unequal status and position. The trick is to recognize the inequality and seek strategies for managing the conflict – not to seek to resolve it against abstract principles. I want to forge an ethical procedural principle which acknowledges the inevitability of unethical stances.

4 Think in terms of the limits of evaluation, not its rights. Ethics require that we keep our evaluation activities in perspective, that evaluation serves ethics, not the other way around. Experience tells me – and I hope I have illustrated this well – that the temptation is to use ethical calculations and procedures to justify and support the conduct of evaluation where it is brought into question. Sometimes – perhaps often – this is sound. Sometimes it is not. It is judicious to assume from the outset that it is not and look for divergent cases.

5 **Never defend the evaluation**. To defend an evaluation against complaints is, at least implicitly, to attack or undermine the complainant – and an evaluator has no reason to be attacking anybody. In any event, evaluation almost always has trump cards in any struggle over legitimacy (who do people believe – the evaluator, or the complaining teacher?) and it is almost always unfair and, therefore, unethical to join in argument as though on an equal footing. Evaluators should, that is to say, be required to fight with at least one hand tied behind their back. Nonetheless, this should be taken in conjunction with the rule that evaluators should always be prepared to lose data, but not the evaluation.

One complexity of this principle is that I can invoke it just as easily as a weapon against plaintiffs in evaluation contests. To accept, frontally, all charges laid against an evaluation can be a very powerful play: it disarms the plaintiff, curries favour for the evaluator who emerges looking less bellicose and probably more reasonable than the plaintiff, it strengthens the legitimacy of the evaluation by demonstrating its responsiveness and, therefore, its undeniability, and it tends to reduce the force of the complaints by making them look sufficiently insignificant as to be instantly assimilable. We find ourselves back in that uncertain terrain where ethics and exploitation conjoin.

8

People in Change

UNSTABLE STATES

One of life's deeper tragedies which we come to know with the loss of innocence is that there is no such thing as a stable state – what Schon (1971: 9) calls 'an afterlife within my own life . . . belief in the unchangeability, the constancy of central aspects of our lives'. Once more, we confront mortality. Historically, the fear of the 'mutability' of experience – its inherent instability – has been a powerful theme and a driving force for social theory (Dollimore, 1998). It has frequently found expression in a desire for the resolution of death (Heidegger, Schopenhauer, Freud) as an escape back into constancy and certainty.[1] Dollimore traces the conflation of death with desire back into the ancient world (Socrates embraced his enforced suicide) and forward to the modern world (Heidegger's philosophical contribution to the Nazi death camp project).

The fear of mutability finds other forms of expression and other kinds of death-wish. The yearning for the persistence of experience is institutionalized in all social domains as custom and tradition, and these serve as the basis for resistance to innovation. We write our personal insecurities large on the walls of our institutions and through their unchangeability we live the existential lie of immortality – or at least a vicarious immortality in which we recreate ourselves through our children. Institutions – perhaps especially schools – are bent to the task of sustaining old realities and we mobilize their energies to create what Schon calls a 'dynamic conservatism' – that is, energetic strategies to

---

1 'Influential developments in modern thought internalise death as never before . . . one of the most fascinating paradoxes of modern philosophies of human identity: death is taken into consciousness in a way which is at once an expansion and a nullification of consciousness' (p. xxii).

protect us from the inevitability of change and to maintain the fiction of unchangeability. As the French aristocrat is supposed to have said to another on the brink of the French Revolution, 'if we want things to stay the same we'd better start changing'.

But, still, one thing the school curriculum rarely deals with is contemporary social change. Far from it. In the UK (perhaps, in due course, even in the USA), we have a national curriculum for schools which, by increments, reaches forward into university education and back into pre-school education. This statutory framework all but seeks to eradicate mutability in knowledge. At the time of writing the Secretary of State announced that certain poets were to be removed from the list for approved study and others – Derek Walcott included – were to replace them. It was not until this announcement that teachers and pupils were free to choose to study Walcott – but now they were to be denied those removed from the list. There was, in fact, public controversy as a result of which the removed poets were reinstated – along with Walcott. The ethical absurdity of such fine-grain tuning of official knowledge masks a more insidious erosion of democracy – the denial of the individual – what Dollimore calls a process of 'self-disidentification'. The denial of the individual and the flight into universal treatments (for example, 'entitlement programs', 'equality of opportunity') is opting for a form of death – that is, the death of possibility and creativity – and is a flight from change and uncertainty, for the unpredictability of individual intent is the best guarantor of change.

There is, then, a fundamental clash between the modernist optimism and commitment to progress on the one hand, and the existential fear of change and mortality on the other. Innovation inhabits that uneasy territory between the two and 'feels the force' of the contradiction. The problem is that we cannot, by definition, know of the world on the other side, as it were, of change; change worth its name implies altered states of being. We have a natural tendency to stick with what we know and to shy away from what we cannot know. The void of moral and political uncertainty is too risky to enter. Schon's work, written in the midst of the post-war epoch of social and educational reform programs, is one of those few theses on innovation which links individual psychology (and morality) with social psychology and those with social change theory.

> The power of social systems over individuals becomes understandable, I think, only if we can see that social systems provide for their members not only sources of livelihood, protection against outside threat and the promise of economic security, but a framework of theory, values and related technology which enables individuals to make sense of their lives. Threats to the social system threaten this framework. (1971: 51)

Similarly, Dollimore documents the impact of the concept of social death on individuality. Earlier (Chapter 2) we saw this fear of social death – the erosion of society itself – as giving rise to 'praxis', to social programming. Mutability, death, incompleteness could be ironed-out of the system by social engineering. But praxis has an impact on the individual, too. Dollimore points to Marx's insistence that the revolutionary world was to be characterized by the parallel energies for changing society and changing the self. Indeed, across the education system and accompanying the 'experimenting society' we are moving into – a society committed to piecemeal social engineering and the innovatory program as a routine experience – has been all the paraphernalia of self-change and scrutiny of the individual: performance appraisal, action research, behavioural testing, psychological profiling, payment-by-results and, above all, allegiance to mission statements. The danger is that this network of control – the panopticon society – becomes an orthodoxy and becomes part of the dependency culture of the individual. Once we assimilate control mechanisms into our daily routines – as we have to do – they become part of our custom, we learn how to excel in methods of compliance and turn them to our career advantage and we even seek out opportunities to express ourselves through compliance.

Schon's view, for any evaluator charged with understanding change, is a useful analytic device. It allows us to look at individuals and through them to *see* the impact of social systems – and to chart the limits of change. Innovation is a test of the dependency culture. One question for the evaluator is how to measure just what is the dependency relationship of individual on social system, for this provides one index of change potential. It also, of course, renders operationally useful the data we often generate on how people apparently lead contradictory lives. Contradictions, for example, between beliefs and action, are often evidence of the strains of personal change management and, therefore, direct sources for insight into the balance between change and resistance.

The personal experience of innovation is as often one of confusion as of purposeful belief and action. Innovation tends to render people 'incompetent' (MacDonald and Walker, 1976) in that it generates new data on life and work which has to be ordered and familiarized. Listen to Maureen, one of the Guildhall student-innovators, talking about the MPCS innovation in a moment of such destabilization:

One of the things – I don't know if it's done me good or bad – is that, it's like MPCS is supposed to teach you to *not* think, to be spontaneous and all that. At the same time – in my first term particularly when we had all those long talks over lunch – it was like, it forced me to think, and in a way, I think it's done me a bit of harm. Well – no – it's probably done me good because I've probably never thought before – but it's done me harm in that I think too much now, and I don't *not* think enough – I can't get a balance between being spontaneous and thinking . . .

Serious stuff for a musician. This is a highly personalized account, of course, but it is typical noise from the engine-room of change. We are with Maureen inside the learning process as she works through her own 'incompetence'.

Maureen is forced to consider some basic strategies for making music – perhaps, in the process, using a single conceptual dimension (say, 'think/not-think') which may well vary in meaning across contexts. It may be that this innovatory course is giving her an alternative to spontaneity; though it could also be that there is no tension at all between being spontaneous and thinking – that is, thinking could provide a different set of conditions in which to be spontaneous. Whatever the case, there is an uneasy tendency for innovations to raise questions of fundamentals for the individual and to do so in contradictory ways.

But we have to picture Maureen talking in her institutional context as a student of music – that is, in the conservatoire. Once we so picture her we can juxtapose what she is saying with the culture and values of the institution. Perhaps she is sitting in the Guildhall foyer alongside one of her friends who is not taking the MPCS course and who does not have the same opportunity to raise questions like this within a support structure as represented by the innovatory course. What does each of these two people mean for the Conservatoire? Perhaps we get a sense that merely on the evidence of what appears to be radical re-thinking, Maureen may be becoming somewhat disengaged from the institution – that reflection at this level represents a degree of institutional autonomy.

For education and training institutions need their students to think for themselves – though perhaps not too much. Autonomy of thought at the level of questioning the fundamentals is assumed to be something reserved for the exceptional student who represents a special and cherished moment in the routine life of the institution. 'Being spontaneous' can amount to a problematic independence from pedagogical authority. Whether spontaneity is 'good' or 'bad' for the Conservatoire is hostage to too many forces and phenomena to consider briefly, but we can be sure of saying that as an individual Maureen represents a small force for change. Her thinking will almost certainly (did, in a small way) recast the struggle between student and the Conservatoire for dominance over who she was and what she played. In a small but not insignificant way, the relationship between the Conservatoire and its students is changing here.

There is, in the light of this argument, a form of mutual dependence between individual and institution (or program). Just as innovation forces the individual to consider their relationship to the sustaining frameworks of their social system, so that social system has to consider the degree to which the continued loyalty of the individual is one of its key sustaining forces. Innovators learn to tread carefully in making their demands for change, often tempering the impulse for change with the need to maintain a power base within the status quo and to maintain esteem among peers and supporters.[2] The relationship between the Conservatoire and Peter Renshaw, Director of the MPCS innovation, represented a resolution of the competing needs for mutual dependency and change. The Conservatoire was involved in a *realpolitik* within which it was well aware of how potentially radical Renshaw could be with his vision, but how necessary it would be to have him as a resource. (For some in the Conservatoire, a case of 'if we want things to stay the same we'd better start changing . . .'.)

None the less, the degree to which the innovatory potential embodied by Maureen and others like her is controllable by the institution is open to question. There is no obvious way to determine a 'direction' to Maureen's thinking and development, or those of other students on that course – no way of predicting the outcome and scale of clashes between these people and the Conservatoire – the host social system. We know only that innovation processes represented by the thinking of these young innovators is complex and sometimes radical, and that they are potentially explosive for the conservatoire. We know that it is perfectly possible for institutions to live with their members in a state of dissonance for lengthy periods, since we commonly live in tension with the institutions of which we are a part. Reducing to the level of daily complaints, our sense that our institutions fail to live up to our personal and peer-group learnings merely bottles up innovatory thinking at the lower reaches of the organization and serves as a release valve for explosive energy. It also means that innovation resources like Maureen remain uncoordinated, less purposeful and, therefore, less predictable in their effects than they might be were they known and embraced by the organization. The innovatory impulse passes, as it were, from those who conceive and manage innovations to those who work with them on the

---

2   See, for example, MacDonald and Walker (1976), who document the way curriculum innovators manage and negotiate such tensions in the context of curriculum reform initiated outside of the school system. Reformers and developers have to alter their message when negotiating access to teachers and when seeking intellectual esteem from peers, for example.

ground, and in the passing, there is a loss of control (notwithstanding House's, 1974, argument that the costs of innovation are devolved down systems to be carried by the less powerful – both are true).

Let me take a second case from the Royal Opera House. At the Royal Opera House, many of the artistes engaged in schools work were there to promote a love and respect for the given vision of operatic or balletic excellence, but were excited by the opportunity to step out of the hierarchical and discipline-based approach to opera or ballet production. The Education Department at the Royal Opera House mounts a range of school activities based, usually, on collaborative workshops. In these school-based workshops members of the chorus, say, work closely together with members of the orchestra, with a writer and, perhaps, with a costumier and a pianist. These are quite unusual pairings. Most large performing arts institutions are no different to other educational institutions in that they are fragmented organizations with highly differentiated and specialized labour. As in schools and universities, people who move across units (here, say, a chorus and set design) tend to be the artistic managers – not the members of those units themselves. Once inside an outreach workshop, however, a member of a chorus, say, might find herself making professional, that is, artistic, decisions she is unaccustomed to make. She may take the role of producer, for example. Not only that, when she performs with the children she may find herself doing strange but nonetheless legitimate things. One singer talked of taking a lead role in one of the school operas and in the final performance finding herself pushed to the back of the stage, having to elbow her way through the chorus of children to reach the front of the stage and then finding herself singing with her back to the audience – but with relish. Here is that singer speaking:

> . . . it's easiest to take things as they relate to you – and I think for most of us who work with the [Education] Department it gives us a chance to break out of the mould – because this is a job. You do get a bit jaded – not always – there are still those wonderful moments . . . I would never get the chance to sing *Carmen* in this House, I'm not that good, not that famous, nobody would pay to see me do the *Carmen* here. But the chance of doing the *Carmen* somewhere else appeals to me . . . you get a chance to perform.

Cast into unusual settings, and with sufficient commitment to stay there and make sense of them, people will sometimes seek alternative strategies – even in the absence of curiosity, which also serves to propel people into novelty. Typically, these activities allow individuals to recast their relationship to the institutions in which they live – and, talking to them, we hear of alternative visions of what that institution might look like. Here is where the dependency culture is under review, as it were, and people make calculations about how far they might stray. Institutions notice the threat. Said a senior manager of the Royal Opera House Education Department:

> . . . in a sense, the organization very much feels that it is often criticized by issues that the Department throws up. I think that may be the key as to why it's difficult to have it from within and – I've even heard the word 'irritant' applied somewhere and that's what it is.

There are, here, two distinct innovatory impulses for the main organization. One is the individual artiste who returns from educational experiments with different skills, ideas – as a different kind of resource for the institution. Each individual potentially carries innovation with them. The second, is the department itself, which promotes, coordinates, archives – husbands – innovatory resources. Of course, neither of these addresses the problems of host organizations adapting to their innovatory offspring, something we now know – after many years of sustained observation – to be complex and difficult to achieve. But this discussion is limited, for the time being, to 'innovation' and not to 'change' – that is, to the laboratory in which we try to 'cook-up' change in a relatively stable environment; not to the far less predictable and more unstable world of normal experience in which change occurs, often, apparently, in spite of our volition.

So Schon's characterization of innovation becomes more complex once we look into personal experience. People clearly are prepared to take risks with their stability, take themselves close to those 'unstable states' and even sometimes relish them. Dependency cultures are not, themselves, immutable. Even so, his principal observation holds that innovation must overcome the inertia of our dependency relationship with our given social systems. In the data on the Conservatoire we recall that students who had called for more exposure to innovatory activities were asked by their Principal which of their routine activities they would give up – none was prepared to go that far. A feature running through the data of each of the three evaluations referred to in this book was of a regression to a common sense of conservatism. I referred earlier to that feature of Conservatoire experience which one student described as 'the dream', that is, of success-with-excellence, of recognition . . . another striving for immortality, both the fiction and the slender possibility sustained by the Conservatoire, by the 'social system'.

This came as an aside during a conversation in a crowded, noisy bar in the City of London after a hard day's innovation-work. The conversation, typically, was driven by Peter Renshaw, the Director of MPCS, who was provoking the students into thinking critically (not dismissively) of the Conservatoire tradition and of a classical music career. The argument turned and turned about as students sought to resolve their yearning for careers with their equal desire to be free of the yearning. The student, Tony, reaching over to pass a pint of beer to Peter Renshaw had quipped, 'it's not just the institution you're fighting – it's the dream!'

UNSTABLE ACTS OF MEANING

In order to evaluate a project or a program we need to hold some view of what innovation means and how it both links and drives apart people and institutions. The success of case study in evaluating programs has been its capacity to operate at a level of meaning. Schon points to the obvious: that conventional ('rational/experimental') forms of enquiry are useless since they assume that 'knowledge derived from experiment can apply to the next comparable instance' (1971: 201) – whereas innovation assumes an erosion of comparability and the possibility of the 'explosion of surprise'. His is a cogent argument for the use of case study – for a methodological approach that allows us to document the existential struggles people wage with change; how that struggle is manifested differently in thought, speech and action; how these struggles are contextualized in embracing systems of community, organization, culture, politics. In the end innovations are acts at the level of meaning – that is, of significance for the construction of group and individual identities.

Innovations are acts of meaning – but there is no reason to imagine that the meanings are stable across individual lives. We tend to think of innovations as agency, things that are *done* as options, as an expression of political choice – we characteristically use purposeful concepts like 'planning', 'implementation', 'goals', 'process' to analyse them. Innovation programs are proactive things. But this is to see innovation from the perspective of the program advocate – not that of the people touched by the program, including its participants. For many of these people innovations are things that *happen* to them, often unasked for and usually unexpected. More appropriate concepts might be 'surprise' rather than planning, 'carried along' rather than implementation, 'confusion' rather than goals identification and 'disconnected episodes' rather than process.

And, too, there is no reason to assume that the *purpose* of innovation is novelty – although this is typically the claim of innovators. To accept the claim uncritically is to be coopted into a program's own – inevitably narrow – definition of itself. The claim to novelty is complex and needs to be carefully questioned, for there are events which are novel for some and not for others, just as there are many reasons for mounting or joining an innovation which may be to do with anything but novelty. For example, the systematic removal of public subsidy from the arts has fostered an enormous amount of innovatory projects – largely to do with broadening access – many of which are motivated by the most modest and conservative of goals, survival, because funding depends increasingly on demonstrating community links.

This is not to say that innovations, even those designed for conservatism, do not often *result* in experiences that are novel for some in ways neither predicted nor sought. The Adopt-a-Player Scheme had a conservative goal at its heart, which was to foster understanding and appreciation of its art form and to generate future audiences for orchestral concerts. Like many arts outreach projects, its primary function was to protect and project the artistic ideal. For the children involved, it took its place among the familiar, routine array of adult offerings; for some teachers it offered opportunities for pedagogical experiments, while for others it offered a chance to pass on onerous National Curriculum responsibilities; for the LEA Adviser who helped conceive it, the scheme was the realization of an ambition and a principle held and nurtured for many years; for an orchestral player it was an opportunity to reaffirm his status as a musician.

There is a clue here that major innovations are not just personalized and plural in their meanings, but in addition are rarely blind leaps into uncertain futures. They are more often distillations of experience, the realization of thoughts and aspirations that have been harboured for many years. They involve what Schon calls 'a rejection of the literal past' but an 'acceptance of the past as a projective model' (1971: 237). Innovation is a mix of biography with aspiration – innovations are, in spite of common assumptions about 'colonising futures', often backward-looking.

Successful innovations are likely to be more conservative than we might otherwise expect them to be, in the sense that they are rooted in personal histories and in what existing institutional politics will allow. But the key implication supports what Schon would argue – that to understand innovations we have to understand the individuals who people them. Let me take the Guildhall project as a case example. Here is a lengthy extract from the final evaluation report, which attempts to show how the innovation represented the coincidence of multiple biographies. It is an example of the point I made earlier about avoiding the trap of locking individuals into discrete accounts of life histories. Here we see the growth of an idea through the confluence of lives, and both the individuals involved and the idea itself can only be understood (for these evaluation purposes) in combination.

Peter Renshaw described this innovation as an 'idea whose time had come' – he was referring to the readiness of professional music communities to contemplate change – a generalized sense of dissatisfaction. That dissatisfaction represents the pre-history of the MPCS Project, and we can get a glimpse of it by looking at some individuals and their backgrounds. We will make them converge on a particular moment – see how they meet in this Project. We start with two students, Vicky and Wendy, and continue with others who became associated with MPCS.

Vicky is a 'cellist. She recalls with affection her early introduction to music back at school. There she would spend her lunchtimes with a friend, locked away in the music room, knowing that their peers were sceptical of their self-enforced isolation, but revelling in the tranquillity of a room which looked across landscaped fields. It was here that she developed her love for music, and decided to make a career of it. She went to London to attend the Conservatoire. The transformation was dramatic, as old associations with musical experience were substituted by the ugly, daily routine of dragging her 'cello through the crowded tunnels of the underground and locking herself away for hours in windowless practice rooms to emerge occasionally for a lesson. By the end of her second year she was thinking seriously about leaving the Conservatoire.

Wendy, also a student at the Conservatoire, is a flautist with a national reputation. She has grown up in the classical music world – she remembers sitting listening to her father rehearsing with his professional orchestra. Winner of a Shell Competition, she has anticipated what others have anticipated for her – a life as an orchestral player – or even as a soloist. But it is recently that she had begun to question unchallenged assumptions about her career. Are there no alternatives? 'Why,' she asks, 'does the fact that I want to be in an orchestra represent what is right for me?'

Peter Renshaw, Director of MPCS, has a career path which combined twin passions of music and education. Until recently Principal of the Yehudi Menuhin School for talented young musicians, Peter has taught philosophy in a university education department and history in a college of education – whilst maintaining an active performing life on the violin. Some events from his life loom large in his memory and continue to guide his motivations. There was a time when he found himself playing music to refugees in a TB sanatorium in Austria. In the open air there had been a woman – a Hungarian woman – weeping. He watched her, and remembers feeling the power of music to elevate the sensibilities, even in such unremitting contexts. This memory, he says, underpins his desire to change music cultures, to make them more responsive and responsible to communities.

Next, let us look at a professional musician – a tuba player with a leading national orchestra. He has an international reputation and many accomplishments to his name. Like most musicians, he teaches, but he feels privileged to choose precisely whom he teaches, how and when. He works in a professional context where, it is said, a great many orchestral players are forced into the use of beta-blockers by the unusual combinations of routine and tension, and the high level of individual skill with submission to a musical hierarchy. He is anxious to sustain the high levels of skill required for orchestras, but sceptical of the forced-feeding pressures on young musicians to develop those skills. He sits as a judge on major competitions and, increasingly, feels the incongruity of giving tacit support for the 'fast-fry' training system – so far from the long cooking 'casserole' approach that he would like to see. But he gets a lot from his teaching and he can still learn from his students – new elements of technique. The Conservatoire? Here he is ambivalent. Music colleges can only teach mediocrity, he feels, since they are adapted to the training of the majority, middle-band of ability. A contradiction works its way into his views – a scepticism towards the current elitism of music, allied to a suspicion of the institutional mechanism for broadening that elite.

Finally, let us look in a hospice. The hospice is part of a movement seeking to produce fundamental change in attitudes towards the terminally ill. Whereas doctors are often thought to abandon the dying patient through the implications of failure, this hospice seeks to emphasize the potential still there in a life of as little as two weeks. They are, they say, seeking ways to 'help people to live until they die'. One of the doctors, in particular, is exploring ways of using the Arts to enrich the life experience of the terminally ill – poetry is prominent, and music is an obvious and attractive source.

Here is some of the raw material of innovation, represented by a confluence of biographies and associated conditions – indeed, here we hear aspirant 'social engineers'. The confluence happened within a particular context which allowed it to happen. Peter Renshaw had approached the Guildhall Conservatoire – John Hosier was the Principal. This was a time when the conservatoires – the London-based ones in particular – were facing increased competition for good students and funds, pressed by a government urgent for spending cuts and increasingly sceptical of what appeared to be needless duplication in sponsoring a musical elite. At the same time, all conservatoires were concerned with the decline in audiences for 'serious music', something whose backwash effect – through growing unemployment among orchestral players – would be felt by the training colleges. With shrewd foresight, and reflecting the dependency of system on individuals, Hosier embraced what looked like becoming a headline-grabbing innovation.

'An idea whose time had come' was an accurate characterization. Renshaw articulated the broad collective concerns that were widespread across the music world, coordinated the collaboration of isolated players – sponsors, students, institutions – and conceived the means to realize the attempted solution. These latter involved, as we have seen, taking students out of the sterile environment of the practice room and placing them in contexts where they would have to fend for and defend themselves and their music, reconsider their relationship to their music and the whole social and personal basis of their creativity. It was a preemptive realization of the theory of the 'reflective practitioner'. Though no one associated with the innovation had studied the work of Donald Schon, these ideas (and a more elaborate extension of professional development into, for example, institutional politics) had been current on the British scene for many years in the form of educational action research (Elliott, 1991). Peter Renshaw had been a player on that scene and had an intimate though intuitive understanding of how to link professional and organizational change.

The means, however, were not the innovation – though they were novel enough. The innovation was far more. It was the learning from bitter and rich experience; what was innovatory was conceptualizing the project as a set of pedagogical and learning activities set in an institutional framework; it was an estimation of what tolerances that institutional framework might have and how hard not to push; it was knowledge of the resources at hand in the worlds of music and how to exploit them in novel ways; and it was an understanding of which values to appeal to in people and how to engage them. In short, what Peter Renshaw brought as the chief innovator was a practical theory of change. The change he sought was a mixture of the novel and the conservative – much of the innovation, as we can see, was an affirmation and a reconstitution of deeply embedded values.

But we can read more into this to develop a more complex view of the innovator within the innovation. Earlier I suggested that novelty was not to be assumed to be the purpose of innovation. This is too hard on the innovators, for it wrongly implies that they need neither creativity nor courage. Far from it. Schon ends his book with a characterization of the innovator within what he calls 'an ethic for existential knowing'. Existential in the sense that innovators are constrained to think and act in the 'here-and-now', though innovation requires 'leaps' away from (albeit rooted in) the past. They are leaps, he says, in that 'they cannot be justified except by what happens after they are made' (1971: 235). Freed from the constraints of conventional practice and the theories of action that bind us to conventions, the innovator can think and act afresh in response to the situational characteristics she confronts. She must be able to be guided by the past but ready to discard its lessons; be committed to an experimental activity but capable of seeing it as merely one point of view; she must be able to reflect back on a situation while acting in it; and flexible enough to think in a theory-debunking mode while synthesizing and discovering new theory. The innovator, says Schon, has to resolve 'engagement with others, with ultimate reliance on the self recognized as the internalization of others' (p. 237).

I will return to this latter attribute shortly. As for the others, we can see these in, for example, Peter Renshaw, creator and major advocate of the Guildhall innovation. At the end of the second year of the evaluation I published an account which documented the regular amendments Peter was making to the innovation objectives. The first such was the deletion of 'music therapy', since he discovered early on that this might create territorial disputes with that discipline. As the opportunity structure for his project (and his wider set of values and ambitions) changed, so he made commensurate changes to project objectives.

This was far from cheating. Here was evidence of a project that was alive to its experiences and with a proven capacity to learn and develop – a project, in fact, which was alive to the state of the dependency culture it was working with. At a simple level it was evidence of creative opportunism in the innovators (one of the beneficial characteristics of 'temporary systems' which are not bound by the conventions of their institutional hosts, argues Miles, 1964) – but this is to partly miss the point. I referred earlier to Lindblom, who suggested that change (new values) derives from action, not, as we conventionally think, the other way about. Here is evidence of this. Each amendment to project objectives represented the emerging theory of change which Peter Renshaw was developing. Here was Schon's 'learning agent', proving flexible in balancing pasts with futures, in an apparent pragmatism, holding off from making major values commitments until the ground has been explored. Throughout the project he juggled with conventional appeals to legitimacy (insisting on high musical and artistic standards) while searching for new ones (involving leading orchestra players and his students in weekend improvisation workshops and asking his students whether hours of practice for technical mastery didn't stunt creativity).

I don't want to create a new orthodoxy – certainly some elements of the traditional training for certain people are probably pretty good, pretty sound. One wants to provide another element which, in itself, is intrinsically valuable – but which can also help an institution respond to certain changes.

At the same time he could talk of his project as an alternative to putting more police on the streets by helping to model a sense of commitment to community. By the close of his project he had generated a theory of change and music development that allowed him to move fluidly in many contexts, including in-service training for orchestras and opera houses; national curriculum design; management education; and conservatoire policy as well as curriculum and staff development. At the heart of his thinking lay a generic model linking development of the individual to development of practice and development of the organization. Crucial to the emergence of this intellectual accomplishment had been sitting on the floor in youth clubs, schools and prisons playing the bongos.

Renshaw travelled extensively with his students to almost all their events – ostensibly, to keep an eye on happenings and to monitor the students' actions and learnings (subsequent searching debriefings were a regular feature) and for the obvious enjoyment he derived. But these were learning experiences for him, too and they fuelled his conversations. Amendments to objectives were indices of advancement, of learning, of the slow emergence of understanding of what the innovation was about.

He did not accomplish this alone, clearly. He spent very many hours with his students (some of whom he had known since childhood at the Menuhin School), often questioning as well as leading them. The students, for their part, tended to treat him as more than a course Director, responding to his combination of charisma and social intimacy with their own intimacy. They tended to bring problems and arguments to him that seamlessly linked their music and their selves. And when they expressed frustration or dismay they seamlessly targeted the man and the innovation.

The pressures on innovators can be incalculable. The demands they have to make on their collaborators (in the light of Schon's analysis) both to confront their own fears and to withstand the attacks of others who will not countenance an exposure of theirs can only be justified by success. What succeeds (and fails) is the idea. It is the innovator – it was Peter Renshaw – who is on trial. Central to the success of an innovation is often the spouse and family of the innovator – that the durability of innovations can be measured against the tolerance of a family for the temporary loss of a mother or a father. They are on trial at home, too – indeed, innovators like Renshaw are often on soft money and *have to* succeed. Finally, on trial are the innovator's theory and hopes for themselves. Innovators have often rhetorically abandoned their past – publicly. If their envisioned future doesn't work, they have nowhere to go.

Let me choose just one more illustration which provides a slightly different angle on the personalization of innovation. This is from the report on the Adopt-a-Player Scheme (AaPS), from a section tracing its origins. Here, once more, we are in the engine-room of innovation as we look into the personal biography of a key member of the innovation community.

The AaPs originated as an idea shared between the education authority and the orchestra – the prime mover was Martha Loman, the General Music Adviser. Martha has a background in music education (and dance) in middle schools – trained in one of those pockets of the teacher-training world influenced by R.S. Peters, one of the progressive educational philosophers associated with the 1960/70s 'golden age' of curriculum reform. She was also taught by Peter Renshaw, who is now one of the leading figures in bringing professional music makers into interaction with communities. 'It was terrific groundwork,' she says, 'I'm not a 'systems' person and I never was.' People, she says, share values, not views.

She left that phase with beliefs that have never left her. At the core of these beliefs is respect for children as individuals and a theory of personal change. Children are to be treated as individuals with independent value systems, free to evaluate for themselves, free to make their own 'connections', encouraged to use music to think about themselves – not just to play music. Connections are important. 'How can you help that child to see what they've done in a wider musical context, in a wider cultural context, in a wider arts context, in a whole world context?'

So music has to be interactive, based on one-to-one relationships. 'If the kids could get to know the player as a friend, then musically all sorts of things would happen.' Hence, schools would 'adopt' a player, invite a more intimate relationship than one in which the player was allocated to a school randomly.

Central to her view of individual change is the notion of 'sparking' a child – a momentary realization, a condensation of experience, a catharsis. 'It may be just something internal, you may not even see it happen, you may have to work on a hunch, it might be a look in the eye . . .' Such a concept is common enough in conversations with musicians – the 'moment' a person decided to become a musician. Martha talks of it in personal terms, recounting such a moment when she was dancing to a violin concerto – a life-changing moment. She clicks her fingers and narrows her eyes to describe its spontaneity and impact. A moment on a course when she felt she attained a level of expression hitherto denied her on her instrument. 'It was something intangible.' Her dance teacher came over to her and said he knew something had happened to her. 'It was probably the most moving experience of my life.'

EXPERIENCE AS REHEARSAL FOR CHANGE

Here, the impulse behind the AaPS innovation was less serendipitous than in the case of the MPCS course, less a coincidence of experience and values. There is a sense of network, of a latent capacity that had been built into the educational system by the semi-concerted work some years ago of educational thinkers and practitioners. There is a purposive, theory of change view implied here – that certain views might be 'seeded' into a system and, some years later, bear fruit.[3] Clearly there was what is often spoken of as an 'epiphanous moment', but prudence demands that we think of that moment of awakening as being rooted in a life process – that Martha had been educated to respond to that dance moment. Martha's experience had generated for her a context of meaning within which she could locate an innovatory project when an appropriate one came along – here is the state of 'readiness' Renshaw so accurately identified.

We can reconcile this, perhaps, with some of the principal preoccupations of this chapter and Chapter 2 – the fear of change, mutability and uncertainty, and the retreat into dependency and inauthenticity. Renshaw does not leap blindly into brave new worlds; Martha does not immediately yield herself up to the full implications of her 'epiphany'. Both allow experience and ideas, dissatisfactions and insights, failures and learnings to build up sediment and to create a bedrock. Experience has, for them, been a rehearsal and a preparation for entering into change processes. This is, perhaps, how people best confront change.

Insofar as people constitute the principal resource for innovation and social reform – for models of praxis – this has important implications for policy. Clearly it undermines contemporary aspirations to a rapid pace of change and almost certainly erodes away the basis for its expectation. But it also asks us to recast the policy process more in terms of discourse

---

3 What is compelling about the number of years it took for Martha's education to bear fruit in the AaPS is that it confounds the contemporary fad for time-limited measurement of educational impact.

(Cohen and Garrett, 1975) than episodes or decisions. The reality of policy development is that it is, likewise, a process of sedimentation and learning – of creating bedrocks of experience on which to construct projective models. The current fad for evidence-based practice embodies the principle, if not the nature of its proper expression. Educational evaluation addresses the basic point that to understand how to effect change we need to understand how people learn, not what will make them comply. Educational evaluation is more or less, the study of people.

Coda

Robert Campbell and Cultural Standards in Curriculum Evaluation

A.S. Neill (1915), founder of the Summerhill progressive school, started his unofficial log of his early teaching career with a self-questioning about curriculum values. He worked in a rural school in Scotland with the children of the poor who were destined to work in factories and farms and to 'live in hovels', and he was required to teach them about Henry VIII, times-tables and the geography of Africa. 'What does it all mean? What am I trying to do?' His answer came quickly – his aim was to develop in his students an 'attitude'.

> Most of the stuff I teach them will be forgotten in a year or two, but an attitude remains with one throughout life. I want these boys and girls to acquire the habit of looking honestly at life. (1915: 13)

'Looking honestly at life'. The 'honesty' of the gaze consists in a tolerance for reviewing contested evidence, a taste for seeking out alternative explanations of events relevant to real dilemmas in living. This is a state of cognitive awareness that stands as a curriculum goal for schooling of all years and which concerns itself with autonomy of thought. But it also stands as a professional goal for educational evaluators who are concerned with the notion of authenticity in representation. The link between personal autonomy and authenticity – both needing to make society transparent – is part of the binding which makes evaluation *educational* and which links the work of educators with the work of educational evaluators – insofar as both teachers and evaluators are less concerned with educational outcomes than with the quality of educational process. The procedural and ethical principles which guide the practice of evaluation are drawn from the same source as those which guide the curriculum role of the teacher in a democracy. The teacher either remains impartial as she presents evidence to her pupils or she imposes an authority which is, effectively, arbitrary and threatens the hope of autonomous judgement. So, too, with evaluation. When arguing for a privileged role for the evaluator I have merely been arguing that we are warranted to look honestly at life (I am aware of, but momentarily dismissive of, the extent of play and controversy we might mount over that word 'honestly').

We are in Britain as far from such honesty in education, however, as we are from the end of poverty. In 1999 the Chief Inspector of Schools for England published a newspaper article[1] in which he called for the books of John Dewey to be banned from teacher training. His reason and his complaint was that Dewey preached that classrooms should be places where democracy was subject to reflection, and that pupils should be prepared to play their role as autonomous citizens within it.

The significance of this article cannot be underestimated. This is the Head of a Department of State issuing a public warning to universities to censor works of political philosophy so that they are no longer available to inform school curricula. The warning has teeth, for the same man sends his inspectors to scrutinize university departments of education in close detail, motivated by what he has already declared to be an animus against those departments – and the consequences of a failed inspection are financially catastrophic and summary. The political and intellectual context within which both educators and educational evaluators seek options in pursuit of their educational principles is becoming straitened.

The cusp years of the millennium mark a period of largely unquestioned national consensus over the nationalization of curriculum, test-based

---

1 Chris Woodhead, 'Millennium reputations', *Daily Telegraph*, 25 April 1999. This article is worth reproducing in full: 'The battle to raise educational standards is ultimately a battle of ideas. For 50 years the influence of "progressive" thinkers has damaged the quality of education our children receive. No one writer has done more damage than the American philosopher John Dewey (1859–1952). Dewey, the great apostle of child-centred education, believed that the classroom should be a sort of democracy in miniature. The teacher, he argued, ought to work with children as a "leader of group activities" and never again exercise authority as "an external boss or dictator". The point of these activities was to initiate children into quasi-scientific techniques of problem-solving. Everything that went on in the classroom had to connect with the child's own immediate needs and aims, for, in Dewey's view, traditional approaches to education amounted to little more than the sterile attempt to transmit barren residues of old knowledge to passive, unmotivated students. Dewey is still revered in some university Departments of Education. As a consequence, too many children waste too much of their time on meaningless activities. Too many teachers continue to think that didactic teaching is outmoded and ineffective. The words of John Dewey ought to be banned from all teacher-training institutions.' The paradox is that at virtually the same time the Secretary of State for Education announced an initiative to stimulate citizenship education in schools.

accountability, competency-based education (behavioural objectives), absolute standards of attainment, politically defined notions of excellence and outcome-driven measures of effectiveness. Educational enquiry is fiscally confined to a narrowing policy agenda and there is a corresponding intensification of intolerance for independent critique. All of these things are seen as necessary and reasonable for measuring and enhancing the productive efficiency of schooling to support social reform – they will enhance the achievement of large groups of pupils. But they are counter-productive to effective personal education. We can, for example, encourage young people to pass more criterion-referenced assessments or to strive for intellectual autonomy – they cannot do both at the same time, for these demand mutually exclusive curriculum strategies and they emanate from opposing ethical positions. One demands compliance with a predetermined set of principles (in exchange for credentials); the other exposes those principles to critical scrutiny – that is, one accepts the authority of government, the other challenges it. We might have the right methodology, but we apply it to the wrong problem. Perhaps most prejudicially, where educational leaders are concerned with educational process it is now with 'teaching and learning', that is, those elements which are most susceptible to measurement and control and where knowledge is given. We risk losing sustained enquiry into curriculum – that is, the level at which we have to confront questions of the ethics, morality, politics and validity of the educational experiences we offer to young people.

Curriculum in Britain is in a parlous state, for it is seen as essentially unproblematic by a government that is committed to its nationalization and control. Knowledge having been rendered 'manageable' by statutory limitation, now finds itself squeezed between and subordinated to two management instruments – 'qualifications' and 'authority' – which prejudice its independence. This is the title of the body which carries responsibility for it – the Qualifications and Curriculum Authority. And, too, the largest integrated program of educational research ever funded in Britain (paid for with money top-sliced from university research budgets as a reminder of the politicization of research funding), managed by the Economic and Social Research Council, bears the title 'Innovations in Teaching and Learning'. In an epoch in which knowledge has been subjected to statutory limitation it might have been anticipated that the role of the leading independent sponsor of educational enquiry would have been to stand back and take an 'honest look' at this period of curriculum reform. Instead, the leading brief for this program is to support the national curriculum and to discover and disseminate techniques for improving attainment.

This is happening in British schools, colleges and universities, but worryingly, it extends beyond the education system. In work there is little respite as we return to unregulated and exploitative forms of labour – young people burning out at the end of 'call-systems' or mindlessly producing food and services to the automaton regime of indicators. We increasingly live the enforced myth of flexible labour and the multiple career – euphemisms for inert pools of labour. The New Deal, minimum wages and the withdrawal of benefits for young people are transferring poverty into the workplace as we rediscover the practice of 'tied labour' clothed in its modern industrialized form. As labour is once again defined as cost rather than resource, so compliance (camouflaged as 'responsibility') has replaced self-realization as the immediate goal.

The pathology is little different to the one bemoaned by A.S. Neill – the irrelevance of curriculum to future life as a citizen. 'The "Three Rs" spell futility,' he said. In a moment of mortal dismay he wrote in his log:

> Robert Campbell left the school today. He had reached the age limit. He begins work tomorrow as a ploughman. And yesterday I wrote about introducing Eurhythmics! Robert's leaving brings me to earth with a flop. I am forced to look a grim fact in the face. Truly it is like a death; I stand by a new made grave, and I have no hope of a resurrection. Robert is dead . . . I have tried to point the way to what I think best in life, tried to give Robert an ideal. Tomorrow he will be gathered to his fathers. He will take up the attitude of his neighbours: he will go to church, he will vote Radical or Tory, he will elect a farmer to the School Board, he will marry and live in a hovel . . . I am as pessimistic as any Schopenhauer . . . (1915: 58)

The crisis in curriculum makes for a corresponding crisis in self-realization. The universal treatment at school and at work, the pressure to surrender individual need to competition within the group threatens to squeeze out educational resources for the discovery of autonomy – something that made the Guildhall project something of a refreshing anachronism. But intriguingly – no doubt partly in response – the educational research community has at the same time developed a close interest in perspectives which I have broadly been trying to reflect in this book – the documenting of experience through reasserting the voice of the individual with qualitative methodologies and often driven by concerns with social justice. There has been, over the past ten years, an explosion of research and publication rendering educational issues through life history, biography, narrative accounting and the promotion of the marginal voice. This has divided researchers, for other significant elements of the educational research community have pursued the systems route, to service the information needs of those who are preoccupied with social engineering agendas. So the same period has seen the return to dominance of productivity theories of education – school effectiveness, school improvement, payment-by-results research (i.e. teacher appraisal), theories of attainment, behavioural objectives development. Nor does 'quantitative/qualitative' adequately account for this division, for school improvement enthusiasts, for example, have relied heavily on case study; teacher biography lends itself to appraisal; action research can be used for that for which it was not originally designed, to persuade teachers to self-scrutinize in order to focus on productivity; and applied research is yielding 'evidence-based practice' (the fossilization of practical ideas into context-less formulae).

The latter – the systems-orientated group – have found ready acceptance and favour in government, largely for their confidence in asserting the universality of standards and the uniformity of change requirements. The government, after all, is urgent in its pursuit of social reform. The former – the experience-orientated group – have tended to rely on the patronage of research councils and charitable sponsors, and find it hard to attract the attention of politicians, who tend to be dismissive of the complexities they insist upon in defining educational standards. There are, in effect, two distinct bodies of knowledge being generated about this volatile period of educational reform and change: crudely, these are the individual perspective and the systems view. This bi-polarity is not a bad thing, were they to collide in ways that are constructive in developing sophisticated notions of educational worth. But they rarely do. Educational policy is largely denied the insights of those whose research speaks of direct experience. Robert Campbell passes unnoticed, camouflaged in the general category, 'pupil'.

There is, over much of this, a vacuum of informed public and educational debate, for it is increasingly difficult for evaluation to find the resources and the political space to address these issues. In that vacuum historical 'ratchets' have been allowed to slip back from learning gains that were made through previous waves of educational reform (partly, it has to be said, due to the success of the postmodernists in dislocating the present from its historical sources). We have largely lost contact with what were once considered to be central educational issues of how to develop teacher judgement and the pupil's intellectual autonomy, how to democratize schools and universities and how to generate community-based discussion of curriculum and educational ideals. These are all controversial and so call for what those divisions in the research community compromise – public contestation, a sensitivity in managing conflict and an acknowledgement from 'experts' that their views are partial and provisional upon broad agreements. All of these implicate the work of evaluators, who carry responsibility for accomplishing these things – for looking honestly.

Above all, managed public contestation and the liberation of teachers and pupils calls for more modesty over what counts as a standard and some caution over invoking it. Robert Campbell was a casualty of, among other things, absolutist standards, that is, universalist criteria which ignored the particular threats to his self-realization. The best way to accomplish some relaxation over what counts as a standard is to define it from within a professional community rather than from outside it – but also to take a process view of standards. Let me explain, with reference to Lawrence Stenhouse and his cultural approach to under-standing educational process.

Stenhouse (1967: 13) viewed culture as 'the medium through which individual human minds interact with each other in communication'. It was the quality of such communication which most preoccupied him, and it is this which make his ideas so relevant to evaluators, for we, too, are primarily charged with improving the quality of exchange. For Stenhouse, conversation was all.[2] A central part of Stenhouse's take on this issue was the concept of the 'standard'. By standard he referred to 'criteria which lie behind consistent patterns of judgement of the quality and value of the work' (p. 70), that is, a standard is a procedural principle, not an outcome measure; it governs how we interact with Robert Campbell, not with what we insist he learns. The 'medium' for communication was regulated in such a way as to produce consistency in judgements about how to proceed and about what to accept as evidence towards emergent views. Elsewhere, (Stenhouse, 1963: 124) he talked of this 'consistency' in communicative interaction as 'a climate of expectation . . . all action takes place within this climate'. It is that notion of consistency – the possibility of expectation – which evaluators seek when they look for the qualities of a program and which we are always in danger of interrupting by introducing our own (or others') view of what is significant or relevant. Externally imposed standards – criterion-referenced measures – will always interrupt that consistency, the continuous flow and evolution of judgement over what is worth saying and achieving.

This, in effect, shifts consideration from the *quality* of a program or a process towards it *qualities*, as summative judgements are subordinated

---

2 Not alone, of course. The most prominent curriculum theorist who placed conversation at the heart of his philosophy (and, incidentally, who pre-figured the role of evaluation in promoting educational principles) was Joseph Schwab (1970).

to the formative. We could talk about the quality of a classroom, for example, anticipating a judgement as to its being a 'good' or a 'poor' educational setting against some criterion which that classroom shares in common with others. When we talk of the quali*ties* of a classroom, however, we merely seek to characterize it – to make it distinctive from others. Our judgements, therefore, are *comparative* rather than *absolute*, to use Glass's (1978) characterization.[3] Stenhouse (1967: 75) illustrates the point like this:

> When we say that we regard the work of one class as better than that of another, we are not simply judging it to reach a 'higher' standard. Such a conception implies a common measure against which both classes can appropriately be assessed, but in fact standards can be qualitatively different. When they are, a comparative assessment is not a matter of measurement but a matter of value-judgement. For example, we may opt for creativity or correctness . . . Such choices are founded upon conviction rather than demonstration. The sources of standards in school work lie in the teacher's values.

This leads us into the need for more description, and for enhancing the diversity of views over the worth of educational events – that is, bringing into question the values and intentions underlying curriculum. Here lies the route away from measurement and back into judgement – where we rely on understanding of individuality. Where standards are treated as guides to action, mediators of judgement, evaluation can discover a role of feeding and managing educational debate in particular contexts and in relation to given programs – but with the thoughts and aspirations of individuals. Just as A.S. Neill looked at his class of 'bairns' and *saw* Robert Campbell, not simply another pupil – and so could bring judgement to bear to guide his actions – so evaluators can look at classrooms, see the individual and produce corresponding accounts that feed the situational judgement of the teacher. Throughout this book I have tried to illustrate the 'messiness' of the social milieu which evaluators portray and the inevitability of methodological individualism. There is no urgency to resolve these confusions – in fact, I have argued that, for the most part, they are irreducible. Where the standards evaluators are responsible for are taken as guides to action, we can comfortably set aside the question of resolution. The responsibility of evaluators is to enhance

---

3 'In education', he argued, shifting the debate from fixed levels of achievement to a discussion of changing states, 'one can recognize improvement and decay, but one cannot make cogent absolute judgements of good and bad' (Glass, 1978: 259).

the quality of intellectual journeys, not to confirm, much less to rule on, destinations. The aim is to 'look honestly at life', not to see life in a particular way.

Evaluation is a cultural pursuit and it demands cultural methodologies – approaches to evaluation that portray with impartiality and respect the nature of experience and conflict over social ideals. Characteristic of all definitions of culture – with Stenhouse's definition, too – is the tension between individual and collective, between the here-and-now and tradition. If culture stands for anything, it is to give identity to a collective; but any collective identity threatens the autonomy of the individual . . . and, thereby, the death-in-aspic of culture. To say that all evaluations are case studies of culture and that evaluation needs to adopt cultural methodologies is to say that methodology must have at heart the unresolved struggle for meaning between individual and collective; between actor and organization. Evaluation needs to document both sides of the tension and then to analyse them in interaction. But it is by asserting the significance of individual experience in policy debates that we engage in evaluation as a form of political action. To favour the individual voice over the official voice is to 'take sides', to opt for affirmative action, to adopt a Rawlsian position on how to act justly.

Evaluation should not be promoting absolute standards on behalf of other authorities: it should be part of the process of defining standards as principles of procedure in structuring debate about our society and its institutions – that is, we should take a sceptical stance towards policy, holding it to account against criteria drawn from direct experience. Personalizing evaluation means offering evaluation as a service for the expression of individual and collective views about culture; that service lies in creating conditions within which agreements can be reached about what is worth talking about and how – that is, deriving criteria for holding policy to account. If we follow Stenhouse, this means evaluation must concern itself with conversation, with the 'interaction through language of human minds'. We need to interact with the mind of Robert Campbell.

Bibliography

Adelman, C. (1996) 'Anything goes: evaluation and relativism', *Evaluation*, 2 (3): 291–305.

Apple, M. (1993) *Official Knowledge: Democratic Education in a Conservative Age*, London: Routledge.

Benne, K.D. (1990) *The Task of Post-Contemporary Education: Essays in Behalf of a Human Future*, London: Teachers College Press.

Benney, M. and Hughes, E. (1984) 'Of sociology and the interview', in Martin Bulmer (ed.), *Sociological Research Methods: An Introduction*, London: Macmillan.

Bentz, V.M. and Shapiro, J.J. (1998) *Mindful Enquiry in Social Research*, London: Sage.

Berger, P. (1963) *An Invitation to Sociology*, London: Penguin Books.

Berger, P. (1974) *Pyramids of Sacrifice: Political Ethics and Social Change*, London: Allen Lane (Penguin).

Berk, R.A. and Rossi, P.H. (1990) *Thinking About Programme Evaluation*, London: Sage.

Bresler, L. (1996) 'Towards the creation of a new ethical code in qualitative research', *Bulletin of the Council for Research in Music Education*, 130 (Fall): 17–29.

Brooks, H. (1965) 'Scientific concepts and cultural change', in G. Holton (ed.), *Science and Culture*, Boston: Beacon Press, pp. 70–87.

Bruner, J. (1979) *On Knowing: Essays for the Left Hand* (expanded edition), London: Belknap/Harvard University Press.

Bruner, J. (1990) *Acts of Meaning*, London: Harvard University Press.

Campbell, D. (1999) 'An inventory of threats to validity and alternative designs to control them', in D.T. Campbell and M.J. Rosso (eds), *Social Experimentation*, London: Sage.

Campbell, D.T. and Rosso, M.J. (1999) *Social Experimentation*, London: Sage.

Chelimsky, E. and Shadish, W.R. (eds) (1997) *Evaluation for the 21st Century: a Handbook*, London: Sage.

Cheshire, G.C. and Fifoot, C.H.S. (1964) *The Law of Contract*, London: Butterworths.

Cohen, D. and Garrett, M.S. (1975) 'Reforming educational policy with applied social research', *Harvard Educational Review*, 45 (1): 17–43.

Cook, T.D. (1997) 'Lessons learned in evaluation over the past 256 years', in E.

Chelimsky and W.R. Shadish (eds), *Evaluation for the 21st Century: a Handbook*, London: Sage, pp. 30–52.

Cronbach, L.J. (1975) 'Beyond the two disciplines of scientific psychology', *American Psychologist*, 30 (2): 116–27.

Cronbach, L.J. (1984) 'In praise of uncertainty', in R.F. Connor, D.G. Altman and C. Jackson (eds), *Evaluation Studies Review Annual*, vol. 9, London: Sage, pp. 693–700.

Cronbach, L.J. and Associates (1985) *Toward Reform of Programme Evaluation*, London: Jossey-Bass.

Danziger, K. (1990) *Constructing the Subject: Historical Origins of Psychological Research*, Cambridge: Cambridge University Press.

Dollimore, J. (1998) *Death, Desire and Loss in Western Culture*, London: Penguin.

Donaldson, M. (1978) *Children's Minds*, London: Fontana.

Eisner, E. (1979) *The Educational Imagination: On the Design and Evaluation of School Programmes*, New York: Macmillan.

Eisner, E.W. (1985) *The Art of Educational Evaluation: a Personal View*, London: Falmer, p. 71.

Eisner, E.W. and Peshkin, A. (eds) (1990) *Qualitative Enquiry in Education: The Continuing Debate*, London: Teachers College Press.

Elliott, J. (1991) *Action Research for Educational Change*, London: Falmer.

Ericson, D.P. (1990) 'Social justice, evaluation and the educational system', in K.A. Sirotnik (ed.), *Evaluation and Social Justice: Issues in Public Education*, New Directions for Program Evaluation, 45, Oxford: Jossey-Bass, pp. 5–22.

Everitt, N. and Fisher, A. (1995) *Modern Epistemology: a New Introduction*, London: McGraw-Hill.

Feinberg, W. (1983) *Understanding Education: Toward a Reconstruction of Educational Enquiry*, Cambridge: Cambridge University Press.

Fetterman, D. (1997) 'Empowerment evaluation and accreditation in higher education', in E. Chelimsky and W.R. Shadish (eds), *Evaluation for the 21st Century: a Handbook*, London: Sage, pp. 381–95.

Fine, M. and Weiss, L. (1996) 'Writing the "wrongs" of fieldwork: confronting our own research/writing dilemmas in urban ethnography', *Qualitative Enquiry*, 2 (3): 251–74.

Fontana, A. and Fry, J. (1994) 'Interviewing: the art of science', in N.K. Denzin and Y.S. Lincoln (eds), *Handbook of Qualitative Research*, London: Sage, pp. 361–7.

Glasersfeld, E. Von (1991) 'Knowing without metaphysics: aspects of the radical constructivist position', in Frederick Stierer (ed.), *Research and Reflexivity*, London: Sage.

Glass, G. (1978) 'Standards and criteria', *Journal of Educational Measurement*, 15 (4): 237–61.

Guba, E.G. and Lincoln, Y. (1989) *Fourth Generation Evaluation*, London: Sage.

Guba, E.G. and Lincoln, Y.S. (1994) 'Competing paradigms in qualitative research', in N.K. Denzin and Y.S. Lincoln (eds), *Handbook of Qualitative Research*, London: Sage, pp. 105–17.

Hamilton, D., Jenkins, D., King, C., MacDonald, B. and Parlett, M. (eds) (1977) *Beyond the Numbers Game: a Reader in Educational Evaluation*, London: Macmillan Educational.

Harré, R. (1983) *Personal Being: a Theory for Individual Psychology*, Oxford: Blackwell.

Harré, R. (1989) 'Social construction of selves as a discursive practice', unpublished paper for the London Mental Models Group (available in mimeo from the author).

Hazen, R. (1988) *Superconductors: the Breakthrough*, London: Hyman.

Heussenstamm, F. (1973) '. . . On not exceeding our grasp', in *Evaluating the Total School Art Programme*, Papers presented at the National Art Education Association Study Institute, San Diego, California, April.

House, E.R. (1974) *The Politics of Educational Innovation*, Berkeley, CA: McCutchan.

House, E.R. (1980) *Evaluating with Validity*, London: Sage.

House, E.R. (1990) 'Methodology and justice', in Kenneth Sorotnik (ed.), *Evaluation and Social Justice: Issues in Public Education*, No. 45 of New Directions for Program Evaluation, Oxford: Jossey-Bass, pp. 23–36.

House, E.R. (1993) *Professional Evaluation: Social Impact and Political Consequences*, London: Sage.

Howe, K.R. and Dougherty, K.C. (1993) 'Ethics, institutional review boards and the changing face of educational research', *Educational Researcher*, 22 (9): 16–21.

Hutton, W. (1995) *The State We're In*, London: Vintage.

Jenkins, D. (1986) 'An adversary's account of SAFARI's ethics of case-study', in M. Hammersley (ed.), *Controversies in Classroom Research*, Milton Keynes: Open University Press.

Karier, C. (1974) 'Ideology and evaluation: in quest of meritocracy', in M.W. Apple, M.J. Subkoviak and H.S. Lufler, Jnr (eds), *Educational Evaluation: Analysis and Responsibility*, Berkeley, CA: McCutchan, pp. 279–319.

Karier, C., Violas, P. and Spring, J. (1973) *Roots of Crisis: American Education in the Twentieth Century*, Chicago: Rand McNally.

Kushner, S.I. (1992) *A Musical Education: Innovation in the Conservatoire*, Victoria (Australia): Deakin University Press.

Kushner, S.I. (1995) 'Learning from experience: the construction of naturalistic methodology for evaluating music education', *Bulletin of the Council for Research in Music Education* (University of Illinois), No. 123, pp. 97–111.

Kushner, S.I. (1996a) 'To have and have not: critical distance and emotional proximity in music education evaluation with a critique of "connoisseurship"', *Bulletin of the Council for Research in Music Education* (University of Illinois), No. 130, pp. 52–64.

Kushner, S.I. (1996b) 'The limits of constructivism in evaluation', *Evaluation*, 1 (2): 189–200.

Kushner, S.I. and MacDonald, B. (1987) 'The limits of programme evaluation', in R. Murphy and H. Torrance (eds), *Evaluation: Issues and Methods*, London: Paul Chapman (Open University).

Lincoln, Y. (1990) 'Toward a categorical imperative for qualitative research', in E. Eisner and A. Peshkin (eds), *Qualitative Enquiry in Education*, London: Teachers College Press, pp. 277–95.

Lindblom, C.E. (1990) *Inquiry and Change: the Troubled Attempt to Understand and Shape Society*, Newhaven, CT: Yale University Press.

Lindblom, C. and Cohen, D. (1979) *Usable Knowledge: Social Science and Social Problem-Solving*, Newhaven, CT: Yale University Press.

MacDonald, B. (1985) 'The portrayal of persons as evaluation data', in N. Norris (ed.), *SAFARI Two: Theory in Practice*, CARE Occasional Publications No. 4, University of East Anglia, Norwich.

MacDonald, B. (1987) 'Evaluation and the control of education', in R. Murphy and H. Torrance (eds), *Issues and Methods in Evaluation*, London: Paul Chapman, pp. 36–48.

MacDonald, B. (1996) 'How education became nobody's business', *Cambridge Journal of Education*, 26 (2): 241–9.

MacDonald, B. and Kushner, S. (eds) (1982) *Bread and Dreams: a Case Study of Bilingual Schooling in the USA*, CARE Occasional Publications No. 12, Norwich, UK: CARE, University of East Anglia.

MacDonald, B. and Walker, R. (1973) 'Re-thinking evaluation: notes from the Cambridge Conference', *Cambridge Journal of Education*, 3 (2): 74–82.

MacDonald, B. and Walker, R. (1974) *SAFARI One: Innovation, Evaluation, Research and the Problem of Control*, CARE, University of East Anglia, Norwich.

MacDonald, B. and Walker, R. (1976) *Changing the Curriculum*, London: Open Books.

MacLure, M. (1995) 'Mundane autobiography: some thoughts on self-talk in research contexts', *British Journal of Sociology of Education*, 14 (4): 373–84.

Macphereson, C.B. (1968) *Hobbes Leviathan*, London: Penguin.

Maxwell, J.P., Bashook, P.G. and Sandlow, L.J. (1987) 'Combining ethnographic and experimental methods in educational evaluation: a case study', in W.R. Shadish and C.S. Reichardt (eds), *Evaluation Studies Review Annual*, Vol. 6, Newbury Park, CA: Sage.

McNeil, L. (1996) 'Local reform initiatives and a national curriculum: where are the children?', *The Hidden Consequences of a National Curriculum*, American Educational Research Association (AERA) Monograph.

Mellor, P.H. (1993) 'Death in high modernity: the contemporary presence and absence of death', in D. Clark (ed.), *The Sociology of Death*, Oxford: Blackwell.

Miles, M. (ed.) (1964) *Innovation in Education*, New York: Teachers College.

Mishler, E. (1986) *Research Interviewing: Context and Narrative*, London: Harvard University Press.

Neill, A.S. (1915) *A Dominie's Log*, London: Herbert Jenkins.

Newman, D.L. and Brown, R.D. (1996) *Applied Ethics for Program Evaluation*, London: Sage.

Norris, N. (1985) *SAFARI Two: Theory in Practice*, CARE Occasional Publications No. 4, CARE, University of East Anglia, Norwich.

Norris, N. (1990) *Understanding Educational Evaluation*, London: Kogan Page.

Norris, N. (1995) 'Contracts, control and evaluation', *Journal of Education Policy*, 10 (3): 271–85.

Parlett, M. and Hamilton, D. (1977) 'Evaluation as illumination: a new approach to the study of innovatory programmes', in D. Hamilton, D. Jenkins, C. King, B. MacDonald and M. Parlett (eds), *Beyond the Numbers Game: a Reader in Educational Evaluation*, London: Macmillan, pp. 6–22.

Patton, M. Quinn (1997) *Utilisation Focused Evaluation, the New Century Text*, 3rd edn, London: Sage.

Pawson, R. and Tilley, N. (1998) 'Caring communities, paradigm polemics, design debates', *Evaluation*, 4 (1): 73–90.

Peshkin, A. (1988) 'In search of subjectivity – one's own', *Educational Researcher*, 17 (7): 17–21.

Peters, R.S. (1966) *Ethics and Education*, London: George Allen & Unwin.

Peters, R.S. (1973) *Authority, Responsibility and Education*, 3rd edn, London, George Allen & Unwin.

Phillips, D.C. (1990) 'Subjectivity and objectivity: an objective enquiry', in E.W. Eisner and A. Peshkin (eds), *Qualitative Enquiry in Education*, London: Teachers College Press.

Pinar, W.F. (1992) 'Cries and whispers', in W.F. Pinar and W.M. Reynolds (eds), *Understanding Curriculum as Phenomenological and Deconstructed Text*, London: Teachers College Press, pp. 92–101.

Pinar W.F. and Reynolds W.M. (1992) 'Introduction: curriculum as text', in W.F. Pinar and W.M. Reynolds (eds), *Understanding Curriculum as Phenomenological and Deconstructed Text*, London: Teachers College Press, pp. 1–16.

Poole, R. (1972) *Towards Deep Subjectivity*, London: Allen Lane, Penguin.

Popkiewicz, T.S. (1988) 'What's in a research project: some thoughts on the intersection of history, social structure and biography', in *Curriculum Enquiry* (OISE, Canada), 18 (4): 379–400.

Rivlin, A.M. (1973) 'Social experiments: the promise and the problem', *Brookings Bulletin*, 10 (3): 6–9.

Robinson, D.N. (1995) *An Intellectual History of Psychology*, 3rd edn, London: Arnold.

Rossi, P.H. and Freeman, H.E. (1989) *Evaluation: a Systematic Approach*, 4th edn, London: Sage.

Schatzman, L. and Strauss, A. (1973) *Field Research: Strategies for a Natural Sociology*, Englewood Cliffs, NJ: Prentice-Hall.

Schon, D. (1971) *Beyond the Stable State: Public and Private Learning in a Changing Society*, London: Temple Smith.

Schratz, M. and Walker, R. (1995) *Research as Social Change: New Opportunities for Qualitative Research*, London: Routledge.

Schwab, J. (1970) *The Practical: A Language for Curriculum*, Washington: National Association Centre for the Study of Instruction.

Scriven, M. (1967) 'The methodology of evaluation', in R. Tyler, R.M. Gagni, M. Scriven (eds), *Perspectives on Curriculum Evaluation*, Chicago: Rand McNally, pp. 39–83.

Scriven, M. (1974) 'Evaluation perspectives and procedures', in W.J. Popham (ed.), *Evaluation in Education: Current Applications*, Berkeley, CA: McCutchan.

Scriven, M. (1993) *Hard Won Lessons in Programme Evaluation*, New Directions for Programme Evaluation No. 58, San Francisco: Jossey-Bass.

Scriven, M. (1999) 'The meaning of bias', in *Proceedings of the Stake Symposium on Educational Evaluation*, University of Illinois, Urbana, IL (May, 1998).

Seery, J.E. (1996) *Political Theory for Mortals: Shades of Justice, Images of Death*, London: Cornell University Press.

Shadish, W.R. (1987) 'Sources of evaluation practice: needs, purposes, questions and technology', in W.R. Shadish and C.S. Reichardt (eds), *Evaluation Studies Review Annual*, Vol. 6, Newbury Park, CA: Sage.

Shadish, W.R. and Reichardt, C.S. (eds) (1987) *Evaluation Studies Review Annual*, Vol. 6, Newbury Park, CA: Sage.

Simons, H. (ed.) (1980) *Towards a Science of the Singular: Essays About Case Study in Educational Research and Evaluation*, CARE Occasional Publications No. 10, University of East Anglia, Norwich.

Simons, H. (1987) *Getting to Know Schools in a Democracy*, London: Falmer.

Sirotnik, K. (ed.) (1990) *Evaluation and Social Justice: Issues in Public Education*, New Directions for Programme Evaluation No. 45, San Francisco: Jossey-Bass.

Smith, L.M. (1990) 'Ethics in qualitative field research: an individual perspective', in E. Eisner and A. Peshkin (eds), *Qualitative Enquiry in Education*, London: Teachers College Press, pp. 258–76.

Stake, R.E. (1967) 'The countenance of educational evaluation', *Teachers College Record*, 68 (7): 523–40.

Stake, R.E. (1975) 'To evaluate an arts program', in R.E. Stake (ed.) *Evaluating the Arts in Education: a Responsive Approach*, Columbus, Ohio: Charles E. Merrill.

Stake, R.E. (1977) 'An approach to the evaluation of instructional programmes (programme portrayal vs analysis)', in D. Hamilton, D. Jenkins, C. King, B. MacDonald and M. Parlett (eds), *Beyond the Numbers Game: A Reader in Educational Evaluation*, London: Macmillan Educational, pp. 161–2.

Stake, R.E. (1980) 'The case study method in social enquiry', in H. Simons (ed.), *Towards a Science of the Singular*, CARE Occasional Publications No. 10, University of East Anglia, Norwich.

Stake, R.E. (1986) *Quieting Reform: Social Science and Social Action in an Urban Youth Reform*, Chicago: University of Illinois Press.

Stake, R.E. (1995) *The Art of Case Study Research*, London: Sage.

Stake, R.E. (1997) 'Advocacy in evaluation: a necessary evil?', in E. Chelimsky and W.R. Shadish (eds), *Evaluation for the 21st Century*, London: Sage, pp. 470–8.

Stenhouse, L. (1963) 'A cultural approach to the sociology of the curriculum', *Pedagogisk Forskning* (Scandinavian Journal of Educational Research), pp. 120–34.

Stenhouse, L. (1967) *Culture and Education*, London: Nelson.

Stenhouse, L. (1978) 'Case study and case records: towards a contemporary history of education', *British Educational Research Journal*, 4 (2): 21–39.

Stronach, I. (1999) 'Shouting theatre in a crowded fire: educational effectiveness as cultural performance', *Evaluation*, 5 (2): 173–93.

Van Maanen, J. (1988) *Tales of the Field: On Writing Ethnography*, London: University of Chicago Press.

Walcott, H. (1990) 'On seeking – and rejecting – validity in qualitative research', in E. Eisner and A. Peshkin (eds), *Qualitative Enquiry in Education*, London: Teachers College Press, pp. 121–52.

Walker, R. (1974) 'The conduct of educational case study: ethics, theory and procedures', in *Innovation, Evaluation, Research and the Problem of Control*, SAFARI 1 Papers, CARE, University of East Anglia, Norwich, pp. 75–115.

Walker, R. (1980) 'Making sense and losing meaning', in H. Simons (ed.), *Towards a Science of the Singular*, CARE Occasional Publications No. 10, University of East Anglia, Norwich, pp. 222–35.

Walker, R. (1991) 'Making sense and losing meaning', in I. Goodson and R. Walker (eds), *Biography, Identity and Schooling: Episodes in Educational Research*, London: Falmer, pp. 107–13.

Wax, M.L. and Cassell, J. (1981) 'From regulation to reflection: ethics in social research', *The American Sociologist*, 16: 224–9.

Weiss, C. (1983) 'The stakeholder approach to evaluation: origins and promise', in A.S. Bryk, *New Directions for Programme Evaluation*, No. 17, London: Jossey-Bass.

Weiss, C. (1987) 'Where politics and evaluation research meet', in D.J. Palumbo (ed.), *The Politics of Program Evaluation*, London: Sage, pp. 47–70.

Weiss, C. (1998) *Evaluation: Methods for Studying Programs and Policies*, 2nd edn, Englewood Cliffs, NJ: Prentice-Hall.

Weiss, C. and Rein, M. (1969) 'The evaluation of broad-aims programmes: a cautionary case and a moral', *Annals of the American Academy of Political and Social Science*, 385: 133–42.

Wildavsky, A. (1979) *Speaking Truth to Power: the Art and Craft of Policy Analysis*, Boston, MA: Little Brown.

Yin, R. (1994) *Case Study Research: Design and Methods*, 2nd edn, London: Sage.

Index